Bases
to
Bleachers

A Collection of Personal Baseball Stories from
the Stands and Beyond

7/20/2019

to chuck

I hope you enjoy this collection of baseball
stories and that you have great baseball
memories of your own. Tell me your story!

Eric C. Gray

Eric C Gray

Palmetto Publishing Group
Charleston, SC

Bases to Bleachers
Copyright © 2019 by Eric C. Gray

First Edition

Printed in the United States

ISBN-13: 978-1-64111-179-9
ISBN-10: 1-64111-179-8

The game of baseball is timeless, and so are our memories. The worst day of my life occurred in October of 1960 when the Pirates' Bill Mazeroski homered against New York Yankees' pitcher Ralph Terry in the ninth inning of game 7 to win the World Series. The game was historic -- because the Yankees lost, and Casey Stengel was fired. This 14-year-old learned the lesson that nothing ever stays the same. Time marches on.

"Everyone who loves baseball has a story like that. This wonderful book by Eric Gray compiles them.

-- Peter Golenbock, author of *Dynasty, The Bronx Zoo* (with Sparky Lyle) and *Number 1* (with Billy Martin)

I love baseball till this day. I have loved this game since I could remember and that was at the age of 4 years old when my Dad took me to my first baseball game at Lane Field in San Diego to watch the Pacific Coast League San Diego Padres play. I was the Batboy for my brothers' team in San Diego when I was 6 years old and caught the bug. I saw a lot of players come and go when I was the Batboy for the Padres at 10 years old in 1961...

Baseball, what's it mean to me? My first pitch, able to play in front of Mom, Dad and family, getting out of games before the end to beat the traffic and listening to game on the way home on the radio. Learning the history of the game, Past, Present, and Future. Being a part of the changes and seeing baseball adjust to the times. Fundamental baseball and how it was the quintessential part of the game. Watching teams manufacture runs and all the different tricks they played on each other to win. Remembering your favorite stars like Mickey Mantle and Roger Maris. Watching two of your favorite pitchers, Sandy Koufax and Juan Marichal, battle it out time and time again. These are the times, the history of Baseball. The romance between the Fan and Player. That most important game 7 of the World Series that will leave an indelible mark on your mind forever. Yet the most electrifying part of that romance was the love of the game. Being able to sit and watch the human chess match unfold in front of your eyes. The signs from the coach to the hitter, that stolen base to advance the runner in scoring position, the knockdown pitch on an 0-2 count. The ensuing brawls that broke out due to fierce competition... All of this wrapped up into a tight little package that could explode at any time like a 500 mega ton bomb, leaving everyone speechless... Ah the love of the game.

Most books that are written are by baseball players to the fans. This book by Eric Gray is written by a fan of the game of baseball. It is a complete disclosure of his beginning as a fan through the changes of World War II and the Korean Conflict that allowed the Women to play the game and continue the great legacy for the fans. As well as the breaking of the barrier of color in our country. The proverbial acceptance of the Negro Leagues players, like Jackie Robinson, Josh Gibson and Satchel Paige, Monty Irving, Willie Mays, and Wille McCovey, all the great, talented players that we know and remember today. These are changes in baseball that have weathered the test time. Baseball has made it through some of the most difficult times a person could imagine. Yet it is still America's Past-time.

Baseball is about life in general. It is about moving forward from base to base before you score the inevitable run. It is explosive, demanding, traditional, colorful, and very exciting to watch. As I said earlier, that it is "The LOVE" that keeps this great game moving forward through the years.

Baseball has ignited many around the world. From Japan, to Puerto Rico, to Venezuela, Columbia, Mexico, Dominican Republic, Canada and even Europe with Teams from Italy, Netherlands, Israel, Germany, Russia, China, Taiwan, Korea, it is everywhere. The bug has caught everyone to feed the cheers of competition around the world with the World Baseball Classic. No wonder it is America's Past Time and now the Past Time of the World

The fan will always find a way to listen to a ballgame, whether on the Radio or Television or at the Ball Park of their choice. It is a legacy of LOVE, it is the fan base of the world; which ignites those fires of competition and keeps the fans coming back for more. It is this never-ending love that is instilled in this book. This book would not have been written unless

Eric had a strong love for this game and wanted to share his story about the love he has for baseball.

So, I end here with this final statement This Book is a remarkable read I hope you can enjoy it as much as I have. Remember that LOVE is the strongest power we know today. It has broken hearts, made them strong, and instilled respect for one another it has also brought Nations together. Baseball has done that to us all. Yet we still love her, and she will always be our LOVE of the GAME.

-- John D'Aquisto, author of *Fastball John*
1974 The Sporting News National League Rookie Pitcher of the Year

CONTENTS

Introduction· ·ix

Generation to Generation: Family and Baseball · · · · · · · · · · · · · · · 1

Let's Beat the Traffic · 19

Love and Baseball · 34

Women in Baseball · 61

The Negro Leagues · 78

Baseball: The International Game · 96

Not Quite the Major Leagues · 127

What Baseball Means to Me · 146

Bunts · 169

Singles · 178

Doubles · 197

Triples · 211

Home Runs · 236

Mickey, Can I Have Your Autograph? · · · · · · · · · · · · · · · · · · · 262

My Time on the Field · 282

Famous, Historic, and Memorable Games · · · · · · · · · · · · · · · · · 302

Mini-Chapters: A Sneak Preview · 319

Afterword And Acknowledgements · 327

INTRODUCTION

I think baseball fans would generally agree that one either likes, or doesn't like, watching baseball because of the slow pace. That being the case, you have lots of time to talk with your companions, gaze mindlessly out at the field, or—on those rare occasions when they're not shooting pizzas and T-shirts into the stands or showing absurd games on the Jumbotron—just think. These circumstances—the ability to just sit in the sun (a rare occasion at a San Francisco Giants game) and think—ultimately became the impetus for this book. It happened at a game late in the 2011 baseball season, sitting in our regular seats at AT&T Park, home of the 2010 World Champion Giants. The losses were coming regularly, and it was apparent that there would be no repeat of the previous magical season, but as a fan of the team, it didn't dampen my enjoyment of just going and watching a game with people I love. Gazing out at the field, I turned to my wife Lynn, daughter Rachel, and friend Cheryl, and asked simply, "So, of all the games you've been to, what is your favorite?

Remarkably, Cheryl and Lynn cited a game the three of us shared, the game in which the Giants finally beat the Padres in the last game of the 2010 regular season and went on to win the World Series. However, the answer wasn't really the important thing. I began thinking about which of the many hundreds of games stood out in my memory, for any of a myriad of reasons. Of course, I really wasn't thinking that deeply about it; the question had just simply rolled out of my mouth.

Several weeks later, I sent an email to about thirty of my friends and family members, asking them to send me their favorite baseball moments. I told them it could be a momentous event, such as a no-hitter or a triple play, or when a player broke a record, or a World Series seventh-game victory. Perhaps it was their first game with dad or grandma, or first game with the person they would marry, or when they took their kid to their first game. Maybe it was something funny or bizarre, such as the Candlestick Park hot chocolate incident (remember what I said before about the weather at SF Giants games?), or the DC sunscreen episode. The reason didn't matter; it was simply which game stuck out fondly—or perhaps not so fondly—in their memory.

In my email, I listed six of my favorite games—at least those I was able to quickly identify without real consideration. No story, no explanation, just a list. Some of the responses I got were also just the mention of a game. But some were explanations of something momentous, or, as in my friend Andy's case, the person who is less interested in baseball than anyone I know, something really personal. It was at that moment that I decided I wanted to compile a book of fan recollections.

I embarked on a mission to obtain as many stories as possible from people representing a wide diversity of ages and places. As a native New Yorker and longtime San Francisco resident, knowing so many people in those two areas, it would have been easy to fill this book with stories of the Yankees, Mets, and Giants, from people primarily my age or my kids' ages. However, that would have excluded tales about Ted Williams or Rod Carew, or a Kansas City/George Brett moment, or something from the Pittsburgh Pirates/We Are Family era. There wouldn't be a Chicago Cubs' Ernie Banks tale, or a memory about Coors Field. There certainly wouldn't be any recounting of the Houston Astros, who, back in the eighties, had perhaps the worst uniforms in history; or the Seattle Mariners, with Ichiro; or the Cleveland Indians, with their great pitching staffs of the 1950s.

So, I began reaching out. A lot. To friends and their friends. At ball games, in airports, and train stations. Waiting in line at a movie, or at a restaurant or demonstration. And then on Facebook (thank you, Ian Kahanawitz and Bill Shelley), which provided me with tons of great stories and new friends. Many of those who gave me a story probably recall how I hunted and tracked them down. I pretty much do. (I've occasionally felt I've cheated fans from areas other than San Francisco and New York, despite my efforts to grab stories from people from other places). I furiously hunted people down at games or approached them on the street if they had a Twins or Tigers cap or Marlins T-shirt on. I've really tried. I have included at least one story relating to each of the 30 major league teams (or one of their players). Story contributors came from almost every state, with 37 states represented in stories used in this book.

One huge surprise was how many stories had little, or nothing, to do with the actual game; they were simply personal memories. As you'll see, for many of these stories, it really doesn't matter where they took place. They don't involve the players or the team. Playing the National Anthem before a game could have taken place in any stadium. Seeing the wide expanse of the outfield grass for the first time could have taken place in any town. Please fight an initial impulse to think this book is bicoastal-centric.

I'm lucky that my lifelong love of baseball has been easy to nurture and continue, because my entire family loves the game. Some of our most wonderful times together have been at ball games, watching them on television, or just talking ball. We would speculate on who would make the opening day roster, and who would be the first to be released. We would figure out who the starting pitcher would be for the game we had tickets to two weeks ahead of time, and we would guess who, if anyone, would make the all-star squad. We would have to guess if it would be cold at the park, and how many layers to bring, or perhaps have a lucky day when we could just take a light jacket. That my son David has always played baseball and loved his Giants is no surprising thing for a boy. But my daughter, Rachel, fell in love with the game *literally* at first sight, and has worked for the Giants since she was fourteen. That inspired Lynn's interest, and she ultimately insisted that we buy into a season ticket partnership. It's been easy, and a real joy. From spring training to the World Series, it's been a great unifying pastime. Even in those rare moments when there was family turmoil, we knew we would have a good time at the game.

I honestly don't know what my most memorable moment at the park is. Like many of us, I have so many memories. There was a game at Wrigley when the four of us could only get seats in different sections, getting ever closer to each other as the innings passed by. Perhaps it was the one at Fenway when we got the royal drunk-filled/beer-spilled treatment from the guy behind us. Maybe it was experiencing different weather systems within the confines of Candlestick Park, or the eighteen innings first game of a twi-night double header at Shea Stadium between the Mets and the Phillies. Every time someone describes a story, I am reminded of something. As a child who lived for every Mickey Mantle at bat, for me, it's the day they retired his number. As a baseball fan, maybe a World Series game with my daughter. As a father, I would have to say it was taking my kids to their first game. This might change if someday I have grandkids.

For a game that I think isn't terribly passionate in play, when compared with the raw emotion of football and basketball, my experience is that fans follow the game, their teams, and players with an unlimited amount of passion: the statistics they remember, the books they write and read, the plays they will never forget. Who beat who in the 1960 World Series (Pirates over Yankees, Mazeroski's home run), or who gave up Hank Aaron's 715th home run (Al Downing). New York Mets' Ron Swoboda's catch against the Orioles in the 1969 Series, Carlton Fisk's waving his home run ball fair during the 1975 Fall Classic versus Cincinnati. The Herb Score and Tony C. tragedies. Joe Nuxhall and Satchel Paige (oldest and youngest to play in the major leagues). Was Mantle or Mays the better ballplayer? Or who *would* have been without Mantle's injuries? Should Pete Rose be in the Hall of Fame? Was the Ryan-Fregosi trade worse than Sadecki-Cepeda? And how about the trade of Babe Ruth for it-doesn't-matter-who? Should the designated hitter be eliminated, or brought to the National League? Do we really need to speed up pace of game? And, as argued a question as any, should the winner of the all-star game *really* have home field advantage in the World Series? (Thankfully, that's no longer an issue). There will never, ever be a shortage of topics that fans will debate and argue about, on talk radio, at backyard barbecues, on Little League fields, wherever at least two baseball fans meet.

There have been unexpected outcomes from this endeavor. One involves the people I met, the great conversations I've had in person, or nice email and Facebook exchanges with some I didn't even know. Some of these have turned into real friendships. Another was how often I smiled, laughed, or had tears reading peoples' stories. That was generally because they cited something I could relate to, an experience or a player they discussed, or just some amazing moment. Sometimes the stories were just so happy or sad. I'm guessing that many of you will have similar reactions.

As this project progressed, I realized that I would have to adjust format to fit content, rather than the other way around. You'll get it when you read Sarah W.'s story, which didn't have a place in the book's original plan. People asked for "guidance" about what I was looking for, and inevitably totally disregarded that guidance and provided stories of a wide and unimaginable variety. Little League and baseball outside the country; falling in love and wacky stuff in the stands. Meeting the players and *not* catching the foul ball. Most stories were short, as I wanted; some were longer, but riveting, and I could only cut a little bit. I'm incredibly grateful that people simply ignored my guidelines; it made this book much, much richer.

In the seven years since I started this project, I've collected over 1,250 stories from more than seven hundred contributors. It wasn't possible to use every story I received; the book would have been as large as the Encyclopedia Britannica that AJ Jacobs read, wrote a book about, and shared a story from. However, I enjoyed reading every single one, and that is the touch-all-the bases truth. I remember meeting most everyone who sent me a story, if we weren't friends already, those I met in "the field" and online. I'm honored and grateful for the generosity of people who gave their time and spirit, to share their experiences, in some cases pretty intimate memories, and allow me to share them with you. This has brought me a tremendous amount of joy, and even greater appreciation for the power of baseball to make a difference in so many peoples' lives. It's one thing to enjoy this game; it's another completely to be so connected because of it. I send a huge grand slam of thanks to everyone who sent a story.

Believe me when I say (and those of you who know me personally understand this quite well), that it was an agonizing process figuring out which ones I could fit into a reasonably sized book. Knowing I was omitting the stories of close personal friends was like watching your team load the bases with no outs in the last of the ninth, one run behind, and have three consecutive players strike out. I truly could have thrown 1,250 pieces of paper in the air and, with a blindfold on, picked up 250 of them at random, and it would have turned out great. Some stories could easily fit into one of two or more chapters (Robin's could be in "Love and Baseball," or "What Baseball Means to Me"). I tried to find balance among which stories are in which chapters; for example, male and female authors, teams, the natures of the stories. If there were stories of a similar experience, or even the same game, again, it was hard to choose. There were too many great ones to include; it was like choosing which album I like better, The Beatles' Abbey Road or Jackson Browne's Late for the Sky. I mean, come on. I had an embarrassment of riches, stretched it as far as I could, like the one triple I had which I tried to turn into the home run I never had (Lynn Held's story). If yours didn't make it, I hope you understand. There will be a second volume.

I hope you enjoy reading this book as much as I've enjoyed collecting the stories and putting this all together. (Finishing this project is the only time I have played Santa Claus: Like his list, I have checked every name, spelling and correction many times, please forgive me for a misspelled name or city), I think you'll find this to be a very different kind of baseball book. I love reading biographies, or books about teams, seasons, eras, or accomplishments. Like other baseball fans, I enjoy and remember the stats, and love good analysis. But this book is different. It's from the fans' perspectives (or players, or coaches, or umpires). It's a human interest book in a baseball setting, rather than a baseball book. These are the stories of everyday folks like me, who aren't in the public's consciousness. I have been fortunate enough to get stories from some great, known writers, a couple of ballplayers, and a few other famous folks. But the essence of this book revolves around the experience that students, working people, and retirees have had regarding their love of our national pastime. I hope you laugh, cry a little, and shake your head in amazement at these stories, like I did.

Here are some themes that emerged, and often shared memories in the stories I received, whether they are included in this volume or not. Going to games with family, wanting that one last catch with Mom or Dad, loving tributes. The experience of the first game, seeing the wide expanse of the field, the crowd size, the brilliant green grass, the white chalk on the dirt, and smell of popcorn and beer and cigar smoke. Mom tossing out baseball cards (me), and kids using and losing autographed baseballs. The

Maris and Mantle home run chase as well as Aaron and Bonds home run records. Team futility, notably the Cubs. Red Sox, and Mets. What a great guy or jerk a favorite (sometimes the same) player was. Loving *and* hating the Yankees. But most of all, the myriad ways that people talk about their love, devotion and gratitude for this great game.

Following, for the baseball uninitiated, is a short index of common baseball terms and abbreviations used in the book:

AL/NL: American League/National League

AL/NLDS: American/National League Division Series; round two of the playoffs

AL/NLCS: American/National League Championship Series; round three of the playoffs

AS/ASG: All-Star/All-Star Game

BP: Batting practice (taken prior to ball games)

Batter's count: Number of balls and strikes on a batter, in that order, for example, 1-2

Batter's "Game line": Number of hits in official at bats, e.g. 1-3, one hit in three at bats

HoF: Hall of Fame

ML/MLB: Major League(s)/Major League Baseball

MVP: Most Valuable Player (an award voted on at the end of each season)

RBI: Run batted in, when a batter does something positive that results in a run being scored

Score: Final, or mid-game score, with the winning/leading team first, for example, 4-3

ST: Spring training

WC: Wild Card; the first round of the playoffs; one game, loser go home

W-L: Win-Loss record (in that order), for a team's record or a pitcher's personal record

WS: World Series; round . . . oh, everyone knows what this is

These stories were collected over seven years. Thus, some things have changed, and will continue to change before this book is published. People's ages, and the number of years married, will change. Kids will have been born; some people will have passed away. The Red Sox will have won a fourth World Series title. I didn't see the need to amend even the stuff I knew about, as the stories captured a moment in time. And finally, for the Cubs fans—quite a few who bemoaned the lack of a championship in their stories sent to me before November 2016— You have your World Series title! Batter up!

For the first pitch:

In August of 1992, I took my kids to their first baseball game, Giants versus Pirates. A transplanted New Yorker since 1975, and still a rabid Mets fan, I had previously visited Candlestick only when the Mets were in town; in those days, twice a season. Rachel was eight, and David, four. We were with David's friend, Kenneth Frankel, and Kenneth's dad, Eric. We sat in the upper deck, first base side, surrounded by a lot of empty seats.

Many people remember their first game (I don't) or taking their kids to their first game. But this was special. Rachel had tried her hand at Tee-ball, and it wasn't for her; she felt she wasn't "as good as the boys" (in some cases, true; in other cases, not). When I took Rachel to a movie, a dozen or so books always accompanied her, so she wouldn't waste a minute from the time her tush was on the seat cush, until the movie started. So, knowing how bored she would be, she brought an entire library with her.

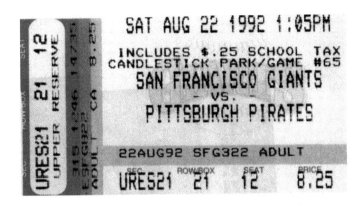

SAT AUG 22 1992 1:05PM

INCLUDES $.25 SCHOOL TAX
CANDLESTICK PARK/GAME #65
SAN FRANCISCO GIANTS
- VS. -
PITTSBURGH PIRATES

22AUG92 SFG322 ADULT

URES21 21 12 8.25

By the fourth inning, David and Kenneth were *done*. They were still having a good time, but that involved running up and down the stairs to the top of Candlestick. I frequently looked at Rachel sitting next to me; her eyes were transfixed on the field, as if she had just seen, I don't know, the Mona Lisa, or the Beatles in concert (right there, almost twenty-six years earlier to the day), or the Leaning Tower of Pisa in the full moon. Take your pick of astonishing sights. Anyway, she had it. The only things her eyes read during the full nine innings were the program I bought, and the scoreboard. And then she started listening—*really* listening—to Kruk and Kuip, Mike Krukow and Duane Kuiper, and learned about the game. She immediately loved baseball as much as her dad did. I will never, ever forget that day. I only know who the Giants played that day because it is on the ticket stub. I don't know who won; none of that is important to me. The story is how a lifetime of family baseball burst forward in an unexpected way.

Seven years later she began working for the Giants in guest services, first handing out giveaways, and now operating the press elevator. She knows, seemingly, everyone. David, of course, grew up to be a huge Giants fan as well, and almost every year I go to Washington DC to take him to see his beloved team (usually) lose to the Nationals. In 2000, when the Mets faced the Giants in the playoffs, Rachel and David essentially called me out, saying, "Okay, old man, which is it? The Light side or the Dark side?" (Star Wars, of course.) I still love my Mets, but the Giants are now number one. I will always remember that day as the one that made it very, very easy to be a family man *and* a huge baseball fan.

—Eric Gray
San Francisco, California

GENERATION TO GENERATION: FAMILY AND BASEBALL

The primary motivation in writing this book had to do with my experiences of going to baseball games with my family, and what great memories and shared bonds and interests this regular and frequent activity has given us. However, what sparked my thinking about these experiences was the story that my friend Andy sent to me, about the only game he had gone to with his dad. In the course of story collection, the single most frequent theme that has emerged is the shared enjoyment of going to games, following teams, with family; carrying on the traditions, the joys and heartbreaks of being fans and following teams. Whether it's the routines of getting to the park, the food that's eaten, games played during the game, the discussion on the rides home—all families have their memories and traditions. Parents, grandparents, uncles and aunts, brothers and sisters, these family relationships are important in our lives, and sometimes they help foster the love of baseball. Perhaps, then, it is fitting that this theme constitutes the first chapter of this book or, in baseball parlance, leads off.

***

My best memory of a baseball game happened just recently. I'm in my mid-twenties, and in a desperate attempt to find my dad the perfect Father's Day present, I bought tickets to the firefighters' appreciation night at the Giants' AT&T Park (he's been with Vacaville Fire Department since I was six months old). I hadn't been to a ball game with my dad in close to twenty years. It felt good to show him how grown up and independent I was. I drove to the park, bought the tickets, and even got him a cold beer.

It's difficult to find common ground these days, as I'm a grown woman and he's working on retiring, but there's something about a ball game with your dad that blurs the lines of time and distance, and just puts you in the now. While everyone around the park was celebrating firefighters and their selfless acts of heroism, I was celebrating the biggest hero in my life—my dad.

—Michelle Bowman
Sacramento, California

***

I was a young immigrant teenager, having come to New Jersey from South Korea when I was about ten years old. We reunited with my father after seven years, and I felt like I didn't know him. He certainly wasn't a very emotional person; I didn't really know whether he cared about me any more than he cared about my passion, the Mets—which was not at all.

When I told him that I wanted to get a baseball glove, he surprised me by saying he wanted one, too. I was skeptical but decided to give it a try. We bought our gloves and went to play catch that night. I knew how to do so from gym class, but Dad clearly had no clue. He would catch the ball in the palm of the glove, rather than the webbing, and I knew how much that hurt. He was so awkward, and his hand was very red from catching that way. I called off the activity, less out of mercy than embarrassment.

When the Mets played the Red Sox in that remarkable game six of the 1986 World Series, my father, exhausted from a long day at the family business, sat down to watch with me. I couldn't see at the time that it wasn't because of his interest in baseball, but in being with me. He started dozing off, but my loud yelling when Ray Knight came home with the winning run woke him up, and he started clapping.

Dad passed away eleven years ago. He never told me he loved me. But he watched that game with me, a game he didn't understand. And the sound of the baseball landing against the thinly guarded soft flesh of his hand over and over again—that spoke its own tender language. All I felt was shame at the time, but now I feel a strange combination of regret and happiness.

—Sung J. Woo, author of *Love Love*, as told to Eric Gray
Washington, New Jersey

***

In 2010, the San Francisco Giants went to the World Series versus the Texas Rangers. In addition to our two regular tickets for game two as part of our season ticket partnership, I was able to score a pair for the series opener. I told my wife, Lynn, that I really wanted to go to the game with our daughter, Rachel, who works for the team in guest services; she completely understood.

The game started with both teams scoring runs in the early innings, but in the fifth, the Giants stormed ahead with six runs on the way to a romp. The energy in the stands was electric, as ecstatic fans watched them get hit after hit, run after run. Everyone was yelling and screaming, smiling and giving high fives to everyone seated (or standing) within reach. Rachel and I were hugging and cheering along with everyone else, with the activity on the field simply providing an opportunity to share many moments of extreme joy and affinity with my daughter. Rachel and I have had our share of difficulties over the years, with lots of evidence that differences and annoyances can sometimes overshadow the love between family members. I won't say that game changed our relationship around completely and forever, but the experience we shared that night did have a big effect on how we felt about being together for a little while, and a smaller but lasting effect on how we did together for a long time afterwards. The next game with Lynn, in which the Giants were in command from the beginning, was also great, and we were all overjoyed that the Giants swept the Rangers. But that game one, I will never forget how I felt that night. It was spectacular.

RACHEL AND ERIC

—Eric Gray
San Francisco, California

***

My dad was a surgeon, and that seemed to be his reason for not doing things around the house. Making repairs, little maintenance chores, these were off-limits to him because he didn't want to "hurt his hands." We all knew this could have just been an excuse, but he was a good dad, provided well for his family, and we loved him.

Dad loved baseball and had season tickets for the Mets at Shea Stadium, box seats behind home plate. His name was actually on the back of the seat, a common practice at Shea. I loved having time with him alone and would often go to a game with him. One day when I was a young teen, a pop-up foul ball came right towards us. He instinctively reached up and caught the ball with his bare hands. What?! I looked at him in astonishment, and he gave me a look with a smile that said, "You never know what to expect"; perhaps, "This is between us!"

Several years later, I went to a game with a friend, my first in a long time. We had tickets, as it happened, just two rows behind Dad's seats. Dad had since passed away; when I arrived, I went to take a look at our old seats, and there was his name, still on the back. It was, of course, an emotional moment for me, sad and happy at the same time. If only we'd had cell phones at that time; I would have taken a photo!

—A. Karp
San Diego, California

***

Growing up, my favorite thing in the world was spending time at my Gram's house. Many afternoons and nights were passed listening to WJR Radio, Ernie and Paul broadcasting Tiger baseball. My love for the game, and spending time with Gram, continued into my teens, and even adulthood. I often fell asleep listening to the Tigers on my clock radio, waking up hearing Ernie yelling "Looong Gooone" in the recap of the game early the next morning; that is how I found out if they had won when they were on the West Coast. We would often call each other to talk about what had happened in the game or find out who'd won because the newspaper had not yet been delivered. Of course, I called her every April on that special day to wish her a happy opening day. Two years ago, after insisting she be allowed to go home from the hospital on time to see the first pitch, Gram passed away in her apartment just two hours later watching the Tigers. We think she knew it was coming and wanted to be home doing what she loved so much, watching Tiger Baseball.

—Jason Temple
Toledo, Ohio

***

I grew up on the North Side of Chicago—Cubs territory—but my dad, Bob, and his dad were Sox fans, and that's how we were raised. We were *big* fans of the Sox; going to games was something we always did as a family, so of course I have lots of wonderful memories.

In 2005, when the White Sox made the playoffs, I was living in Arizona with my now wife, Julie. We got tickets for the two American League Division Series games versus Boston to be played in Chicago. I went to the first with my dad, a 14-2 destruction of the Red by the White Sox. For game two, Dad and I went with my sister Michelle and her boyfriend, Andrew. The Sox swept the series, their first post-season series win since 1917, and then went on to beat the Angels to advance to a World Series showdown against the Astros.

Back to Chicago: Julie and I headed for the World Series, game one, with my mom Lou Ann, and dad. On the train to the game, Dad was in some pain; he thought it was kidney stones but insisted on going to the game. The Sox won, and dad was so excited that he started chanting "Sweep!"

ROBERT AND GREGG

On the way home, he was again clearly in agony, but nothing was going to get in the way of watching his Sox, and the whole family watched game two on television. Back in Arizona, my friends and I watched game three on television. At some point we decided to drink a shot after every inning; this turned out to be a bad decision, as it became the longest Series game in history with respect to time and tied for the longest in terms of innings.

The next day, I got the call no one ever wants to get. Mom told me that Dad had gone to the doctor and was diagnosed with stage three pancreatic cancer. He was given one month to live. I immediately flew to Chicago to be with him, which of course included watching the series from his hospital room. Dad was so happy about the Sox that he even wrote a song about their hoped for, and then realized, championship. On October 26, the Sox completed a sweep of the Astros. A few days later, I went to the championship parade as Dad was moved to a bigger room for chemotherapy treatment. Just a couple of days after that, on Halloween, Dad passed away. My dad, a doctor, was way too young, and this was much too sudden. We were so close, sharing so many things, particularly our love of the White Sox. We were all so grateful that he lived long enough to see his cherished team win the series.

As it happened, the organization was replacing the seats at Cellular Field after the season. I contacted someone, and we were able to get the actual seats that Mom and Dad sat in for that first game. I have them in my home. We were able to spread his ashes on the warning track. Every year on October 31, we set off balloons towards heaven. Julie's and my kids, all boys, didn't have a chance to know their grandpa, but of course we tell them stories, set off those balloons, and make sure they're rabid White Sox fans.

RYDER. AYDEN. AARON. ALYSSA

—Gregg Levine
Phoenix, Arizona

***

Baseball has always been a family affair for me. My brother Joel played baseball through high school. I played competitive level fast pitch soft-ball. When we weren't playing, you could find us in front of the TV or at the stadium. My grandma has been an avid Rockies fan for as long as I can remember and passed that on to my mom, Betty. I got my love of the Rockies from them. My dad, Herb, was born and raised in a Chicago suburb and is a big Chicago sports fan. Joel took after dad and grew up loving Chicago teams. Dad prefers the White Sox, but they don't come to Colorado regularly so every summer we go to one game as a family when the Cubs are in town.

Dad always manages to get tickets in a Cubs section. One year, Mom and I stuck out like sore thumbs in our purple and black in a sea of blue. I was 20 at the time, fair game to the hecklers in blue. The game was a back and forth battle. The Rockies were winning and then the Cubs went on a roll and made a comeback. As a Rockies fan, I was used to seeing them blow leads, and ready to accept defeat. Cubs fans around us started to get louder and louder, Dad and Joel included. Houston Street entered the game in the ninth and threw a perfect inning. That was when true magic was ready to happen. The Rockies sent Carlos Gonzalez to the plate in the bottom of the ninth with the game tied. He was 3-3, a homerun shy of the cycle. I turned to Joel, whose favorite Rockie to this day is Car- Go, and said something along the lines of, "I hope your favorite Rockie hits one out of the park to beat your favorite team." Soon after, Car-Go unloaded on a pitch for a walk-off homerun to complete the cycle. To this day I have never seen a ball hit so far at Coors Field. The ball landed in the third deck where the Rooftop is now located.

The whole family remembers this moment. Mom and I might have been totally outnumbered in our section; in the end we got the last laugh, in our purple and black. Joel and Dad couldn't even be too mad since we witnessed a cycle, something none of us had seen before.

—Kristi Small
Greely, Colorado

***

Baseball, fathers, and sons: It is nothing philosophical or existential, just one of life's opportunities to share time and create memories. I'm lucky enough to be on both sides of the relationship, with stories about the love young boys have for baseball, and shared experiences and perspectives with their dads.

I grew up on Long Island with a dad who had no real rooting interest in either New York team. Shea Stadium, the home of the Amazin' Mets, was an easier destination than Yankee Stadium. I lived and died for sports, as did my older brother, Eric. We loved playing, devouring box scores, and especially going to games, which we did a few times a year. If going to one game was great, a doubleheader was ecstasy. In the sixties, the Mets hosted a yearly Banner Day doubleheader; two years in a row we convinced Dad to take us to this event, each time against the Houston Colt 45s. We were in heaven; Dad, not a patient man to begin with, had trouble sitting through one game, and went crazy sitting through two, strung out with between-game activities, fans parading around the field carrying bed sheets painted with clever sayings like "Tommy and Billy of Plainview love watching Hot Rod Kanehl MOTOR around the bases."

Thirty-six years later, I took my son Josh to his first Major League game, on an outing with his Little League team. Tickets in the nosebleeds, five-year olds more concerned with hot dogs, cracker jacks, and cotton candy than the little ants running around hundreds of feet below in the Giants new AT&T Park. By the fourth inning, these kids had eaten as much as they could handle. Needing a new distraction, off they went to play in the mini ball field in the left field pavilion.

"Josh, do you want to go?" (No response) "Josh do you want to go with your friends?"

"No, I wanna watch the game." (A response given without taking his gaze off the field for an instant.)

"Josh, all of your friends are going." (No response).

We stayed in our seats and watched the rest of the game.

—Kevin Gray
San Rafael, California

(It took years for me to realize that cousins Josh and Rachel had the same first experience of total rapture at their first games.)

***

It was Memorial Day 1962, and I was a teenager still in high school. The Mets were playing the LA Dodgers in a doubleheader in the Polo Grounds. It was before they built Shea Stadium for the Mets, and it was the first time the Dodgers had come back to New York after moving west. My father took me to the game. Dad was legally blind, and had a terrible time seeing anything. We got seats in left field; it was a hot day, and the place was sold out. In the sixth inning of the second game, the Dodgers got runners on first and second, with nobody out after singles by Murray Wills and Jr. Gilliam. Willie Davis hit a liner to Elio Chacon at short; he caught it and threw to Charlie Neal at second to double off Wills, and Neal threw it to Gil Hodges at first to double off Gilliam. Triple play. The crowd went nuts. The awful Mets had done that.

When the noise died down, my father said, "Lowelly, what just happened?" "There was a triple play, Dad." He looked happy.

—Lowell Cohn, former sports columnist, *Santa Rosa Press Democrat*
Oakland, California

***

My grandpa was my hero. He was a tough-as-nails veteran and he never took any shit from anyone, but he loved his grandkids so much. My family is full of bubbly, artsy, happy people, who I love, but I don't always relate to well. Grandpa was another story. We shared a common love of all my favorite things: family, barbequing, and most of all, *baseball*.

My family visited Grandpa in Utah every summer from the time I was a little girl until he passed away when I turned eighteen. I never went to a ball game with him; there was no major league team near where he lived. My most vivid memories of him involve him sitting in the kitchen next to his mini-fridge that had a little radio on top of it. Inside the fridge was his beer; next to him on the table was his dip spit cup. He could sit forever listening to games, grumbling to himself when his team wasn't doing well. I don't even know if he had *a* team, one he listened to; it didn't matter. I loved to sit at the table with him, listening to those games. He was a man of few words, but I cherished those times. I loved Grandpa.

I miss him so much and am sad my kids will never meet him. Sometimes people ask me, "Where the hell did your love of baseball come from?", especially if they know my family. I happily tell them about my kick-ass Grandpa, and how I'm so proud to have inherited that love from him.

—Sheree Barrios
Houston, Texas

***

My mother, a British War Bride and my dad, an American soldier from Chicago, met in a Liverpool blackout in 1944 and called Chicago home after the war. Unlike so many women of her time, Mom became a baseball fan. While others watched soap operas, she tuned in to WGN Channel 9 to watch Jack Brickhouse call Cubs games. Sadly, Mom never saw a Cubs World Series, having arrived in the United States in 1946, the year after the Cubs' last pennant. I inherited my love of baseball and the Cubs from Mom.

My first game, at Wrigley Field, was on August 14, 1953, when I was seven years old. Watching on TV since I was four, the excitement of seeing them play in person was almost too much. When we got to the ballpark (*not* stadium!), I was struck by two things: how really big it was, and that it was in color; all my previous images, on TV and in sports pages, were in black and white. On October 13, 2015, in Chicago for a family visit planned long before any hint of a Cubs' playoff possibility, I got a ticket for the fourth game. To be in Wrigley for a game in October was mind-blowing. Who in Cub-dom would expect an RBI single by pitcher Jason Hammel? When Javy Baez came up, I said to the guy next to me, "If he hits one, this place'll explode." He did. It did. Schwarber hit his monster homer over the new right field scoreboard! The Cubs beat the Cards 6-4, the first time in sixty-five years of fandom that I personally attended a Cubs post-season series victory. I was as proud of the fans as I was of the team and its effort. We hung around for over an hour. On the walk to the car, everyone sang "Go, Cubs, Go!" There was no rowdiness typical of sports celebrations these days.

Mom was alive for the 2016 season, turning a healthy ninety-eight on July 3. Her health began to slide in mid-September, and she passed away on October 24, the day before the World Series began. She knew they had won the National League pennant, and we figure she and Dad had sky boxes for all seven games. The next week was a double roller-coaster of emotions. We watched the seventh game on TV with friends and family, including my granddaughter, Rebecca. Real Cubs fans are optimists, but realists; the mood in the house ebbed and flowed, as the game did. In the top of the tenth, just before Schwarber's leadoff single, Rebecca said, "I just got a message from GG [great-grandma], and it's a *good* one!" They went on to score two runs. It mattered not that the Indians came back with one in the bottom of the tenth, or that Bryant slipped as he threw over to first for the final out. Nothing could get in the way of the Cubs' destiny. In Jack Brickhouse's and Harry Caray's immortal words: Hey Hey! Cubs win! Holy cow!

My daughter Michelle sent me a post three and a half months later: The Cubs haven't won the World Series in 108 . . . *days*!

—Lou Harris
San Mateo, California

***

I was born into a baseball family and have my dad to thank for everything. While my mom is a huge fan in her own right, it was really Dad who turned us, including my sister Rachel, into a baseball family. Whether going to Giants games at Candlestick Park, and then Pac Bell Park (aka SBC Park, aka AT&T Park, now Oracle Park), avoiding the freezing nights at Candlestick and watching games at home, going to baseball card stores, talking baseball over meals, arguing about favorite players, playing Little League, or watching Dad play softball and my serving as the bat boy, baseball has always been an integral part of our family dynamic.

My favorite team has always been the Giants. Growing up in San Francisco, it's pretty easy to understand why that is, but even before I knew why I should like them, they were my team. I liked them because of Dad (even though he then had a deep-rooted allegiance to the Mets, he knew which team *I* should root for). It's the same reason I'm also a Red Sox fan (and thanks for that, as well; between the Sox and Giants, it's been a hell of a run the last thirteen years!). In fact, I've taken a number of cues from Dad over the years; it's why I'll always have a soft spot for the Phoenix Suns, and why my favorite number to this day is seven (Mickey Mantle's number).

Throughout the ups, downs, lulls, and excitements in our relationship, baseball has been a steady constant we can always talk about. We've had too many memories and experiences to share in one story, ranging from the exciting (countless Barry Bonds milestone homeruns) to the disappointing (I was at game three of the 2002 World Series, the Giants first Series game at the new stadium, their first since 1989, and, of course, the only home game they lost in that series) to the mundane (I still remember him buying me my first beer at a Giants game after I turned twenty-one, and though not much of a drinker himself, he loved that) to the frustrating (when the all-star game was in SF in 2007, he drove all over the city to make sure I could get tickets to as many of the events as possible, including the Futures Game, the Home Run Derby, and the actual game with Rachel, using Mom and Dad's tickets). When I was twelve, Dad let me skip school to go to the very last Giants game at Candlestick. How cool is that?! I still have the ticket and pack of tissues they handed out "to wipe away the tears at the last game at the Stick." He even comes to DC every miserable, hot, and humid summer to take me to see the Giants play the Nationals.

Baseball has had such a huge impact on my life, and I owe it all to my dad. Thanks, Dad, I love you.

—David A. Gray
Washington, DC

(Yep, "Dad" is me. I am happy and humbled. What dad wouldn't long to see those words?)

***

My story is a simple one, about my family's love of baseball. I was born and raised in the Cleveland area, and lived there until I was thirty. Both my parents' families were big baseball families; they each had six siblings, many of whom also had large families with almost everyone growing up in the area. Baseball was a common link for all of us; for example, we would often play pickup baseball games at family picnics. But after moving away from Cleveland, I lost touch with most of the family, with few exceptions. My wife Ellen's family are also big baseball fans, from her parents to sisters to cousins.

Ellen and I raised a family with two children, a boy and a girl. I believe the love of baseball must be in our genes. Our son is a great athlete, and somehow baseball rose to the top as his favorite sport. He probably would have been a high draft pick in his high school senior season, but a stress fracture in his right ulna bone scuttled that, though only for a short period of time. He was fortunate to have a backup plan, a baseball scholarship to a great academic as well as baseball school. He spent three years in college, getting drafted in the fourth round of the draft after his junior year.

His time in the minors had its ups and downs; he didn't fly through the farm system. Each season he seemed to start out well, getting a promotion to the next level, where he didn't initially have success. This was the story for three years after his initial season; stay at the same level he finished at, get promoted, and then stumble. That changed, only slowly. One year, at the July 31 Major League Baseball trade deadline, he gave us a call. Ellen and I answered the phone at the same time; I said go ahead and talk to Mom, then I'll take it from there. He said "No! I need to talk to you both. I just got traded to the Indians!" Can you imagine what went through my mind at that moment? Joy, shock, amazement that he would now be part of my favorite team's organization! I called my brother, who lives in Germany, to tell him the news. When he heard it, he dropped his phone, screaming with joy. That trade re-opened the door with relatives I hadn't been in contact with for years.

His time in the minors with Cleveland was similar to his earlier seasons. He had big league call-ups in a couple of seasons but didn't stick. Things clicked the third time around, and he was there to stay. During these years, my circle of family and friends with whom I had lost touch continued to grow as his success grew. It is simply mind-boggling to me how much the love of baseball has brought us all back together.

By the way, my son is Corey Kluber, two-time Cy Young Award winner for the Cleveland Indians! Do I have a favorite moment from his career? At this point it is hard to choose. If pushed, I would say game one of the 2016 World Series, where he was the starting pitcher at home for the Indians, striking out eight of the first nine outs, and going on to win the game 6-0. Sitting in the stands, I couldn't help but think Ellen and my parents, and all of our other relatives who have passed, were watching the game from above.

—Jim Kluber
Centerville, Massachusetts

***

In the sweltering heat of a southern summer, my grandparents, Burl and Mary Alice, would load the Mercury with all that was needed for a month or so at the beach house. My grandfather had named the house Costalota. I was buried in the back seat with a box that contained neither food nor water, but the number one essential item to my grandmother: radios, four of them, just in case, each older than the last. There were coat hangers to ensure reception from Atlanta. The car was unpacked, and shrimp was boiled and cooling in the old monitor refrigerator, along with the sweet tea.

The sleeping porch offered the coolest place to enjoy the new hammocks. That was fortunate, as it was the best place to pick up Braves baseball. If a game went into extra innings, we would tag team it. Grandmom slept, and I listened, tapping out every fifteen minutes. My grandfather never listened with us, yet he had a vested interest in the outcome. When the Braves lost, Mary Alice took it hard. Burl knew that until the next Atlanta win, he was on his own. He came to call dinner "cream of lunch."

Flash forward fifty years, and I have the best apps, and all of the big screen baseball any fan could ask for. I would trade it all for one more night in a hammock listening to Ernie Johnson utter the words, "Welcome to the Braves Radio Network," as my grandmother tats lace and offers the team her baseball expertise and colorful insights. I am sure the Braves miss her guidance, and that sweet southern lilt admonishing the manager (I think his name was "Fool") to let "that Black man [Hank Aaron] bat." So many things have changed, most for the best, but I would still rather listen than watch.

Thanks, Mary Alice.

—Viki Short
Southern California

***

It was May 10, 1967, and I was a fifth grader at Albert Schweitzer Elementary School in Anaheim, California. It was time for the annual father-son outing held by the school. That year, we were going to see the California Angels play the Yankees at Angels Stadium, and we had the chance to see Mickey Mantle in person. First, there was a dinner at the school. My brother and I were there, as were all of our friends with their fathers. But my dad wasn't there. We kept looking back at the entrance doors, thinking he'd walk in any moment. Everyone had their dinner finished, and there we were, still waiting for Dad.

The principal announced that it was time to load up on the school buses and head to the stadium. My brother was pretty calm, but the anxiety of waiting for Dad was getting to me, and I started tearing up, thinking he wasn't going to make the trip with us. As everyone started to get up from their seats, the entrance door opened, and in stepped Dad. I proudly turned around and said to my friends, with a grin from ear to ear, "There's my dad." He was running late because of traffic.

We were excited to see Mantle yet hoped to see the Angels beat the Yankees. But what will always stick out in my mind is seeing my dad walk through those cafeteria doors. My hero was not a professional sports figure. I'm a sixty-year-old man now, and my father passed away when I was only twenty-five, but he was—and will always be—my hero. It was one of the best days of my entire life.

—Kelly Taylor
Altoona, Iowa

***

I was six or seven years old and my mother took my brother Tom and me to a Red Sox game at Fenway. It was my first game, I believe 1970. Many kids are taught baseball by their fathers; mine was a musician and college professor who didn't care about baseball. He was brilliant, but not very coordinated. My mother, however, was a star athlete. While in the army as a Captain she played baseball for her various post teams. She was awesome! One article in the base paper read that they all hoped Emily Carpenter would be off the injured list for the big game because, the star player, "she hits like Babe Ruth and fields like Pee Wee Reese." Mom taught me how to throw, catch, and hit. These skills in turn helped me learn teamwork, how to make friends, sportsmanship, and leadership.

Going to Fenway was epic, seeing the Green Monster, seeing a live game. I couldn't believe I was actually there! We were all Boston fans in my family; my brother and I were born in Worchester. Tom's favorite player was Carl Yastrzemski; mine was Rico Petrocelli. We are a little bit competitive. Yaz had a good day, but Rico was the star, hitting a grand slam. I had a good day too…I had bragging rights over my brother on the long ride home!

My mother is gone now…what I would give to play one more game of catch with her.

— Andrew Carpenter
Rochester, New York

LET'S BEAT THE TRAFFIC

When I was a kid, my dad always wanted to leave early to beat the traffic, beat the crowds. Yankees games, Mets games, Knicks games. If I went to a concert with Dad, we were gone before the first encore. At a movie, we'd be out long before the credits started rolling. At High Holy Day services, our yarmulkes were in our pockets long before the final amen (I think I'm just kidding about those last three, but I'm not really sure). It was annoying, to say the least. I was never aware that I missed anything momentous by leaving early, but of course with the absence of information that is available every second today, it wasn't as easy to know. I swore I would never be the guy who would make his family leave a game early (and I say that as if I'm the one to actually make any *decisions in this house full of strong individuals), and with four exceptions, both for great reasons and with complete consensus, that has been the case. Following are stories of folks who left early, and shouldn't have, and stories of those who perhaps should have left . . . and were glad they didn't. In two cases, the writers never even got to the games they so desperately wanted to attend. I guess I could have named this chapter in honor of the classic Clash song, "Should I Stay or Should I Go?"*

***

I once witnessed history. I wasn't at the Battle of Waterloo. I missed the Crusades. But I did see Reggie Jackson play that epic sixth game of the 1977 World Series at Yankee Stadium. Well, almost.

Here's what happened: When I was nine, Dad somehow scored tickets to the big game. My parents were no sports fans, but they wanted to give me an All-American childhood, so once in a while they'd suck it up and take me to the stadium. So, there I was, with my mitt on my left hand, my Yankees yearbook on my lap, gloriously giddy.

My hero Reggie steps up to the plate in the fourth inning, and bam, hits a home run. Sails it over the right field wall. Awesome. The very next inning, crack! Another home run. Unbelievable. I'm in heaven. Two home runs! And then—Dad decided it was time to leave and beat the traffic. We wouldn't want to be jammed into a subway with all the other people, right?

"But Dad, what if Reggie hits another home run?"

"Oh, he won't," Dad assured me, as he tugged me out of the packed stands.

We were on the subway platform when we heard it, a stadium-shaking roar from the crowd. A roar like I'd never heard before. Reggie had hit his third home run. History had been made. People would be talking about that homer forever. And I would not be speaking to Dad for several days. Though we did have the subway all to ourselves, which was nice.

My attendance at two-thirds of this historical event was in one sense disappointing—like leaving Iwo Jima right before the flag was planted. But it did make me think that I made an impact, ever so slight, on the history. If I hadn't been cheering so dutifully in the stands, Reggie might not have hit those two home runs. The third, I can't take credit for, as we know. [1]

—AJ Jacobs, author of *The Know-It-All*
(passage used with the author's permission)
New York, New York

(Read this book. It is hilarious and great, as are all his works.)

***

My dad took me to my first baseball game in 1937 or 1938. I was eight or nine years old, and I was so excited that I ran around the neighborhood

---

[1] Jacobs, A.J., *The Know-It-All,* (New York, Simon and Shuster, 2004), pp.156-157

telling all my friends that I was going to Yankee Stadium. The Yankees were playing the Washington Senators, and the game wasn't going well for the home team. By the bottom of the ninth inning, the New Yorkers were losing by three runs. Finally, the Yankees loaded the bases, and with two outs, the great catcher Bill Dickey was coming to the plate. The crowd was going wild; after all, Dickey was not averse to coming through with a clutch hit with men on base.

As he approached the batter's box, my father announced that we had to leave if we were to beat the traffic. Begging was useless, and so we left. Of course, we avoided the traffic of the parking lot. My father seemed proud of his decision to leave before the rush. As for me, I sat in the front seat sulking.

I was to feel even worse as we neared home. My friends were in the street excitedly waiting for me. As it turned out, Bill Dickey had hit a grand slam home run, clearing the bases, and the Yankees beat the Senators by one run. Boy was I upset with my father. The other thing that I never forgot about that day was that it was the only time I ever saw Lou Gehrig play.

—Ivan Kusinitz
Melbourne Beach, Florida

***

My team, the Tampa Bay Devil Rays, was playing the New York Yankees on the final day of the 2011 season. The Rays and the Boston Red Sox were tied for the division title. The Yankees were winning 7-0 in the sixth or seventh inning, and Wendy (then girlfriend, now wife) said to me, "Maybe we ought to go home. I'm really discouraged, and we can beat the traffic." I thought about it for a few seconds, and then thought better of it. "Let's hang in a little longer," I said. We ended up tying the game 7-7, and then Evan Longoria hit a home run in the bottom of the ninth to win it. A few minutes later Boston lost to the Orioles, when ex-Ray Carl Crawford, playing left field for the Red Sox, dropped a line drive that let the winning run score for Baltimore. In a matter of a couple of minutes, the Rays were

American League Eastern Division champions, and we celebrated with the team at "The Trop" for the remainder of the evening. Even today, we say to ourselves, "Imagine if we had left?"

—Peter Golenbock, author of *The Bronx Zoo*
St. Petersburg, Florida

(In Madison Bumgarner's great rookie with the San Francisco Giants— straight through to the World Series—he pitched one real dog. I was there. By the second inning, the Reds had hammered him and the Giants to an 11-0 deficit. People streamed out of the park earlier than any time I can ever recall. It never occurred to us to leave. We'd paid for a game, and were going to stay, at least, unless we became violently ill, or extraordinarily bad weather forced us to flee. The Giants did not win that game, but they closed it to 11-10. Had we left, we would have missed one hell of an exciting game.)

***

My first experience at a baseball came at Shea Stadium in September 1969, when I was seven years old. The Mets were playing the St. Louis Cardinals. Uncle Ed, a Flushing native, who was a doctor, was notorious for leaving early so he wouldn't hit traffic. Years later, when I looked up the game for nostalgia purposes, I discovered that the game had been on September 24—the day the Mets clinched their first pennant against the Cards. I howled when I realized it. A few years ago, after he passed away, the next game I attended with my sons, Tony and Matthew, was Opening Day for the Pittsburgh Pirates. We got up and left in the seventh inning in his honor.

—Dave Finoli, author of *Classic Burgh: The Greatest 50 Games in Pittsburgh Collegiate History*
Monroeville, Pennsylvania

***

I'm a lifelong Milwaukee baseball fan; first, the Braves, now, the Brewers. I took my family to a Tigers-Brewers game when Sparky Anderson managed the Tigers. Brewers' players included Robin Yount and Michael Young. Our kids, Faye and Marc, were young; Marc, now an avid baseball fan as well, was four or five. At that time, I was the only fan in the family, and essentially dragged them on a family outing, hoping for a great time that we could repeat. Like any young kid not into the game, Marc was very fussy, soothed only by the next food treat. He loved the red licorice ropes, so I bought him one every time he whined about going home. The game hit a dreadfully long "intermission," when Sparky, the umpires, and Brewers' manager, Tom Treblehorn, conferred for the longest time, with the fans not having the faintest idea about the matter. As the discussion dragged on, Marc got fussier and wanted to go, a sentiment with which my wife Debbie agreed. However, I'd never left a ballgame before it was over, regardless of the score, including this one, in which the Tigers had a seemingly insurmountable lead in the early innings. (We later learned Sparky was objecting to an error on the lineup card that Treblehorn submitted, listing either Young or Youn*t* twice, rather than correctly identifying each of them.) Marc grew more insistent about leaving, progressing from whining to coughing. Debbie became more insistent that it was time to go. I was even more adamant that we stay until the end. By then, Marc had agitated himself to the point where he vomited the day's treats onto the woman next to him. Someone across the aisle said he was getting the paramedics on duty, because he appeared to be vomiting blood, but I explained that it was only the red licorice. We had no choice but to go, tail between my legs, really upset about leaving, even under those circumstances. Of course, as soon as we left, Marc calmed down, acting like the happiest guy in the world. I was fuming, both for having left early, and anticipating Debbie doing the I-told-you-so thing. She remained silent, knowing I was upset. Not a word was spoken during the ride home, as I continued to fume, grasping the steering wheel so hard I thought it might crumble under my grip. As we pulled into the driveway, I turned on the radio to hear Bob Uecker announce that the Brewers had just completed the greatest comeback in their history in the bottom of the ninth. Debbie hustled the kids into the house before I imploded, and I stayed in the car long enough to go back into the house in only a bad mood, rather than a destructive one.

—Dean Zemel
Milwaukee, Wisconsin

***

One windy, chilly night at the 'Stick, in 1973, when I was thirteen, the Giants were playing the Pirates, and getting clobbered. Going into the eighth inning, with the score 7-1, my father leaned over and told me he wanted to leave to get a jump on traffic. I almost yelled at him, telling him, "*No way*! We have to stay. It's our Giants. They can still do it." A huge man behind us said, "You tell him, son," and my dad gave in and stayed. The Giants then made one of their amazing comebacks, with a string of hits and walks, and a grand slam by little-known Chris Arnold, bringing the score to 7-5. Four batters later, Bobby Bonds hit a bases-loaded triple to clear the bases and win the game. And *that* is why you don't leave a game early.

—Joe Diehl
New Orleans, Louisiana

***

My fondest childhood memories took place at the ballpark and around baseball. Elation came in 1969, with the arrival of the Montreal Expos. My family went most weekends, as it was (then) an affordable activity *and* a family passion. At a Dodgers game on my eleventh birthday, seeking autographs, as always, I was talking to Don Sutton, who asked if there was a special reason for me being at the yard. When I told him it was my birthday outing, he told me that since it was my special day, if there was any autograph I wanted, he would bring his teammate over to chat and sign for me. In a heartbeat, I was shooting the breeze with Willie Davis, Wes

Parker, and Ted Sizemore. Sutton then went to the clubhouse and brought me back some sugarless bazooka gum. I was in seventh heaven.

In September 1972, the Expos played a twi-night doubleheader against the Mets. I tried to broker a deal with my mother, asking her to let me go, with a promise I'd leave right after the first game. She said, "Knowing you, that will be unlikely. It is a school night, after all." In that first game, Bill Stoneman pitched the second no-no of his career. Mom felt awful the next day, saying, "Aaach, I should have let you go."

—Ian Abugov
Montreal, Canada

***

It was a bone-chilling only-at-Candlestick weeknight game in 1989, with the Giants playing the Reds. By the ninth inning, there were only about two thousand fans left in the stands, and the game went extra innings. By the top of the fifteenth, about five hundred of us remained. We all moved down to sit by the field, and it felt like being at an American Legion game. The Reds scored two runs, and more people left. It was around twelve thirty in the morning, on a Tuesday night; it was freezing. But it was summer, and we were in college, so we stayed for the bottom of the inning. The Giants pieced together a few singles and scored a run; with runners on second and third, up stepped Brett Butler. He proceeded to line a single to center, and the winning runs motored around. The approximately 250 remaining fans went crazy! I turned to the person sitting behind me to high five him, and I ended up getting hugged by a fan who looked and smelled like a homeless guy. I held on to that guy like my life depended on it. To me, that's what Candlestick was about. It brought people together in a spirit of camaraderie.

—Dan Schmid
San Francisco, California

***

The Montreal Expos came into our city and hearts in 1969. I still have memories of those days at Jarry Park. By the late seventies, they had moved to Olympic Stadium, and baseball was flourishing in La Belle Province. I watched as they fell short in both 1979 and 1980. No baseball fan in Montreal will ever forget the heartbreak of Blue Monday in '81, or the excitement in '82, with Montreal the center of attention, as the all-star game made its first appearance north of the border. However, having witnessed so many exciting moments, none will ever compare to that evening on August 23, 1989, when the Dodgers were in town to play Nos Amours. I headed to the stadium with my brother to catch the game, on this the day of my twenty-third birthday. Flamboyant Pasqual Perez took the mound to face off against Orel Hershiser. They threw zeroes across the board through seven innings. Even with both starters out of the game, the zeroes kept coming. And coming, they did.

In the top of the eleventh inning, Dodger manager Tommy Lasorda complained that Expos' mascot Youppi was distracting his team atop the dugout and had him ejected. It finally appeared over in the sixteenth frame, until an appeal play at third ruled that Larry Walker left early on a sacrifice fly, so on it went. Depending on public transport to get home, I had to leave before this nail-biter was over. As I walked through the door and turned on the television set, I was thrilled to see the game heading into the twenty-second. I quickly made a sandwich and settled down, only to watch Dennis Martinez give up a home run to Rick Dempsey. The Expos managed a baserunner in the bottom of the inning, but it came to an end as Rex Hudler was caught stealing. A 1-0 loss in twenty-two innings. How I had hoped that on this twenty-third day of August, on my twenty-third birthday, this game would have gone on for just one more inning. It will always remain the game I will never forget.

—John Rotari
Montreal, Quebec

***

In 1974, I went with my family to see my Reds play the Atlanta Braves on the last day of the season in Atlanta. Both teams were out of contention, and many of the stars were not in the game. But Henry Aaron played! He had broken the home run record earlier in the year, passing Ruth's 714 life-time homers. During the year, he had announced that he would return to Milwaukee (where he started his career) for the following season. So, this was known to be his last game as a Brave.

In the late innings, my mom was complaining about the cold night air, and we left the park. As we were walking to the car, we heard a loud roar from inside Fulton County Stadium. Once we were inside the car and had the radio turned on, it became clear what had happened. Aaron had homered in his last game as a Brave. I had, of course, missed it.

In later years, Mom would often recall causing us to miss Aaron's "famous home run." This caused quite a stir, because people assumed she meant number 715—an historic event! It was, in fact, number 733. You know what? I miss my mom, who died in 2007, more than I ever missed that home run.

—Mark Stuart
Ashland, Tennessee

***

My dad was an older dad, and he hated when guys he worked with would say, "Wish I did this," or "Should have done that." So, in 1980, during a work shut down, we took off on a month trip across the United States—Buffalo to Disneyland—through the northern states, with the return trip through the South. With baseball schedules in hand, we made several stops along the way. We stopped in St. Louis to see the Cardinals, with the Wizard of Oz; we visited the American League Champs, Kansas City, and saw the players on my baseball cards, Brett, McCrae, Aikens, and Quiz. A schedule change forced us to miss a game in Oakland, so we headed to

Candlestick on June 27, 1980, with Mom complaining about everything. She was sick of Dad and me talking baseball every day, and wanted to leave San Francisco, continuing to complain as we waited for the ticket office to open on a cold, windy evening. Dad believed the saying "happy wife, happy life" applied, so we skipped the game and started towards Anaheim.

We found a hotel, who knows where, and turned the TV on to see how the Giants game had turned out, figuring we should at least see what we had missed. WTF! Jerry Reuss pitched a *no-hitter*, allowing only one base runner in the first inning! *Mother of God*, how did we miss a *no-hitter*? A person can go their whole life and never be at one. It was a very grumpy day and story. We got over it; the vacation was a lot fun, although every so often we would talk about "that game we missed." We saw the Rangers play the Indians, and for the last game of the trip, the Houston Astros versus the to-be 1980 World Series Champion Phillies at the Astrodome. The game had some of the greatest names in baseball: Nolan Ryan, Joe Morgan, McBride, Rose, and Bowa.

On June 27, 2013, thirty-three years to the day of that missed no-hitter, my family took our annual summer drive back to our hometown to visit Mom. Friends got tickets to a Batavia Muckdog/Aberdeen Ironbirds, New York/Penn League short season. We sat next to the Aberdeen dugout and talked with the coach. In the eighth inning, I realized that the kid from Batavia had a no-hitter going into the ninth. Had the planets aligned on this "anniversary," and was my dad looking down on us? The pitcher gave up a double with one out in the ninth. The fates will never allow you joy.

—John Aiken
Bel Air, Maryland

***

I was always a left field bleacher bum until one 1969 summer day, shortly before I would leave home for college. Someone gave me two box seats by the Cubs dugout, and I brought a girl, my senior prom date. I had never brought a girl to Wrigley. It was August 19, seventy-six degrees, wind blowing straight in over the left field wall. Over forty-one thousand jammed Wrigley to see the first place Cubs take on the Braves, Kenny Holtzman versus knuckle-balling Phil Niekro. Ron Santo hit a three-run homer under the wind in the first inning to give the Cubs a 3-0 lead. Holtzman was throwing nothing but fast balls; about the sixth, I was plotting an early exit to beat the crowd, when I realized the Braves did not have a hit. I couldn't leave. In the seventh, Hank Aaron hit a towering shot to left, out over Waveland Avenue; the wind pushed it back in, and Billy Williams caught it in the vines. A miracle! (Aaron later called it the hardest hit ball in his life that wasn't a home run.) In the top of the ninth, the crowd was in frenzy. Holtzman had walked three and no K's (strikeouts), but still no hits for the Braves. The top of the order was coming up: Felipe Alou, Felix Milan, and the Hammer himself, still miffed about the ball he hit earlier.

Two quick outs, and up came Aaron, with Rico Carty on deck. The count went full; after a foul ball, Aaron hit a ground ball to second baseman Glen Beckert's right. Beckert's knees almost buckled; he must have been so nervous. Somehow, he fielded it, threw to Ernie . . . and it was done! A no-hitter for Holtzman, and Wrigley exploded with joy! A lifetime memory for me, my date, and forty-one thousand other ecstatic Cub fans. We were so glad we didn't leave early!

The win put the Cubs up eight games, with only forty to go. They finished fifteen out of twenty-five, and the rest is history. It was the year of the Miracle Mets.

—Bill Hedberg
Ponte Vedra Beach, Florida

***

(Remember the song by the Clash song I mentioned earlier? Doug's stories embody this, once leaving when he shouldn't have, and once perhaps staying a little too long)

I went with my brother to see the 2016 Diamondbacks Opening Day. He was all excited— "Wait till you see Zack Greinke pitch"—describing him as the best pitcher around, a coup for the D'backs to get him. We hauled on up to our seats in the thirtieth row of the upper deck. The Fitbit on my wrist told me we had traveled four flights of stairs before we perched ourselves parallel to the row and began our lateral move to seats thirteen and fourteen, smack behind home plate, slightly lightheaded from our climb, but great seats in which to view the great Greinke's precision.

The seats started to fill in; the smell of new shirts with Greinke's name, and the new team logo, was strong. Larry Fitzgerald threw out the first pitch, and Gold Gloves were presented to honor last year's fielding performances, including one to Greinke for his work with the Dodgers. There was a moving tribute to Joe Garagiola; finally, a cute kid appeared on the jumbo screen and said, "Play ball."

"Hey, brother," I said, "if the great Greinke is so awesome, why all the bat work by the Rockies?" In the third inning, the Rockies' bats came alive. Rookie Trevor Story hit two home runs. Who in the hell is Trevor Story? It had been reported that every pitch Greinke threw cost the Diamondbacks $10,000. Man, was that a painful and expensive pitch count.

We stayed all the way to a 10-5 loss. That is part of our heritage from a tight-assed family. The most interesting thing about the night was the record length of the game—four and a half hours. Wow. And our seats where so high up, neither of us had a desire for food, drink, or pee.

My dad was a stay-to-the-end guy. One time, my wife and I dragged the tribe to Cincinnati. The Reds were getting their asses handed to them, so we left. Sitting in a packed parking lot with all the other early departers, we saw a huge fireworks display. Of course, the Reds came back, and we missed the whole shebang; ironically, we got caught in the early traffic mess! Should have listened to Dad!

—Doug Kremer
Glendale, Arizona

***

On June 4, 1964, I was in sixth grade. My friend Randy Glezerman told me that a World War II buddy of his father, Bill Jackowski, whom Randy knew as "Uncle Bill," was going to be one of the umpires at the Dodgers-Phillies game. Randy thought there would be an extra ticket for me and said he would call me around dinner time to let me know. I came home, told my parents, and made everyone promise to stay off the phone until he called. Despite that, my older sister got on, and stayed on the phone, so that when Randy called to tell me I could come, all he got was a busy signal. Off he went to the game and watched Sandy Koufax pitch a no-hitter. Uncle Bill even took Randy to meet Koufax after the game. The next day at school, Randy gave me a ball that had been used during the game, which I still have. Randy got a ball signed by Koufax. Randy can't figure out why he didn't bike over to my house, since we lived so close, when he got the busy signal. I still hold a grudge against my sister.

—George Kalikman
San Francisco, California

***

In 1986, in the sixth game of the World Series, the Mets seemed like they were toast. My father left, but I was determined to see it to the end and was praying for a miracle. Then, in what seemed like slow motion, a miracle occurred, when, with men on base, Mookie Wilson's ground ball went through Buckner's legs. I don't think I've ever been that happy (except possibly when they won in '69, and the Saints' Super Bowl win).

—Dan Storper
New Orleans, Louisiana

(And that is how to meet both sides of this chapter in the same story, leaving when you should stay, and staying when you should go.)

***

In 1973, I was ten years old, and just becoming a big Indians fan. Unfortunately, my father did not care for sports at all, and to top it off, he hated driving and crowds. *The Cleveland Plain Dealer* newspaper then annually ran "Grandstand Managers," where you sent in an essay, or maybe just your name, I can't quite recall. If selected, you got free tickets to Grandstand Managers day. I got the tickets, and Dad reluctantly agreed to schlep me to the game. The White Sox beat us 15-4 (I have since attended hundreds of Indians games, but this is the only one whose score I remember). Dad complained a lot, and we left early. But I was smitten and have followed the Tribe through thick and (mostly) thin since.

Fast forward to 2006; I was very excited to get two free tickets to see the Indians versus Tampa Bay Rays; I planned to take my four-year-old son, and share a special day at the ballpark with him. As we neared Jacobs Field, the roar of the crowd, and all the familiar sights and sounds of baseball, filled the air. Daddy was very excited. But two seconds after we walked through the gates, Nathan said he wanted to go home. The loudness and stimulation annoyed him. We left after a few innings, as I did not want to torture him. Even a trip to the kids' play area did not help. Thankfully, Nathan does not remember any of this, and by 2008, came around. Like his dad, he's a fan of the Tribe. For me, this is truly a case of like father, like son!

—Craig Dorn
Cleveland, Ohio

***

I attended the game on September 6, 1996, when, one year to the day after Ripken broke the streak, Eddie Murray hit his five hundredth home run, a traditional milestone gateway to the Hall of Fame. Unfortunately, there were two rain delays that night. I was with my daughter Meg, and my two young grandchildren, Jake and Kyra, so by eleven thirty, we decided to leave. At a quarter to eleven, with us in the parking lot, Murray hit his home run, circling the confetti-filled stadium to a nine-minute standing ovation. I always vowed never to leave a game early, but the circumstances this time just dictated that it was time to go.

—Chuck Edson
Chevy Chase, Maryland

***

July 18, 1999 was Yogi Berra Day at Yankee Stadium. My wife was away for the weekend, and I decided to take my kids on their first trip there. My son Jordan had just turned seven, and my daughter Jenna was twelve. We arrived early and went to Monument Park. As we looked at the monuments, I explained to my son that Yankee greats were not buried there. The ceremonies for Yogi were touching, as George and Yogi finally made up, and Yogi was returned to the fold. David Cone was facing the Montreal Expos, and the game was quickly interrupted by a brief rain delay. By the time it started again, my son was reaching his limits and asking to go home. Montreal had not gotten a hit, and I told him that we would leave after the first hit. Inning after inning, no hits and no walks. The crowd grew excited, but my son was chanting, "We want a hit!" By the time of the final out, my son was fascinated by the excitement in the crowd.

—Bob Schultz
Silver Spring, Maryland

LOVE AND BASEBALL

Falling in love at a baseball game, or having that incredibly romantic moment, has eluded me. I have been to countless games with my wife of forty-one years, often on our anniversary, and certainly there have been many moments in which we were able to dovetail being in love at a game, or endure each other's craziness—and that's love, too. She arranged for the AT&T scoreboard to flash a happy sixtieth birthday greeting to me; I somehow managed to handle watching her, with our cousin Andi, down a nightmare in a glass, the Hrbek Bloody Mary, at the Twins stadium. Our family has shared so many great experiences at games, from San Francisco to Boston, New York to Arizona to Seattle, and if sitting in a park on a nice day or evening, and reveling in being with your wife and kids, everyone happy, isn't love, I don't know what is. But I never did have that cannon-firing, fireworks exploding, I've Just Seen a Face I Can't Forget (Beatles) moment. These folks did, with, of course, the exception or two.

***

My birthday is April 2, and on that day in 2009, I planned a birthday party at the San Francisco Giants' AT&T Park. I love baseball and did this to help distract me from waiting for a love, Josh, to return for rest and recreation from Iraq. We didn't know exactly when he would be back, but "ballpark," so to speak, was a few days after my birthday. Sure enough, about noon, I found out that the army was sending him back that very day. His flight kept getting delayed, and then his phone died. He knew I would be at the game, and he arrived smack dab in the middle of the party. He finally found me around the fifth inning. This was straight off three days of flying across the globe in his smelly ACU (uniform). I was dressed for a cold baseball game, so it was not exactly a romantic reunion. I'm sure going to a baseball game right then was the last thing he wanted to do.

We had spent less than ten days in each other's physical presence after meeting before he deployed. This R&R was a test and having the reunion at the ballpark was unexpected. I will always remember our awkward kiss outside the park. But it went well, quite well. Today, we are married with two kids.

—Hilary Jacobs Trout
Claremont, California

***

As either a senior in high school or freshman in college, Caroline and I went to a Yankee-Red Sox game one hot summer afternoon. This goes back before we really thought about our long-term future. We would both go to college near Boston, but that wasn't necessarily by design. Anyway, at this game, I recall that as we sat in the bleachers, a young boy, perhaps seven years old or so, started talking to us. At one point, he said, "Are you guys in love?" I remember that Caroline and I looked at each other, smiled, and told the kid some version of yes, but without really saying it. The fact is that game is etched in my memory as one of the places, and perhaps the first time, when I knew we would be together forever.

—Avi Rodin
London, England

***

In 1980, the Phillies finally got into the World Series. My then-husband managed to get tickets to one of the home games, but I turned down his offer to take me to the game; I already had plans for a business/adultery trip with a coworker. I told him to take a friend in my place. The coworker and I made the trip, checked into a hotel, and during a lull in the proceedings, he turned on the TV to see how the game was going. The screen immediately filled with a tight shot of my husband, jumping out of his seat behind the Phils' dugout, catching a fly ball, and triumphantly holding it up for the camera. This could only be a message from the universe, aimed directly at me.

When I returned home, my torment only increased as my husband showed off his game ball. I had to admire all the signatures he'd gotten on it, and then let him display it in a prominent place, so I had to see it every day. However, the message didn't take. That was my then-husband; I now have a different one, the coworker. To quote Hall-of-Famer Jane Eyre, "Reader, I married him."

—M.
Philadelphia, Pennsylvania

***

Before 1993, I had little understanding of baseball, a strange sport played by beer-bellied Americans. I am from Argentina, and regard myself as a dual Swiss-Argentine citizen. I felt that the only sport that really counted was soccer, and I collected soccer shirts because of the 1986 World Cup, with Diego Maradona leading the team to victory and celebration in the streets of Argentina. At one point, as you would tire of eating your favorite food 365 days a year (for me, ravioli), I started feeling filled up with watching, living, and overall consuming soccer. The United States has four sports throughout the year to balance the interests of viewers; in Argentina, you get soccer all the damn year.

In 1992, at twenty-two years of age, thanks to cable television, my wandering eyes led me to start watching baseball. I was attracted to the many differences: uniforms, rules, surroundings, strategy. There were no goal posts or hoops to score goals or points. In other sports, you score with the ball; you score with your whole body playing baseball. It is a circular game, in a way, around the bases, rather than back and forth. It is a team sport, but in so many ways, an individual one, pitcher against batter. As a deaf person, I particularly liked how plays were communicated, all the hand signals, kind of American Sign Language. This was compelling to me. The 1993 World Series completely hooked me: Toronto versus Philadelphia. If you want to sell baseball to neophytes, use this series as your pitch. It made a lifetime fan out of me.

I started looking for leagues to play in, but they were all far from my hometown of Quilmes, twenty-five kilometers from Buenos Aires. University studies and a girlfriend left me with no time to train and play baseball. Ballparks were of truly amateur, "sub-bush" league, level. Teams of the Metropolitan League in the Buenos Aires area (www.beisbolmetro. com.ar), like Jupiter, DAOM, Nichia (the Japanese community's team), and even the team of American expatriates, the Shankees, competed on bald fields with a few worn-out spectators' benches. (www.shankeesbase-ball.com). The only real baseball stadium, "Estadio Nacional de Béisbol" (National Baseball Stadium), is as big as a Single A (American minor league) ballpark. The local league arranged two or three games, between four or six different teams, each Saturday and Sunday so every spectator who bought a ticket could see all the games.

How did I become a fan of the Boston Red Sox and San Francisco Giants, teams representing cities I have never been to, in a sport I had no knowledge about? I started reading about the history of baseball and became intrigued with these teams. I was shocked to learn about the collapse of the Sox after the sale of Babe Ruth to the Yankees, their resurrection under Ted Williams, and their appearance in the 1967 World Series. The Giants of Mathewson, McGraw, Ott, and Terry seduced me, with particular interest in the 1951 and 1954 seasons. I wear a New York Giants cap everywhere. They certainly weren't playoff teams, like the Yankees, Indians, and Braves; even when they got into the playoffs (Red Sox, 2003) and the World Series (Giants, 2002), they left you with anguish and a bitter taste in your mouth. Yet I must be the only Red Sox fan on the face of Earth who found something wonderful about their defeat in the 2003 American League Championship Series (ALCS).

In 1998, recently degreed as a graphic designer and no longer with my girlfriend, I found a softball team close to home. This "baseball's son" sport is much better organized in Argentina than baseball is, with many leagues and available fields, and every player following Major League Baseball and specific teams for a variety of reasons. I developed many lifelong friends. In October 2003, during the ALCS, I received an invitation from an acquaintance to the birthday party of a woman I didn't know, Romina Rimer. The date was October 25, 2003, the scheduled sixth game of the World Series! What if the Red Sox would defeat the damn Yankees and the Cubbies won the National League pennant? I couldn't afford missing a Series for all the ages! I told my friend I would have to let him know. Of course, the Sox lost to the Yankees, further destroying the soul damaged the previous year by the Giants' unthinkable Series loss. Was there really a Red Sox curse? I did not want to watch a Series with the Yanks probably winning it all, so I called my friend to confirm that I would attend the party.

While the Marlins were beating the Yankees to claim their first title, I met Romina. We got along very well and started dating the next week. Fifteen years later, we are happily married, with seven and three-year-old daughters. And, of course, six Series titles, three each by Boston and San Francisco so far).

What if the Sox had broken the Curse of the Bambino one year earlier? Surely, I would be very happy, but probably would not have the life that I have now. I must to give credit to baseball, because it modeled the course of my life in its own way.

—Ruy G. Pinto Schaffroth
Quilmes, Buenos Aires, Argentina

***

Growing up in Connecticut, I never considered myself much of a baseball fan. Most of my friends and family were split between the Red Sox and the Yankees but given that we were two hours away from either stadium, getting to a game was a full day affair. Plus, I never could understand how anyone could spend three hours watching a baseball game; it always seemed so boring to me.

After moving to San Francisco, I finally realized why people love the game so much. Erin, then my girlfriend, took me to my first Giants game on July 4, 2008, as they hosted the Dodgers on a picture-perfect afternoon. They lost, but I was hooked. The atmosphere of AT&T Park was intoxicating (I was probably also intoxicated, but that's neither here nor there), and I had such a good time watching the game *and* the crowd. My brother and his family came to visit in August 2010, and I took them to see Tim Lincecum pitch against the Padres. Timmy was awful, and barely made it out of the third inning before Bruce Bochy yanked him. However, there was something special about that team, and I told my brother not to be surprised if they made it to the World Series. He said, "Your ace pitcher just gave up six runs in three innings. There's no way you're making it to the playoffs at this rate." Of course, in October, the Giants—with Lincecum leading the way—won their first World Series in fifty-six years.

In 2013 non-baseball related news, Prop 8 and DOMA had been recently repealed, and for the first time, a federally recognized same-sex marriage was an actual option for Erin and me. Unbeknownst to me, Erin had decided it was time to propose. Neither of us is into jewelry, so she thought a shared experience with the people who mean the most to us would be the most appropriate way to propose. She asked our friend Nak to help her out by creating a fake chain letter from his marketing department, saying that he'd won a raffle to "Steal Second Base" at a Giants game. He's an A's fan, so it sounded legitimate that he would give the event to me, given that Erin and I are huge Giants fans. Steal Second Base is an opportunity for a fan to be an honorary crew member and change out the bag during the third inning break. Nak's story started to fall apart the closer we got to the event, and I figured Erin had something to do with it, but I suspiciously went along with it.

Shortly after the second inning started, the Giants staff plucked us from our nosebleed seats to bring us down to the dugout. It was kind of funny, waiting to go out on the field as one of the batting coaches told me, "Don't trip!"—as if I wasn't nervous enough! I ran out onto the field to change out second base (in front of forty-one thousand fans!). I came back to the dugout, carrying the base, to find Erin waiting there on the stairs with a silly orange glass ring. (Aside: As she was waiting for me to return to the dugout, Tim Lincecum looked over at her and the ring box, and gave her the thumbs up—which we both thought was really cool.) She dropped to her knee, but before she could get out her proposal, I said, "Of course!" We kissed, took some photos, and walked back into the stadium. The entire bench and all the fans around the dugout gave us a round of applause, and many players congratulated us. Just a truly special time!

Cain got the win against the Diamondbacks, Posey hit a two run-homer, and Romo closed out the evening. I now have an authentic Major League Baseball second base as my engagement ring—how many people can say that? The night couldn't have ended more perfectly. We re-enacted the moment at the end of the game, and yes, the sign says, "We're way past second base . . . will you marry me?"

ERIN AND VALERIE

—Valerie Gallo
San Francisco, California

***

In the Fall of 1992, Giants owner Bob Lurie negotiated a deal to sell the team to a group that would move it to St. Petersburg, Florida. I took a day off work to take my wife and kids (ages four and eighteen months) to see what was to be the last game at Candlestick Park. Tom Glavine and two relievers shut out a modestly talented Giants squad (featuring Will Clark, Robby Thompson, and not a lot else), 4-0.

When we got home after the game, my wife asked me to take the kids upstairs and put them down for their naps. I did so and came back to discover my wife lying on the staircase, wearing an unbuttoned Giants jersey, a Braves cap—and nothing else. We went at it immediately and fiercely, both celebrating the last Giants game in San Francisco, and releasing our anger and frustration over losing the only baseball team we ever cared about.

That marriage is long gone, and the Giants are still here, but I cannot think of a game I remember with more fondness.

—Anonymous
Walnut Creek, California

***

In 2010, I joined a season ticket holder group (with, among others, the author of this book) for the San Francisco Giants. I had grown up a Giants fan, and had always enjoyed going to games at, what I will always refer to as, Pac Bell Park. I am also a huge fan of ice cream sundaes. Fortunately for me, Ghirardelli (the San Francisco-based chocolatier) serves up some ridiculously good ones at the ballpark. In an effort to put at least a minimal check on my ever-expanding waist line, I limit myself to just one per season (I typically make it to ten or so games a year). One year, I picked the wrong game.

It was 2011, my last game of the year, and I had not yet had my sundae. Between the seventh and eighth innings, I made my girlfriend (now fiancé), Megan, come with me to get my little (okay, gigantic, five-thou-sand-calorie) treat. This also happened to be the time that the Giants did their kiss cam, where they show couples on the scoreboard and get them to kiss to the delight of the crowd. As it happened, while we were getting my sundae, our seat partners (our good friends who invited us into the season ticket group) were featured on the kiss cam, and had we not been off on an ice cream adventure, we would have been shown as well. To this day, every time the kiss cam comes up at a Giants game, Megan reminds me of the time I cost her opportunity to be a featured kisser.

That said, the sundae was amazing; I regret nothing—I just don't tell her that.

—Joe Grasser
San Francisco, California

(I won't, Joe, but you probably shouldn't show her this page.)

***

My exposure to baseball has always been influenced by the men I have liked, loved, and even lusted over. I started as an avid Angels fan; my ex-husband had an eye for the good things in life, and I enjoyed the luxury of a beautiful stadium and prime seats. We didn't talk about the game, mostly because it bored me. I enjoyed the atmosphere, the drinks, and the sun during day games, and I especially loved the occasional fireworks show after a night game. The years passed, and though the luxuries continued, the love faded. We went to fewer games than I wanted, and it was always a "we-can-go-next-weekend" thing. Eventually the marriage deteriorated, and given that I was born into a family of Dodger fans, I no longer had an affiliation with Angels in red.

The first time I sported a Dodger blue baseball cap, I was seated next to a man who, although far from offering me any luxuries or real love, en-tangled me in a lustful relationship, the passion of which easily replaced the comforts and beauty of luxury seats at the Angels' stadium. The excitement of the fans, the crowds, the energy, and the passion experienced before and after each game, paved the way towards my becoming a Dodgers fan. We didn't talk much during the games; unlike me, he grew up playing the game, and was paying attention, while my attention was lost in his gestures and affection towards me. The rollercoaster of the lustful relationship came to a halt, despite his having introduced me to a new playing field, and I loved it.

The years passed, and so continued my dates to various baseball fields. Finally, I met the man who introduced me to the game of baseball, not just going to games. He taught me the history of the LA Dodgers. As my appreciation grew for the team, its history and the culture of "Dodger baseball," I fell in love. I was no longer a cute girl out on a date; my whole existence as a pseudo-baseball fan was transforming, and all of a sudden, those "slow, long, boring games" weren't long enough for me. We not only enjoyed the games, and the drives to and from the park, but he took the time to teach me about something that he was so passionate about. I will never forget that I fell in love with a true Dodger fan while sitting on the field after a Friday night game, while sparks from both heart and the fireworks were in the air. Going to baseball games with him was more than being on a date; it was an experience to be lived. He had me falling in love with him a little more after each game.

—E.
Los Angeles, California

***

It was 1969 or '70, and I was twelve or thirteen years old. The Angels were playing the White Sox at Anaheim Stadium. My friends and I belonged to the Junior Angels club, where kids paid $1.50 to get into the park. They were upper deck seats, but we would always sneak down to the lower deck level because the crowds were usually small, especially when two lousy teams were playing.

We were sitting down near the field along the right field line, and after an inning ended, the White Sox right fielder came over to me. He asked me to go back behind where we were and give the note he had written to a specific lady. Of course, it was some hot chick, and so I did; she thanked me, and then I went back down to my seat. The same player came back after the inning was over and gave me a bat. Using little kids to get some, as Jim Bouton described it, "Beaver!" Ball Four had just been published!

—James Goldstone
Miami, Florida

***

When I first meet my wife Toni twenty years ago, she knew next to nothing about baseball, but we would happily sit and watch Giants games on TV and at the park on a regular basis. She would knit or needlepoint quietly, while I would drone on and on about the game and the situations. All she would offer was that Bobby Estalella and JT Snow were cute. One night after several years of her patience—but what I thought was indifference—toward the game, she surprised me. During some mid-season game in 2000, she suddenly said, "Hey, shouldn't they have called the infield fly rule on that play?" We have loved baseball together ever since.

—Bob Johnston
Salt Lake City, Utah

***

First dates can be an uncomfortable experience. If you go out to dinner, and the conversation doesn't flow easily, there can be lengthy, awkward silences. Movies don't provide much of chance to actually talk, so it may feel like you didn't really get a chance to know the person. Activity dates can be risky. What if you realize you can't stand the person, and are stuck with them in a canoe in the middle of the Potomac River? Not ideal. That's why I think a baseball game has to be the perfect first date. There is built-in entertainment and conversation, and if there are a few too many awkward silences, at least you're watching the game and not staring at her eating a meal.

In April 2012, I started to become pretty crazy about my current girlfriend, Anna. We had met on Thanksgiving Day 2011 in Baltimore, Maryland, at the house of our mutual friend, Amie, but not until the following spring, after Amie had moved away, did I try to ask Anna out on a date. She shut down dinner and movie invites. She thought it was weird dating one of Amie's friends, which is understandable.

Anna is from Columbia, Missouri, a great baseball area, mostly Cardinals territory, but the Royals have a strong backing, too, and Missourians love to cheer for their own. Anna is a lifelong Cardinals fan, but it was actually at Royals game where we had our first "date." After many tries, I was resigned that it wouldn't happen. But one Sunday morning, I got a text asking if I wanted to go to the Royals-Orioles game that afternoon in Baltimore. I was stunned; she didn't look at it as a date, but I certainly did! That day at the end of May was brutally hot; we couldn't get seats in the shade, so we had to sit in the sun, seemingly melting away. One moment when we were drinking beers, I noticed she had some liquid running down her leg. I turned to her and said, "Did you spill some beer on yourself?" She replied, "No, that's sweat." She was clearly not trying to impress me. I felt awkward, but hey, at least there was a baseball game to watch to smooth things over.

After that, I decided to make ball games my way in with Anna. I bought tickets to Nationals (my favorite team) and Orioles games. We went to so many games that her friends nicknamed me "Baseball Billy," as we always seemed to be going to ball games. But I really loved it. Sitting there watching a baseball game with a pretty girl isn't the worst way to spend three hours. It was an exciting summer for the Orioles and Nationals, as both teams went on to the playoffs. We were at Camden Yards for the Orioles' first home playoff game since 1997. You can bet we would have been there for the Nationals-Cardinals National League Division Series that year if she hadn't been on a work trip to Texas.

I work in the NFL, and love football, but there is nothing like being at a baseball game. For Anna and me, it's where our relationship started and developed. Years later, we live in California, and continue going to games; that is, after all, how it all started. We still joke around that those weren't actually "dates," but they sure felt like them. And yes, I eventually graduated from "Baseball Billy" to "Boyfriend Billy."

—Billy Jones
Washington, D.C.

(And you've now graduated to Fiancé Billy, and live with Anna in Washington, DC!)

***

Baseball is something my father Russell and I have shared since I was born. To try and whittle down our twenty-five years of passionately cheering on our beloved Astros to a quick anecdote would be a fruitless exercise. Instead, an example that accurately illustrates the influence our national pastime has on me, comes from my college days. In 2012, I was in the last semester of my senior year at Texas A&M University, counting the days until I finished school and started my time in the army. I had recently started dating a girl, and one of our first dates was an Aggie baseball game on a Friday night. Still early in the season, the main attraction was that the team's ace pitcher was a dominant junior righty named Michael Wacha. I knew that he had a chance to be something special at the next level, and wanted Lindsey to see the same thing.

We had not planned on a weather forecast calling for a cold and windy game. Before someone who lives further north than Nebraska starts telling me to be quiet about cold weather, I must emphasize that it actually does get cold in the southern half of the country; that night in the Brazos Valley was brutal. At game time, it was a mere thirty-five degrees, with high winds viciously dropping the perceived temperature another fifteen or so. It was that special kind of piercing cold aided by stiff winds, and Lindsey had already told me that she did not like the cold. Even I was cold, but I had to keep an upbeat attitude to ensure we enjoyed the date that was all my ~~fault~~ idea. Wacha struck out the side in two of the first three innings, his fastball the only hot thing in town that night, and his command of the zone against the hapless Holy Cross Crusaders was something else to watch. In the third, Lindsey asked how much longer I wanted to stay. I have a personal distaste for leaving before games are over, so early in our relationship, I could either guarantee a good date and continuation of our budding relationship or stick to my guns and say that we were staying despite a bit of chilly weather. Instead, I took the coward's way out and put the onus on her, saying, "We can leave whenever you want, but I don't really like leaving games early." We continued to watch Wacha dominate the lineup for a full seven shutout innings, surrendering only a few scattered singles and racking up eleven K's. It was one of the best outings of his career, including his outstanding first three years in the majors.

My only concern as the game progressed was for Lindsey, who got colder and colder as the night wore on. It was easy to see that she was wholly miserable, wanting to be just about anywhere else, as it had to be warmer than where she currently was. Yet she never complained about staying, and I only *heard* her shiver once or twice (she seemed to be in a constant shiver when I looked over at her). She knew how important this silly little game was to me, and wanted just as much to support her Ags, just maybe on a warmer evening. She even stuck it out when the game went to extra innings, after the classic bullpen collapse in a game that the fans wanted to see over quickly. Isn't that how it always works? As we left Olsen Field that night, my fingers and toes were frozen solid, but my heart was on fire for the girl huddled next to me. I've been married to Lindsey for almost two years now, and always go back to that cold, windy baseball game in College Station as the first time I knew I was dating my future wife (and mother of my son Craig, named after my favorite Astro, Craig Biggio, and another on the way).

LUCAS AND LINDSEY

—Lucas Turner
Colorado Springs, Colorado

***

During the wasteland time period of no DC baseball, my friend and I needed to roam outside of DC to find a game. One day in the early 1990s, we went to experience the Vet in Philadelphia. Living in Washington, DC, I had heard lots of horror stories about that stadium.

Marriage proposals on the Jumbotron were new to us, but suddenly one was taking place. It was on the first base side, second deck; we were on the third base side and could see the proposal in action from across the field and on the screen. Only in Philadelphia could you see a guy get down on his knees, then watch the girl stand up, throw her drink in his face, and storm up the steps to leave the park.

The poor guy, after getting a face full of drink, just collapsed onto the wet concrete. She was booed as she walked out. He stayed for a few more innings, sitting there, wet and stunned and, adding to his misery, the Phillies were losing the game.

—Paul Virostek
Washington, DC

***

(While the stories in this chapter involve romantic love and its connection with baseball—and many of the stories in other chapters do *deal with loving the game—I honestly couldn't imagine any chapter more appropriate for this story.)*

If one's connection with a baseball team is like a human relationship, I confess to being a total hussy. Over the course of my life, I've rooted for every single team in the National League East. Some would be ashamed of this; not me. "Playing the field" may be an overused cliché in the world of human relationships, but it's an accurate one for me. Still, there is hope that at the ripe age of thirty-four, I may have finally conquered my fear of commitment, and pledged undying fealty to one team. After all, my baseball promiscuity is not just some immutable genetic personality tic. It is very much a product of my upbringing. Let me explain.

My father grew up in the Bronx, but inherited from his father, a love of the New York Giants. Perhaps baseball team profligacy is inbred; Dad saw no moral conflict in continuing to root for the Giants after Mays, McCovey, Marichal, and Cepeda fled to the West Coast, while also slumming with New York's new team, the Mets. Dad became a huge Mets fan, and they were huge as I reached pre-pubescent baseball awareness in the mid-1980s. I developed an innocent childhood crush just in time to watch Mookie Wilson's grounder and the Mets epic 1986 World Series (WS) victory.

I grew up in Richmond, Virginia—home of the then-woeful Atlanta Braves triple-A club. That same year, the R-Braves took home the coveted Governor's Cup as champion of the International League. I cheered deliriously with my whole family in the stands when the team rushed onto the field to claim the trophy. Five years later, the Atlanta Braves themselves became good, with players that I'd seen pass through Richmond: Glavine, Smoltz, Avery, Chipper Jones, Justice, Gant, and Wohlers. I waited breathlessly by the home dugout to get their autographs on my baseball cards after every game I attended. For fourteen years, the Braves were not just America's Team—they were my team. I'm sure the Mets kept close tabs on my shifting allegiances, but don't think they were too jealous, as the Braves were then in a different division. It was my first long-term relationship, and things quickly got serious. I got to know my team. I may have even done the tomahawk chop a few times, blissfully ignorant of its offensive implications. I stuck up for them at my northeast college when I was quite possibly the only person on campus rooting for them against the Yankees in the 1998 WS.

Our relationship became stale over time. It was long distance—I never actually went to Atlanta to see a game. It was tough having a team that was excellent every year, but rarely won the championship. Maybe I took them for granted. Boredom set in; I started to feel like Billy Joel waking up to Christy Brinkley every morning and wondering if maybe there was something better out there. I started to stray. First there was a short fling with the Marlins in the 2003 WS. Granted, it was because they were playing the Yankees. But still, it was an ill omen. Even the Red Sox started looking good; so desperate for a change, I had even started looking in another league. I pined for a true hometown team. The last time a major league ballclub resided in Washington, DC, the closest city to Richmond, I was eight years from being born. The nearest team, the Baltimore Orioles, didn't pull me in despite Ripken's pursuit of the consecutive games record. They opened the 1988 season with record twenty-one straight losses. But the real reason couldn't root for O's: Its goddamned owner, Peter Angelos, worked tirelessly for decades to deny a team to DC, where I had migrated after college.

DC always had an allure for me; when it finally snagged a team for the 2005 season, I was at RFK Stadium to see the first Major League game in the city in thirty-one years. Surprisingly good at first, it soon became abundantly evident that the Nationals would be awful for the foreseeable future. In my defense, I grew up lacking the fortitude to endure tough times. I lacked the patience of a lifelong Cubs or Red Sox fan to stand by my team decade after stale decade. Just as it looked like I was finally going to settle down for good, I was swept off my feet by the next shiny object to come along: the Philadelphia Phillies. There were good reasons for this betrayal. My wife Andrea and I, and our kids Eli, Evie and Simon moved to Philadelphia in 2007, as the Phils were getting good. They pulled off a stunning end-of-season comeback against my old flame, the Mets. Howard, Utley, Rollins, Victorino, Hamels, and company were fun to root for. A year later, I found myself climbing a fence to cheer on a Championship parade near my office with two million of my closest friends. I was smitten. The Nats were several area codes and dozen games away in the standings. They didn't need to know of about this affair.

Unfortunately, this particular girlfriend had a tendency to surround herself with batshit crazy friends. Andrea and I quickly discovered that Philly sports fans' reputation for lunacy is richly deserved. We only took our young children to one game at Citizens Bank Park, where we essentially had to apply "earmuffs" for three straight hours to shelter their tender ears from an avalanche of F-bombs. (A year later, notoriously, a blasted fan got into a verbal altercation with an off-duty policeman in the row in front of him, and then forced himself to vomit all over the cop's eleven-year-old daughter.) Sure, the team itself wasn't technically to blame for its psychotic fans. But it felt a lot like seeing a woman with a well-known history of dating serial killers: There was guilt by association.

After three years—for entirely non-baseball related reasons—we decided to move back to DC in 2010. My friends couldn't comprehend why I'd walk away from the greatest dynasty in baseball and re-adopt the city that lost two franchises in the 1970s and been rewarded, after decades in baseball wilderness, with a team that just suffered two straight hundred-loss seasons. Little did they know that the homely team I dated casually a few years earlier was about to undergo an '80s-movie-esque ugly girl makeover. The Nats had drafted Stephen Strasburg with the number one pick; Dad and I snagged tickets to see his scintillating debut in June. For the first time, I had a hometown team that could turn some heads. I fell head-over-heels as they rapidly improved—developing home-grown talent, overpaying big-ticket free agents, and trading prospects for budding superstars. Even better, I converted Dad as well. He finally discarded the Mets and bumped his beloved Giants down the totem pole. By 2012, I was a truly devoted fan following not just the stars, but also the role players and minor roster moves.

As the Nats' 2012 division championship season unfolded, it was thrilling to watch an entire city fall for that team. Curly W hats popped up like crocuses after a long winter. Friends, coworkers, and perfect strangers actually wanted to talk about a Washington baseball club. I bought more Nationals paraphernalia that summer than I had for all other sports teams my entire life combined. Best of all, the Nats hooked my oldest son on baseball at about the same age my father got me into the Mets. You know things are getting serious when it's time to introduce your team to the family. With the Nats on the cusp of bringing playoff baseball to DC for the first time since 1936, I convinced Dad to join me in making the ultimate commitment: a season ticket package. Okay, it was a two-ticket twenty-game package—the bare minimum to be eligible for the postseason ticket pre-sale. Still, this was a big step for a commitment-phobe like me. It was at least a promise ring, if not a full-on engagement.

Twenty-five years into my life as a baseball fan, the first playoff game I ever attended was in the company of my betrothed team. One hundred regular season games had not prepared me for the intensity of taut playoff game with your hometown team facing elimination. In a mid-season game, it's easy for your attention span to wander. (Heck, in my case, I might have even found a new team to root for mid-game.) In the playoffs, you're locked into every pitch. A Werth walk off to win game four was followed by the crushing blow of the Nats coughing up a 6-0 lead in the elimination game. This epic meltdown was followed by a maddening 2013 season in which the team picked by everyone to win the WS slogged through a season of maddening mediocrity. Losses piled up, playoffs slipped from our grasp, but I continued to watch dutifully and attend as many games as I could bear. This was my team now. I was not tempted by a more successful team and hated the playoff teams for doing what my Nats were supposed to do.

I hope this is the end of the story, that I have finally learned to appreciate baseball monogamy. The lesson is that it is far more satisfying to be a truly devoted fan, to stick with your team through soul-crushing heartbreaks, rather than flee into the waiting arms of another, less maddening and frustrating club. I expect to frequently be in the upper deck at Nationals Park each summer, family in tow, whether we're contenders or in the National League East basement. Maybe, just maybe, I can teach my kids the value of sticking with something, or someone, for richer or poorer, in sickness and in health. I suppose there is also my human marriage to hold out as an example. But this is baseball we're talking about.

—Joshua Kaplowitz
Arlington, Virginia

(Josh has maintained his monogamous relationship with the Nats, sticking through playoff flameouts and other disappointments. I think he's in it for the distance.)

***

I had been dating my then-girlfriend, Ashley, for about six years. Always afraid of commitment, I often told her, "We'll get married when the Pirates make the playoffs." I figured that bought me a couple decades. Yet on October 1, 2013, I was sitting high up in the stands behind home plate with Ashley for the Wild Card (WC) game. When they announced the lineups and Andrew McCutchen ran onto the field, PNC erupted to a level I have never heard since. I looked at Ashley, and I'm not afraid to admit I cried. A twenty-eight-year-old crying at a baseball game out of pure joy. I had suffered through two decades of losing, following every game, never thinking a moment like this would happen.

As great a story as it would have been, I didn't propose at that game, even though I had already gotten a ring. It was inevitable, and I officially proposed just a few weeks later, on October 26. There is no doubt, however, that the pennant chase in the final months of the season brought us closer together. We didn't worry about making plans in the evenings, knowing we would either a) be going to the game; or b) watching it on television. Ashley went from not being sure how many players were on the field at a time to knowing the meaning of a LOOGY (left handed one out guy) and the 6-4-3 (short to second to first double play). Baseball was such an important part of my life, and I recognize the point where she adopted its importance and bought into its greatness. We were married a year later, and still both agree that the 2013 WC game was the best moment of our lives. I mean, honestly, how many women would say a National League WC game in the nosebleeds was better than their wedding day?

—Joe Giardina
Carnegie, Pennsylvania

(Joe, on our post-marital vacation, I met my idol, Hubert Humphrey. Among other things, such as saying "I love you," I told him it was the greatest moment of my life. Lynn understood.)

***

On August 30, 2014, my son Gregory married Stephanie. They wanted to have the ceremony on a boat, so they chartered one from Commodore Events, the *Cabernet Sauvignon*. They left Alameda Harbor, went through the ceremony, and then sailed into McCovey Cove, just beyond the outfield of AT&T Park. The Giants were home that day against the Milwaukee Brewers.

At some point, Greg's uncles, Gary and Doc, watching the game on an iPhone, alerted Greg that the game cameras were focusing in on the newly married couple. Jon Miller and Mike Krukow, the TV announcers, gave their best wishes, Kruk noting that the "groom looked like he was in a daze." Back and forth, the cameras went, from game to boat, until they finally caught Gregory and Stephanie kissing, with our daughter Leanna right behind Greg. I asked him how he knew when the cameras would zoom back in; Gregory simply said, "We just kept kissing."

Guests on the boat started to get calls from folks who were watching the game. My husband Russ' cousin Loren, in Japan, playing a rock concert, was watching the game from his hotel room on the Major League Baseball internet site; he texted his brother Ari, who was at the wedding. Another guest got a call from her gynecologist. Texts and calls continued to come in for several days. Our family thanked the Giants' cameraman for making the day unforgettable and creating a memory to share with future generations. The Giants won the game 3-1. As far as we were concerned, though, our party hit the home run.

—Betty Zipkin
Pacifica, California

***

On June 14, 2018, my girlfriend Debbie Bruhier and I went to our first baseball game together, the Minnesota Twins visiting the Tigers at Comerica Park in Detroit. I was a lifelong passionate Expos fan until they became extinct in 2004. Debbie is a maritimer from New Brunswick, Canada, geographically a Red Sox follower, but also a patriotic Blue Jays fan. I was blessed from 1975 to 1999 to become friends with many of the stars of that era through my photography, featured in Jonah Keri's bestselling book *Up Up and Away*, published in 2014. Most recently, I was acknowledged as unofficial Montreal Expos historian in the 2017 Tim Raines biography *Rock Solid*, by author Alan Maimon, and was a guest of Tim's to his Hall of Fame induction ceremony in Cooperstown, New York.

In January of 1998, I left Ontario, returning to the province of my birth, New Brunswick. Debbie and I met in church in May while I was grieving a tragedy in my life. It was a difficult time for me, so I focused on my faith and my photography as a place to channel my emotions and energy. One Sunday, we struck up an instant friendship, and chatted every Sunday in the commons. Soon after, she left for the university in Halifax, Nova Scotia, and I moved to Southern California, and we lost touch. However, in 2010, we connected with the help of Facebook, starting six years of quarterly phone calls, catching up on each other's lives. I returned to Canada in 2013. In 2016, I asked Debbie, "Are all of the men in New Brunswick blind or stupid?" She had never gotten married in all those years since we had met; I always believed she would be an incredible wife and amazing mother. Our friendship turned to romance when I never expected to find love, as I had focused on caregiving for my octogenarian parents. We reunited that December after an eighteen-year estrangement. The chemistry was immediate, and we spent forty-five days together in 2017, despite the thousand-mile long-distance relationship, and Face-timed every night.

In March 2018, I had received a game-used baseball from a Jays versus Cardinals exhibition game held at Stade Olympique in Montreal, when Vladimir Guererro Jr. had hit a walk-off home run to win the game 1-0. The time was right for me to escalate the relationship to a new level; I was ready to ask for her hand in marriage. How could I make this a "Magic Moment"? I decided to make a ring holder out of that baseball. I sawed the ball in two, leaving one piece of leather intact as a hinge. I then converted the inside of the ball, decorating it with red velvet, and finally added a brass fastener with a clasp to close the ball. I put the ring inside the ball, and the ball inside of a plastic cube.

I recruited the collaboration of hip-hop recording artist Annakin Slayd Farrar to help me with the deed. I knew him through the Canadian Baseball Hall of Fame, and he was emceeing this year's event, the induction of Pedro Martinez. With Debbie a Red Sox Fan, it would be perfect. Pedro could sign the ball and have Annakin present it to her. Sometimes the best plans get sabotaged; I received an email that Pedro had taken ill and was unable to attend his induction ceremony. It was time for Plan B to be put into action. Debbie arrived in Windsor, Ontario (aka, South Detroit in the Journey song "Don't Stop Believing") in time for the Tigers' game. What could I do to hit this moment out of the park? A "PAWS" for the cause would be my plan of attack.

An uneventful game, the Twins led 1-0 going into the seventh inning stretch and the singing of Take Me Out to the Ballgame. Slipping out to the concession stand, I arranged for the Tigers' mascot Paws to deliver the loaded ball to Debbie in her seat. As Paws came down the row toward her, catcher John Hicks led off with a triple. Niko Goodrum followed up with an RBI single, tying the game. I told Debbie that Paws wanted to give her a ball. She looked puzzled by the gesture; at just the exact moment when she received the ball and opened the unique hinge, leftfielder JaCoby Jones hit a two-run home run, which proved to be the game-winning hit. It was like lightning and fireworks collided. The fans surrounding us stood up and cheered when they realized what had just happened.

DEBBIE, RUSS AND PAWS

Baseball has always been very good to me. Diamonds are a girl's best friend. Now I can say that *Baseball diamonds are a girl's best friend.* The couple with us asked Debbie, "What did you say?" Her reply was "Yes! Yes! Yes!" I can honestly say that JaCoby and I both had game-changing hits out of the park on that day. I could never have scripted it any better, and we are excited about the wedding plans for 2019.

—Russ Hansen
Windsor, Ontario, Canada

***

I wasn't looking for a relationship when I decided to take an afternoon off to go to an Oakland A's game, but destiny had something else in mind. A series of coincidences put me in a seat next to Kevin Shafer at the Oakland Coliseum on October 10, 1990, at game four of the American League Championship Series with the Red Sox facing the A's. I didn't have a ticket for this game but thought I would be able to find a single ticket for sale. I decided to take BART (the commuter train), rather than drive; the train was crowded, and three stops later, three men boarded, and one of them took the only remaining seat, which happened to be next to me. His name was Kevin Shafer.

Kevin and his friends were discussing the game, which would feature Dave Stewart facing Roger Clemens. After joining the baseball talk, I found out that Kevin had an extra ticket to sell; he wanted to just give it to me, but I insisted on paying for it. His friends were sitting elsewhere, but the extra ticket was for the seat next to Kevin, so we spent the afternoon together. It was an incredibly fun day, and the A's winning the game, which sent them to the World Series, made it even more exciting and special. We exchanged phone numbers, and a few nights later, went on our first date. The next five years included frequent games with Kevin's season tickets.

When we married in July 1995, we celebrated our shared fandom by incorporating an A's theme into the wedding. To guide guests to their tables, we handed out A's tickets indicating their "section." Seating cards were made from A's ticket card stock donated by a friend who worked in the A's front office. Flowers were the A's colors, green and gold (yellow) arranged in A" s helmet vases. The piece de resistance: a baker friend created a cake in the shape of the Oakland Coliseum, and used loaf pans to re-create the BART train where our fateful meeting took place.

We have continued to enjoy our weekend plan season tickets for the past twenty-eight years. We have seen our A's play in stadiums around the country, including Fenway Park and Wrigley Field, but we are doing a ballpark tour to see all Major League Baseball stadiums. We have seen thirty-five so far and have nine to go. You know, though, you can often find us on weekends tailgating with friends and in our seats, watching our A's.

SUNDAY, MAY 11, 2014

HOW WE MET: DORI AND KEVIN SHAFER

A's got couple's ball rolling

Dori Shafer wasn't looking for a relationship when she decided to take an afternoon off to go to an Oakland A's game.

But destiny, fate or whatever you call it had something else in mind. Just consider the number of coincidences that put her in a seat next to her future husband, Kevin Shafer, at the Oakland Coliseum on that October day in 1990.

And this was certainly a game that would allow these die-hard A's fans to meet and bond: The A's were facing the Boston Red Sox in Game 4 of the American League Championship Series.

Dori and Kevin had met earlier that afternoon as strangers on a BART train headed to the game. In the first coincidence of the day, Dori decided to go to the game even though she didn't have a ticket. She figured she would chance it, hoping she would find someone to sell her a ticket — even if she had to pay a scalper's price.

In another coincidence, Dori opted to take BART from her office in Lafayette rather than drive. The train was crowded by the time it reached the MacArthur station in Oakland. Three men got on, and one took the only seat remaining on the car, which happened to be next to Dori. That man, it turned out, was Kevin.

Dori heard the men talking about the game, which had the A's' Dave Stewart going up against the Red Sox's Roger Clemens. As Dori joined in their conversation, she heard that Kevin had an extra ticket he need to unload.

"He wanted to just give it to me, but I insisted I pay for it," Dori says.

The coincidences continued to unfold. The tickets Kevin had were for two seats together. His friends had tickets for elsewhere in the stadium, which meant that Dori and Kevin got to spend the afternoon alone together.

PHOTOS COURTESY OF DORI SHAFER

Die-hard A's fans Dori and Kevin Shafer got to know each other at Game 4 of the American League Championship Series in October 1990.

"We had an incredibly fun time, and the A's won that game, which made it even more exciting," she says. In fact, winning the game sent the A's to the World Series.

Before the game ended, Dori and Kevin exchanged phone numbers. They had their first real date a couple of nights later.

They went out for the next five years, with Kevin making full use of his season tickets for their dates.

When it came time to plan their July 1995 wedding, the Pleasant Hill couple didn't just get into selecting color schemes, they decided to celebrate their shared fandom by incorporating an A's theme into the occasion.

To guide their some 100 guests to their tables at the garden at Scott's Seafood Grill & Bar in Walnut Creek, the couple handed out A's tickets indicating their "sections." The seating cards were made from actual A's ticket card stock donated by a friend who worked in the team's front office.

The flowers consisted of yellow blooms and green leaves arranged in A's helmet vases, while the pièce

For the Shafers' A's-themed wedding, a baker friend fashioned a cake in the shape of the Oakland Coliseum with a BART train circling past.

de résistance was the wedding cake. A baker friend fashioned a spice cake into a replica of the Oakland Coliseum and used loaf pans to re-create the BART train where Dori and Kevin's fateful meeting took place.

Over the past nearly 20 years, Dori and Kevin have spent many of their weekends at A's games and tailgate parties with friends and family, taking in about 40 to 45 home games a year.

Their vacations also take them to A's games in some of the nation's great ballparks, including Boston's Fenway Park and Chicago's

Wrigley Field. A trip this summer will take them to Safeco Field in Seattle.

Dori thinks the A's are looking good this season and says she and Kevin will remain loyal fans forever, even if the A's leave Oakland.

"We hope they stay in Oakland, but if they go to San Jose or somewhere else, we'll be there," she says.

— Martha Ross, Staff

If you want to share how you and your partner or best friend met, email mross@bayareanewsgroup. com with the subject line "how we met."

DORI AND KEVIN

—Dori Shafer
Pleasant Hill, California

WOMEN IN BASEBALL

This chapter began to take flight when I learned of a much-respected female umpire. Then I learned about women who didn't want to play softball, who insisted on playing baseball. Of course, some women coach, and some are in the front office of baseball clubs. For purposes of this chapter—frankly, this book— I'm not making a distinction between baseball and softball. The basic game, positions, strategies, and goals are the same: see ball, hit ball, run, throw, catch, touch home plate. This chapter includes stories from women who were involved with the game in various capacities. I do, however, wish to acknowledge my new knowledge of how some women feel about the difference between playing softball and baseball.

***

Back around 1990, I was assigning umpires to camps down in Florida, and at the request of another umpire I knew, I hired a former American League umpire named Frank Umont to work the Mets Fantasy camp with me. I hadn't met Frank, but I had a copy of an old *Baseball Magazine* with an article about, of all things, a home run call at Yankee Stadium that he had allegedly blown. So, the first time I introduced myself, he was sitting in the locker room at Port St. Lucie with the other umpires, and I walked up to him. He looked at me, totally flabbergasted; I guess Joe, the umpire who'd asked me to hire him, hadn't told him that "Perry" was a woman, much less a petite blonde, who—in her street clothes at least—looked like butter wouldn't melt in her mouth. Right away I could tell he was sort of put off, and I figured, *What the hell, it can't get much worse,* so I pulled out my copy of *Baseball Magazine* and showed him the article, and cheekily asked, "Do you remember that play? Did you really blow that call?" Umont sat there—in his underwear, by the way—thighs the size of ham hocks, his face ruddy with the hue of way too many alcoholic beverages, seventy years old, if he was a day, his twenty-year career in the American League, a distant memory. He stared me up and down, looking as if he was about to swallow me whole and spit me back out in pieces. Then this enormous smile creased his face, and in a voice reminiscent of Eugene Pallette's, he growled, "Baby, I blew a *lot* of calls out there!" It was hilarious. He autographed the article for me, too. I probably still have that issue somewhere in my basement. I'll have to go rummaging one of these days.

PERRY

—Perry Barber
New York, New York

***

My grandmother, Nora Rock, loved baseball from an early age, and was known as "Babe Ruth" on the local playgrounds. She was "Nana" to me, and she and my grandfather, "Pa," often took me to see the Giants play at Candlestick Park. We always had good seats, behind third base. This was in the seventies, when I was about eight years old. She once asked me what I wanted to do when I grew up, and I answered, "I want to be the first girl player for the Giants, playing third base." I held that dream for a long time.

I played Little League, then competitive softball in college, loving the game, loving playing the game. In 1993, I was notified about a tryout for the new women's hardball team, the Silver Bullets. I went to a tryout in Sacramento, took infield grounders, shagged fly balls in the outfield, and took batting practice. The fastball looked like a watermelon compared to the fast, underhand softball pitches I was used to. The hardest thing for me was learning to grip and throw the hardball, much different than how you would the larger softball. I was one of fifty finalists chosen to go to spring training in Orlando in the spring, 1994. We used the Chicago Cubs practice facility. The lockers were huge, chairs for each player. I recall how funny it was that the locker room *boy* had to do the laundry, including panties and bras, for the women players. It was quite a role reversal.

I was selected for the team managed by Phil Niekro, with his brother Joe as a coach. My parents, and Nana, were absolutely thrilled. The schedule was announced; we would play minor or independent league teams around the country. Imagine my joy when I discovered that one of our scheduled sites would be . . . Candlestick Park. On the day of the game, I got to the park, saw a friend who was a security guard, and walked through the players' tunnel. It was just magical. And there, as I went out to take my position at third base, right in the front row were my parents and Nana, cheering me on. I walked my first time up, advanced to third on a fielder's choice, and took my lead. The pitch bounced past the catcher, and I dashed for home. Unfortunately, the pitch hit the umpire's shin guard, bounced back, and I was caught in a rundown and tagged out. There went my dream of scoring the first run in this game, but no complaints from me. I literally lived my dream, with my family supporting and cheering me on.

RACHELLE

—Rachelle "Rocky" Henley
San Francisco, California

***

I've been fortunate to play on the USA Baseball Women's National Team since 2006, but my baseball journey started long before then. I grew up in San Diego, played Little League baseball at Chollas Lake, and eventually was the first girl to play high school baseball in San Diego County when I made the team at La Jolla High School. I played two years of junior varsity, and two years of varsity baseball for the Vikings. There was always some pressure to switch to softball to pursue opportunities in college, but I just couldn't imagine playing anything but baseball. Fortunately, I excelled in volleyball and basketball in high school, and accepted a volleyball scholarship to the University of North Carolina at Chapel Hill.

Volleyball provided me with wonderful opportunities and experiences, but I missed baseball. In my free time, I coached a youth league team in Chapel Hill, but it did only so much to fill the void. In 2006, I stumbled on an announcement about open tryouts for the USA Baseball Women's National Team, which was preparing to play in an upcoming World Cup. My volleyball career had ended, and I was working for the university. I jumped at the opportunity to try out, made the team, and I haven't looked back since.

As a member of the Women's National Team, I've played in seven World Cups and participated in the 2015 Pan American Games, the first time women's baseball was included in a multi-sport international event. Through baseball, I have had the opportunity to travel to places like Taiwan, Japan, Venezuela, Canada, and South Korea. I've played with and against amazing athletes. There is nothing quite like standing along the foul line with USA across your chest, listening to our National Anthem before a game. It gives me chills every time. One of my favorite memories with this team was winning the gold medal at the Pan Am Games. I caught the final out of the game at first base; I so clearly remember the throw from our third baseman, Michelle Snyder, as it hit my glove (she made an awesome play on a slow roller).

I look forward to where the game takes me next!

—Malaika Underwood
Atlantic Beach, Florida

(Malaika was very modest in her story, focusing on the opportunities she had to play for the national team, which receives far less attention than the woman's national softball team. That includes seven World Cups and nine international competitions. What she didn't say is that for the tournament, she led the team in hits, with sixteen, and batted .552.)

***

Cleveland was putting on a city-wide high school baseball all-star game. I was working in the Indians front office at the time, and Phil Seghi, the general manager of the Tribe, came into my office and asked me if I knew where Edgewater Park was, the location of that game. Of course I did, because I was from Cleveland; he said that if I drove, we could cut out of work and go see this game. So, there I was, driving a 1969 Volkswagen beetle with the general manager of the Cleveland Indians sitting next to me!

When we arrived, there were many Major League scouts present, congregating behind the home plate screen. The game started, and Phil came up to me and said, "Let's see how good of a scout you are. Give me a scouting report on the pitcher." I knew the pitcher from a high school in town was being touted as a very high draft pick. I watched the kid and thought to myself that he wasn't that good. Did I tell the truth? Or did I say what I thought was expected of me? I told the truth!

Phil started laughing hysterically, and said it's a good thing you said that, because the kid I'm watching is pitching for the other side. When the side changed, and the kid Phil had come to see came in to pitch, he watched for two or three batters from behind home plate, and also from first base. He came to get me, saying, "Okay, I've seen enough. Let's go." I looked at him kind of quizzically, and he said, "The kid's going to be a first round draft choice." He was—future Major Leaguer, and fifteen-game winner, Ken Kravec.

—Peg Wagner
Olmsted Township, Ohio

***

I am one of the fortunate women who have had the chance to play women's hardball. I was a forty-three-year-old rookie when I started playing and played until I was fifty-nine. I'm from the time when girls were not allowed to play baseball, not even Tee-ball. Anyway, in the late 1990s, I was playing in a Great Lakes League tournament in South Bend at Coveleski Field for the Michigan Stars from Battle Creek, playing teams from Chicago, South Bend, Akron, and Fort Wayne. I played mostly first base and third base, occasionally pitching to give our regular pitchers a rest in blow-out games. I am proud to have been inducted in the National Women's Baseball Hall of Fame in 2003, as well as the Michigan USSSA hall of Fame for slow pitch softball. But my accomplishments are not what this story is about.

During one game in this tournament, every time I came in from the field, or went to the on-deck circle, I had a conversation with a young boy. He was the grandson of the umpire and was chasing down foul balls for his grandfather. At the end of the game, I came out of the dugout to pick up equipment and he was waiting for me, with a ball and a pen . . . just standing there. I finally said to him, "Do you want me to sign your ball?" He nodded yes. As I stood there on a pro baseball field signing his ball, I wondered how any player could ever turn down a little kid.

—Carol Sheldon
Royal Oaks, Michigan

***

For me, fast pitch softball was in my blood. I didn't do it for the competition, or because my dad was a former barnstorming superstar. It was just a part of me. I gave to it, and it gave back. Had I been focused on really excelling, who knows where it might have led. The coolest story for me involved exposing just how little I actually had "thought" about what I had accomplished. I was at my college award night to hear my name being called to the front for my school letter, and found out, to my utter shock, that I had had an .800 batting average. Batting was just natural. I always knew I could hit anything thrown my way. It wasn't ego; it was one of life's simple pleasures.

—Linda Rikli
Larkspur, California

(Linda later played on my co-ed softball team; not only could she hit, but man, she could play the outfield. I remember those throws from her to me at deep short when I turned and threw out runners at home plate. A few great moments for me in an undistinguished softball career!)

***

I had the opportunity to work with a group of young girls this summer, third through fifth graders. They were all learning the game of softball and were of varying skill levels. My job was to use a pitching machine and umpire games. The girls learned everything, batting, throwing, offense, and defense. As the season progressed, I noticed that some of the girls were not progressing with their batting skills as much as the others. One thing I know as an umpire is that it is not my job to coach anyone, but with these girls, it was easy to decide to help with the coaching. I spent one day watching and making recommendations with batting stances, where to stand in the batter's box and how to swing. They were so enthusiastic to learn, and some did improve greatly. The coaches and parents were very supportive of my help. Each week these girls played their hearts out and grew with the game.

It gave me great pride to hear from the parents what a good job I did and the girls that would just come up to hug me when they saw me. To me, it wasn't about doing a job, it was about helping girls learn the wonderful game of softball and being a positive role model throughout the season. I realize this is bridging two different roles, but as a female umpire working primarily in softball, it makes me proud when I walk on a field and an entire dugout of young girls looks at me and says, "We got a lady umpire, so cool." That happened a couple of weeks ago, and it made me stand a little taller, and feel very proud of being a female umpire.

—Brenda Knapp
Champaign, Illinois

***

After Red Sox Women's Fantasy Camp in January, I ambitiously declared 2016 the "Year of Women in Baseball." I had no real concept of the amazing journey ahead. This story contains excerpts from an extraordinary weekend, camaraderie, more than just a specific game or event.

Memorial Day weekend marked the eleventh Diamond Classic Women's Baseball Tournament in Baltimore, hosted by the Eastern Women's Baseball Conference. The EWBC is dedicated to providing opportunities for girls and women to play organized baseball and preparing amateur female players for national and international competition. Major League Baseball rules are used. Yes, women pitch from 60'6" and run and throw 90' between bases. This year's Classic featured eight teams, two from Canada, and at least one player from Australia. The Diamond Classic has become a fixture thanks to Bonnie Hoffman and the EWBC.

For many girls, this tournament, and a couple of others, is the highlight of their year. Some play on teams with boys, often as the only girl. Some have no other opportunity to play baseball and can only play softball the rest of the year. It's a time when new friendships are sparked, and old ones rekindled between players from all over the country. Camaraderie runs rampant; it is a chance to talk baseball with other females who understand and feel as strongly as you do. Players range from fourteen years old to their mid-forties. Parents can talk with other parents who understand what it's like to raise an athletic girl determined to take the road less traveled. At the opening dinner, as the players introduced themselves and talked about experiences, one theme rang true: girls and women continue to face enormous obstacles to playing baseball. Many begin on co-ed Tee-ball teams; as they get into Little League, they are often the only girl on their team, one of a handful who do not follow the others into softball. Once they age out, the options become even slimmer. They might be the only girl in the entire league; they might face tremendous pressure, harassment, and bullying. Or, they can play softball.

One high school sophomore's story echoed the reality for many girls. She doesn't play on a team at home, only at women's tournaments, for which she will travel across the country to play baseball for a weekend. She didn't try out for the "boys" high school baseball team, because she didn't believe she would get a fair shot at tryouts and would receive little opportunity to play in games if she did make the team. She knew she'd be harassed if she was better than some of the boys. Another girl went to a private school for which there was no regulation requiring equal opportunity. She wanted to try out for the baseball team, but the coach told her, "You will not be on the baseball team. I won't allow it."

Listening to these life stories, and knowing my own, was troubling. It made me realize why this tournament was so important to all of us, and why we were willing to make great sacrifices to play in it. We share a deep love for baseball, and an incessant number of obstacles to playing. These tournaments are the only opportunities for many women to play baseball with other women; for many, it is the only way to play baseball in a live game. For too many, our baseball practices are limited to solo experiences in a batting cage, hitting off a tee, pitching to a net, and fielding rubber balls off walls.

I had the good fortune to play for the Great Lakes Lightning with players from all over the US. The anticipation of putting on a uniform makes me giddy. I brought a royal blue belt and socks, and my beloved gray baseball pants, to complement the jersey, undershirt, and hat we were given. The logo on the hat was a baseball with a bolt of lightning through it, reminding me of the Bad News Bears logo. Perfect. I like to wear number twenty-one to honor Hall-of-Famer Roberto Clemente; it is my good luck number. It can't hurt to pick a good one.

A.J. SECOND FROM RIGHT
Photo by Debbie Pierson

Details of the games are not that important. In our first game, we faced the Chicago Pioneers. On the mound was star American women's baseball pitcher Stacy Piagno (at the time of this re-write she had become just the third woman to ever win a professional baseball game, for the Sonoma Stompers). My first thought, "I'm doomed," conflicted with my excitement knowing I was facing a Team USA pitcher, who'd thrown a no-hitter in the 2015 Pan Am Games. Baseball is a mental game; I swung two bats in the on-deck circle, as I watched her throw, to get bat speed but mostly to psych myself up. I had never done this before. I even used eye black to look intimidating, although my goal was partially psychological, to get prepared. Every advantage counts. I suspect she wasn't intimidated.

My goal was making contact, since she throws heat. I asked teammates what she was throwing: "Strikes, and fast," was the unanimous answer. I took a deep breath and walked to the plate. I smoothed the dirt with my foot, striving to focus and take my time, concentrating on Piagno's glove. I fouled off the first two pitches, and felt confident, taking deep breaths between each pitch. On the third, I rolled out to first. As I jogged back to the dugout, I wanted to break into a smile; I had made contact with each pitch, a moral victory.

We lost all four games we played, but again, it really didn't matter. The dinner on the night between two days of game play saw some wonderful moments. Each team was asked to select someone to receive a "10" award for being essential to the the team, embodying the spirit of women's baseball, and doing good unto others. Among the women who were deservedly honored were Bonnie Hoffman, Amy Schneider, and Meggie Meidlinger. Carmen, a cancer victim who was the inspiration for the award, was feted, with lots of adulation and tears. Who said there is no crying in baseball? There were, of course, so many great players that weekend, including Stacey, Marti Sementelli, Donna Mills, Malaika Underwood, Samantha Cobb, and Michelle Snyder. There were some real up and comers, like Denae. I had great teammates like Cameron and Jenn.

There were so many wonderful moments that weekend. When a game was rained out, some of us took a challenge to run and dive on the soaking wet grass outside the stadium, trying to slip and slide. Paige, of the Yankees, amazed us with her ability to do flips, earning the nicknames "Flipper," or "Flippy." With a few dives into grass and dirt during the tournament, I ended up with a baseball nickname: I became "Crash," with bruises and scrapes to prove it was earned. We conducted a Kangaroo Court, issuing "fines" for small, funny indiscretions. We ate and laughed together, joking about age differences, dialects, and word usage. Most of us had an injured finger or rib or aggravation of some body part, but none of us were going to sit on the bench; ice packs were a common sight. We were all exhausted from the heat and giving every ounce of ourselves, to every play but we didn't want it to end.

These enriching experiences to play and be part of a baseball team are rare for women. What I already knew and loved, but had confirmed, was that we are all ballplayers. We are all female. We are all strong.

—AJ "Crash" Richard
Iowa

***

When I first started playing softball, I would play any position. "Put me wherever, coach" is what I would say, just so I could get some dirt on my cleats and touch those laces. When I was ten years old, I discovered my love for pitching, and my confidence grew; as a shy girl, that was something I really needed. I was mentally able to block out the chants and razzing from opposing players. My idol growing up was Jennie Finch. I could watch her pitch for the Arizona Wildcats all day. She inspired me to push my limits and always strive to do my best.

The inspiration Jennie gave me made me want to do the same for a girl wanting to become a softball pitcher. In my sophomore year of high school, I participated in a passion project: teach a young girl about pitching, and the techniques that needed to be learned. I worked with her for many weeks, practicing, over and over again, the precise techniques. I could see her inspiration come to life during this time. Today, she is a senior in high school, and has received a full ride scholarship to play softball for the Oregon Beavers. The mental and physical demands of playing softball can help build confidence for females. I am so proud to be a woman who knows the ins and outs of the game. The love for softball and baseball will be forever with me.

—Roxanne Ray
Chico, California

***

I play in a hardball league, and a few years ago I had the attitude that there was no place in it for women. A young lady, Susan, was pitching against my team, and I thought, "There's no way this girl is going to get me out." Lo and behold, she sent me down two times. She would set you up with a fastball, and then drop an unbelievable curve with great movement on the inside. The next thing I knew, I was walking back to the dugout, talking to myself. I went hitless in four at -bats that day. It changed my mind and attitude forever. Some women can play this game at the same levels that men play. I have played with her, and against her. Some women are just as good, if not better than, men. This attitude that women can't or shouldn't be allowed to compete has got to change.

—Doug Sasfai
Arlington, Virginia

(It starts level by level, Doug—generally at the lower ones—until the ground-swell becomes too powerful to ignore. Thanks for being the guy to acknowledge this.)

***

I grew up in Tidewater, Virginia, baseball deprived. As a ballerina and actress, I had little exposure to, and even less interest in, sports. In 1980, I moved to San Francisco as a member of a comedy troupe. I had a day job, and performed in the clubs at night, which left me only weekend days to find fun things to do. I started going to Giants games and listening on the radio. It was Chili Davis' rookie year, and I became a fan. I remember one morning on the street car reading in the newspaper that Chili had been sent to the minors, and blurting out, "Oh no!" to the surprise (and concern) of fellow passengers. New to the game, I had no idea that this could happen. My burgeoning interest was also fueled by listening to the Giants' great announcer, Hank Greenwald. I started reading the sports page daily, devouring baseball literature, and making spring training a yearly destination. In short, I fell very hard for baseball. I especially loved the players' self-deprecating humor. It was interesting to me how you could fail 70 percent of the time and still be considered successful. I felt that baseball had some kind of deeper meaning, teaching you how to confront failure with grace and humor.

When the Giants were "rescued" from their expected move to Florida for the 1993 season, they held auditions for the stadium PA job. Not planning to go, I woke up that morning, saw it was a beautiful day, called in sick (a decision I would come to regret), and on a lark, went to Candlestick Park. Five hundred people—only eight women—showed up to audition. It annoyed me that so few women had come. I went as a fan, not to win the job, just thinking it would be fun to hear my voice over the sound system.

After almost two hours, I was only the second woman to audition. We all had to announce two batters; I don't recall for sure, but I think I chose Robbie Thompson and Will Clark. I was amazed to find people applauding, and being told, "Good voice," as I walked back to my seat. As I left, I started to realize that it was possible that I really could get the job. It isn't often that you get that walking-on-air feeling, but that day I did. I received a call back, so I, the only woman, along with eight men, returned for a more extensive audition. Of the nine of us, seven either worked in a voice industry, or had vocal training. As a theater major in college, and an actress, I had both training and experience. And thank goodness I knew baseball! As a fan, I had been the scorekeeper for my section at Candlestick. With only bare facts, we had to announce the line-up (with all the tricky names they could find thrown in), the National Anthem, the first pitch, and so on. After a few minutes of consultation among the Giants brass, I was chosen as one of the three finalists; after another audition, to my great surprise, I was given the job.

I was the Giants' announcer from 1993 to 1999. The players and umpires were terrific, but I had to endure some pretty sexist reactions. I heard more than once on sports talk radio, "I go the ballpark to get away from women," and everyone just laughed it up. Letters berated me for taking a job away from a man (I have supported myself all my adult life). If you realize it was only twenty-five years ago, it is amazing that those kinds of sentiments were acceptable, especially in liberal San Francisco, even then. It was just part of the territory, outweighed by the overwhelming support I received from the fans and the great joy I experienced announcing every home game. I am honored to have been the first woman to hold this type of position in American professional sports. I'm very, very thankful to have been a part of baseball, and to have had such a wonderful experience. I urge everyone to dream big, regardless of the odds, and to pursue those dreams. You will never win unless you put yourself in the game.

—Sherry Davis
Vallejo, California

***

In October 1947, I was playing softball in Los Angeles. A scout, whose name I don't recall, saw me and said, "I want you to play pro ball." I replied, "Of course, there is no such thing," and he responded with, "I have news for you. There is." I tried to explain that my mom wouldn't let me go, but he wanted to meet my folks. When he told Mom that I would be paid fifty-five dollars a week, Mom turned to Dad and said, "Go crank up the car!" Off I went to play for the Peoria Red Wings in the All-American Girls Professional Baseball League.

Seventy years later, I vividly recall how I felt the first time I put on the cute team uniform; I felt so proud. Then I put on my spikes and walked up the ramp to the accompanying sound of the clicking of the spikes on the concrete, and then saw all the greenery on the field. It was a thrill I felt, and still feel, all the way through my body.

I remember little things from my time on the team. I had a Cuban roommate, who did not speak any English. It was hard to communicate, of course, but we got along fine. The bus rides to different stadiums were always fun. We always had to wear dresses and lipstick, or else we'd be fined. We learned how to play poker. When one of our teammates broke her leg sliding into second base, she was taken to Catholic Hospital, which had sharp restrictions on visiting hours. We had to climb up a fire escape just to visit her, breaking the visitor's curfew.

The one game experience I most clearly recall involved the first time I came in to pitch. There was a runner on first, and I was so nervous, so excited, so in awe of the moment that as I took my wind up, I forgot to check the runner. By the time my first pitch reached home plate, the runner was at third base! I did not make that mistake ever again.

I played one season, 1948, and made wonderful friendships, some which have lasted until today. We made history, but we didn't realize it at the time. We were being paid for something we loved to do. I don't know if a woman will ever play in the Major Leagues, but over a hundred thousand women and girls are now playing baseball—*baseball*—and they sure need a league of their own.

—Maybelle Blair
Palm Desert, California

THE NEGRO LEAGUES

It should be totally unnecessary to explain the role of the Negro Leagues in the history of American baseball. This is not a sociology book; to go into detail about why these leagues had to come into being, to describe why African-American players were prohibited from playing in the Major Leagues, would be as obvious as explaining why you put socks on your feet before your cleats. At this late date, it's harder and harder to find former Negro Leaguers to speak to, but I was fortunate, through the help of friends, to locate a few. These stories, along with those of folks who have had some story connected with the Negro Leagues or players in various ways, helped make this a viable and interesting chapter. Any little thing to keep these stories alive.

***

In 2004, the Boston Red Sox overturned the Curse of the Bambino, winning their first World Series (WS) in eighty-six years. A wave of pride, excitement, and joy filled the hearts of millions of Sox fans who'd stood alongside their team through decades of ups and downs . . . but mostly downs. Within hours, every store in New England had converted entire aisles to Sox paraphernalia. *The Boston Globe* began issuing collectible pins, Dunkin Donuts had souvenir cups and magnets, and big establishments hosted meet and greets with members of the team. As a ten-year-old baseball player, fan, and amateur collector, this climate quickly sparked an obsession. Within weeks of the Series win, I had amassed quite a collection of Sox-related memorabilia, even waiting over four hours in the snow to meet Johnny Damon at a book signing.

In the coming years, my room began to resemble a mini-museum, housing hundreds of signed baseballs, and thousands of signed photographs, cards, and miscellaneous artifacts. My Red Sox memorabilia? That had long been buried away. My new focus: The Negro League, a professional baseball league for Black athletes denied the chance to play Major League Baseball. How did I stumble upon this era of baseball, and why had I become so obsessed? It started with handwritten autograph request letters to legends like Duke Snider, Sparky Anderson, and George Kell, but everyone had written to those guys. Nobody had written to Stanley Glenn, and from what I heard, he was quite an all-star athlete.

After several dozen mail correspondences, I somehow ended up speaking on the phone with a couple of former players. Within weeks, I'd finish my homework at school so I could come home and immediately call and speak with these players. In our chats (many of which lasted hours), I noticed several key themes: Most of these players hadn't stayed in touch with their former teammates; they had never been recognized for their careers; and they had no articles, baseball cards, or any sort of documentation to back up their careers. I felt like they had been completely forgotten, and I couldn't shake it.

For example, Keith Foulke pitched a couple dozen games for the 2004 Red Sox, and hundreds of people lined up at an appearance to meet him after the Series win. While those days are long over, anyone can quickly pull up anything you might want to know about his career and personal life through a quick Google search. But Joe Elliott, the star pitcher in several Negro League East-West All-Star games in the 1950s? Where was he? Was he alive? Dead? Was Joe even his real name? Your guess was as good as mine. In talking with players, everyone just assumed their teammates were all deceased, and no artifacts existed; if they were around, they would have known by now. While several hundred players were known to be alive, that number seemed awfully low for a league that existed from 1920 to 1963. Using a combination of player interviews, old newspaper articles found in online archive databases, a variety of people-finder websites, and a phone bill that my parents fronted, magic began to be made. By piecing together approximate ages, places of birth, and any additional details gathered through these sources, I began to track down former Negro League players who might have still been alive. In a matter of minutes, I was able to chop down a list of ninety-seven Russell Patterson's in the US to under ten. With a tip from one of his former teammates that Patterson had once lived in Paterson, New Jersey, I was able to locate him. I found his phone number and blindly called him. We spoke for nearly two hours, and he began to cry. Age seventy at the time, Russell was still coaching high-school baseball and football, umpiring full time, and regularly trying to convince his athletes that he played professional baseball with the famed Indianapolis Clowns, even though he had little to show for it.

Now, after having co-organized nearly ten Negro League player reunions, tracked down hundreds of former players, and helping over a dozen acquire pensions, I have come away with something much greater than the joy of a World Series win. If it wasn't for the Red Sox, would I have ever stumbled upon perhaps the most fascinating and unrecognized part of baseball history? I don't know.

#13. BUTCH HAYNES, W. JAMES COBBIN, REGINALD HOWARD, CAM PERRON, GIL BLACK, CLINTON JOHNS, RUSSELL PATTERSON, LEO WESTBROOK, JAYCEE CASSELBERRY.

As for Russell Patterson, well, we have roomed together at the annual reunion since I was fifteen. He can't be found without several baseball cards in his pocket, picturing a young Russell in his Indianapolis Clowns uniform, which I was able to locate in an old program (you know, the ones everyone thought didn't exist). And Joe, his real name was Albert; no wonder I could never find him. He now works as a security guard at the TKTS discount Broadway tickets booth in Times Square and was able to collect a six-figure pension from Major League Baseball for his lengthy career in the Negro League. While neither has a Wikipedia or Baseball-Reference page, a new sense of pride, like that felt by those lifelong Red Sox fans in 2004, fills their hearts.

—Cam Perron
Los Angeles, California

(In my quest to find stories about the Negro Leagues, Will Clark suggested I contact Cam, who, at a ridiculously young age, had started to contact former players. What he's accomplished is only slightly touched on in his story. What he's done to help gain some attention for these players, help connect former teammates and friends, and help keep this era alive, is monumental. I can't think of a better lead story for this chapter. Thanks, Cam, and I know I'm not the only one saying this to you.)

***

During Christmas 2012, I was home in Kansas City, Missouri, visiting family. On the first Tuesday of the New Year, I found myself in the historic 18th & Vine district. I had just finished breakfast, and was driving away from the area, when something in my head said, "Turn around and go to the Negro Leagues Baseball Museum." I flipped a U-turn and made my way to the museum. Browsing in the gift shop, I heard a guy ask about items for the Newark Eagles. I literally stopped in my tracks and turned around to see who this person was. I had lived in Jersey City, New Jersey for twenty-two months, and was not aware there had been a Negro

Leagues team there. I made my way over to him and we struck up a conversation. Within seconds, he was telling me about the legendary pitcher Leon Day. Being from Kansas City, the only pitcher I'd ever heard of was Satchel Paige. I was drawn into his story as he told me about Day's strikeout record, and how every time he faced Paige on the mound, Day won. He said he was from Hammond, Indiana. I thanked him for visiting our museum, informing him I was a Kansas City native but living in Laurel, Maryland. We chatted some more, and then he said, "Did I tell you I live in Baltimore?"

Time was getting long, and I had to rush to my next appointment. We exchanged numbers and vowed to stay in touch. I kept thinking how cool and random it was to meet someone from Baltimore in Kansas City at one of my favorite museums. I realized that I had left some material I had picked up for my grandfather, so I texted my new friend to see if he was still there. He replied he'd picked up my items and asked if I wanted to retrieve them here or when we returned to Maryland. We agreed to meet up later that day. His name was Michael Rosenband, and he is the historian for the Leon Day Foundation. From that afternoon, a remarkable friendship formed. Once I returned home, I started volunteering with Michael at Leon Day Park. Soon, I was invited to become a board member for the Leon Day Foundation, Inc. Through this journey, I have learned so much about Leon Day and his contributions to baseball, met some amazing people, and become involved in programs that impact the lives of young people. In January 2015, I was elected president of the Leon foundation! My friend and I would have never met in Maryland, but a chance encounter at the Negro Leagues Baseball Museum set us upon a trajectory neither of us could have imagined. The work that we have done in West Baltimore has been featured in *The Baltimore Sun*, Dick's Sporting Goods, and the Baseball Factory! It has been an amazing ride, and I look forward to more memories!

—Michelle Freeman
Laurel, Maryland

***

Just before baseball returned to DC in 2005, I was working as Washington correspondent for the Norfolk *Virginian-Pilot*. Norfolk had been in the running to get the Montreal team, so my editors had an interest in stories about the transfer. I learned of a group of people working to name the team the Washington Grays, to honor the Homestead Grays who had played in DC through much of their glory days in the Negro Leagues. I tracked down some former players and a lot of background on Black baseball.

One afternoon in 2004, the phone rang. "Dale," the voice on the line said, "this is Buck O'Neil." In thirty-seven years as a reporter, I had occasion to interview presidents and presidential candidates, Supreme Court justices, generals and admirals, and all manner of other politicians. None of those stick in my memory like ten minutes on the phone with Buck. He painted word pictures of daytime crowds at Griffith Stadium, and nights on the town at clubs with performers like Louis Armstrong and Count Basie. I was awestruck. He talked about how DC fans had embraced the Grays, and how the team took some pride in knowing that their games routinely outdrew the Senators, who, of course, also played at old Griffith Stadium.

He also talked about how much the players looked forward to coming to DC, where there was a large black population, and a black middle class that could and did support good restaurants and nightlife. He thought that giving the Grays name to the relocated Expos might aid his pet project: getting more inner city, African-American kids interested in and playing baseball. It would take a lot more than a name to do the job, he reminded me, but reviving the Grays and their tradition would surely help.

When people ask me what was the high point of my time in journalism, I never hesitate: "I talked to Buck O'Neil," I tell them.

—Dale Eisman
Springfield, Virginia

***

During the summer of 1999, I took my son Austin to a Royals game. It was one of many games we attended in a season that saw the Royals surrender 5.72 per game runs per game. You don't win many games with that kind of pitching and defense (they finished 64-97). One of the few advantages to being a fan of a bad team is you can walk up to the ticket booth right before game time and purchase a seat directly behind home plate. We brought a baseball to the game in case we had a chance to get an autograph, but as is often the case, the few athletes who make themselves available draw a huge crowd, and it's difficult to get a signature without making a fool of yourself. I didn't want to model foolish behavior for my son, so we took our seat to watch infield practice and wait for the game to begin.

While contemplating whether to purchase peanuts or a frosty malt the next time a vendor walked by, I noticed that Buck O'Neil was sitting five or six rows in front of me. I didn't know that was his usual seat, and that he attended almost every game. I thought it was a pretty special occurrence, and I wanted to take advantage of the situation. I said to Austin, "Do you remember the man we talked about who led the Negro Leagues in hitting three times, and was the first African American coach in the major leagues, the guy who lives right here in Kansas City?" Buck is a Kansas City icon, and I didn't want to make a spectacle of myself, but it seemed important for Austin to see him. I pointed down the aisle and said, "That's him."

Feeling the "autograph-less" baseball still jammed into my pocket, I had an idea. I told my ten-year-old son to walk down the aisle and hand the ball to Buck, instructing him to say, "Mr. O'Neil, may I have your autograph, please?" As Austin approached Buck, I could see that a stadium attendant had spotted him and moved quickly to intervene and prevent him from making an autograph request. I immediately realized that Buck likely encounters hordes of adoring but obnoxious fans pestering him at every game, and stadium personnel work hard to keep everyone away—the reason he hadn't drawn a crowd.

Not wanting to appear as insensitive, autograph-seeking jerks, I jumped to my feet and began to hustle over to stop him. Before I could get there, the stadium attendant grabbed Austin by the shoulder and said, "Sorry, no autographs. Please return to your seat." I was so busy watching Austin and the usher and becoming embarrassed that I had sent him to breech the protective barrier Royals security had created, I didn't notice that Buck had stood up, walked over to Austin, and reached his hand out for the ball. He said, "He's fine, please let him come here. I'll be happy to sign the ball."

While signing the ball, Buck asked Austin if he played baseball, what grade he was in, and who was his favorite player. As he finished signing, he asked Austin to step back. I wasn't sure what he intended to do, but I loved the way Austin's face lit up when revered icon Buck O'Neil tossed the ball back to him.

I know this sounds corny, but if you don't know Buck's touching story, or the history of the Kansas City Monarchs, the Negro Leagues Museum, or what a fantastic all-around great guy Buck was, it's hard to appreciate this. But the sight of Mr. O'Neil gently tossing a baseball back to my ten-year-old son is a vivid and timeless sports memory that I will always cherish. I have met a number of famous people, but no encounter is burned into my memory like the day I met Buck O'Neil.

Over the ensuing years, I watched Buck share his disarming and incomparable wit and humor with David Letterman, and saw him bat in the Northern League All-Star game at ninety-four years old (he was forced to duck an inside pitch!). I remember how sad I was when he passed away, and how proud I felt when I learned the Royals had honored him with the red legacy seat. There has never been, and never will be, another Buck O'Neil. I'm thrilled and grateful that we were able to spend even a brief moment with him.

—Alan Barrington
Kansas City, Kansas

***

I have been interested in Philadelphia baseball since the early 1950's, first following the A's because of their style and personality. The game I will always remember took place in 1953. The St. Louis Browns were in town to play the A's at Connie Mack Stadium, and a member of that team, denied the chance to play and excel in Major League Baseball because of racial prejudices, was the great pitcher, Satchel Paige.

There were very few people in attendance, and as I recall, they were mainly white men. It was clear to me that most of them did not really know anything about Paige or the Negro Leagues. However, I had read about his career, and became very excited when it was announced over the stadium loudspeaker, that coming in to pitch was Satchel Paige. I definitely heard some snickering in the stands. Paige came sauntering in from the bullpen to the pitcher's mound, limbs loose, a forty-seven-year-old player obviously past his prime but still an effective relief pitcher. A baseball legend deprived of the opportunity to thrive in and make the Hall of Fame based on his performance in the Majors, he is a legend, nevertheless.

I don't recall how he pitched that day; to me, it isn't important. Having the chance to watch this legend play was inspiring and unforgettable to me. Because of my affection for the underdog, borne from my love of Paige, I also loved Richie Allen, the first Black star in Philadelphia who also endured his share of difficulties because of his race. I am involved in a movement to put Richie Allen into Cooperstown.

—Ken Shuttleworth
Haddon Heights, New Jersey

***

I recall Satchel Paige warming up in foul territory at a Cubs game, with my mom explaining to me that he was the greatest player of all time who had been prevented from playing in the majors because of racial segregation. This seemed like a ridiculous notion—anyone could see that there were plenty of good ball players who weren't white. Of course, I was young then, and didn't have a historical perspective.

—Shary Rosenbaum
Pleasant Hill, California

***

Visiting the Louisville Slugger factory a couple months ago, I was in their store and came across a selection of autographed bats. I perused the offerings (actually hoping to encounter something from my all-time favorite player, Ted Williams, or second favorite, Hank Greenberg), and saw many names I recognized. I came across a bat signed by Cool Papa Bell; as soon as I touched it, it was like an electric shock ran through me. I was stunned, thrilled, and amazed. "Cool Papa!" I shouted to my husband, who looked completely bewildered. I explained who he was (Negro Leagues, 1922 to 1950, legendary speed), and Andy replied, "That's great," as he wandered away with the friends we'd brought along. I looked at the bat for a while longer and then joined them. As they headed toward the hats and T-shirts, I had to turn back to hold that magical bat again. I returned to Andy and told him again how thrilling my experience had been finding and holding that bat. We walked around a bit more, and I told him I just had to go see the bat one more time. I did, then found our friends, and helped them shop a little longer. They checked out and I went in search of Andy to tell him we were ready to leave. As we headed for the door, Andy brought his arm from behind his back and handed me *the bat*! He'd bought it for me! I burst into tears (I'm almost crying now as I write this) and startled my friends and all the other shoppers in the store. I wept for quite a while, and then we left.

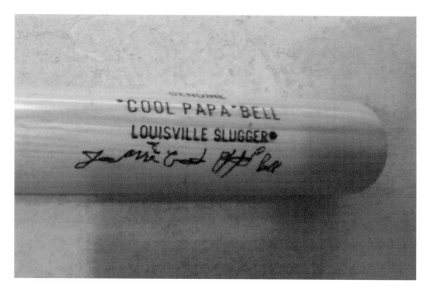

SALLY

For readers who don't know about Bell, here is a Wikipedia entry I like to share with students:

"In Ken Burns' *Baseball*, Bell was described as so fast that he once scored from first on a sacrifice bunt. In an exhibition game against white all-stars, Bell is said to have broken for second on a bunt and run with [Satche] Paige at the plate. By the time the ball reached Paige, Bell was almost to second and rounded the bag, seeing the third baseman had broken towards home to field the bunt. The catcher, Roy Partee of the Boston Red Sox, ran to third to cover the bag, and an anticipated return throw from first. To his surprise, Bell rounded third and brushed by him on the way home; pitcher Murry Dickson of the St. Louis Cardinals had not thought to cover home as the catcher moved up the line, and Bell scored standing up." [2]

---

2 Wikipedia contributors, "Cool Papa Bell," *Wikipedia, The Free Encyclopedia,* https://en.wikipedia.org/w/index.php?title=Cool_Papa_Bell&oldid=882122305, last revision: February 6, 2019 (accessed February 8, 2019).

The bat now hangs in our dining room, next to a signed Andy Warhol print of Pete Rose and across from our Velvet Elvis purchased in Tijuana. A perfect display of *treasures*.

—Sally Harrison-Pepper
Cincinnati, Ohio

***

Minnie Minoso used to hang out at a bar near Wrigley, Sluggers, in Chicago. In truth, I was never sure if he was a part-owner or just enjoyed being there and talking with people. There were batting cages above the bar. I often visited with him; I had known he was the first Black player on the Chicago White Sox and discovered that he had broken in with the Cleveland Indians, for a few games in 1949 and then again in '51, but traded to the Sox that year. I knew Minnie was from Cuba; doing some research, I learned that not only had he played in the Cuban baseball league, but that he played for the New York Cubans in the Negro Leagues. That team won the 1947 Negro League World Series against the Cleveland Buckeyes. He was the starting third baseman in that league's all-star game. He went on to have a long all-star career, mostly with the Sox, until 1964. He also made brief appearances in the major leagues in 1976 and 1980, making him a five-decade player.

My most interesting experience with this legend, however, was an almost ride on the wild side. Minnie loved Ted Williams, and would often say that without him, it would have taken another 20 years for Negro Leaguers to be allowed in the Hall of Fame It upset him how Williams' remains had been fought over by his family (for those who don't know, his head was detached from his body and frozen); Minnie wanted to take a road trip with his son and me to the facility where the remains were being kept, liberate him, and give him a proper burial. He was serious about this; I asked him if he had a plan to accomplish this goal, and he admitted that he hadn't thought it through. I told him I would go with him…but did not want to go to jail for him. Fortunately, this interesting but shaky plan

89

never got past the talking stage. It was certainly an interesting time for me, getting to know this wonderful man, and talking out this wild scheme with a former great Negro and Major Leaguer.

—Margie Lawrence
Chicago, Illinois

***

I grew up in Savannah, Georgia. I loved baseball, and spent most of my life playing the game, on "town" teams, in semi-pro leagues, and in the Negro Leagues. At sixteen, I started playing for the Savannah Bears. I could hit, pitch, and had a good outfield arm, but my size, five feet nine, and the fact that I was Black, limited my chances of playing in the Major Leagues. I was told several times by Major League scouts that my color held me back, and of course that was true for so many great Black players of the era.

One time the New York Yankees came to town and played the Bears; I was young and sat in the dugout as I watched my teammate, big left-hander Larry Norris, strike out Yogi Berra and Mickey Mantle. In 1958, I went to Lakeland, Florida, to play in the Detroit Tigers' instructional camp. There were two hundred players, only three of whom were Black. Future Baltimore Orioles Manager Billy Hitchcock told me, after I struck out five batters in a row, "As long as you are the color you are, you are not going anywhere." I didn't feel that was something he personally felt, just his view of the reality of the time. Another scout told me that I had a better screwball than Louis Arroyo, who went on to be a good relief pitcher with the Yankees. But, again, there was the issue of race. You'd think that wouldn't still have been an issue by then, but it was.

In 1960, I went to the Minnesota Twins' instructional camp. I knew I had the ability to play in the majors, but knowing the odds were against me, I signed with the Indianapolis Clowns instead. I played for them in 1960 and 1961 and was given the nickname "Crazy Legs." Being on the ball field was joyous for me, and I loved to dance. Some thought I took some of the spotlight away from the team's star, "Nature Boy" Williams.

It wasn't a luxurious life, but it was baseball. We received two dollars a day meal money, and often had to sleep *under* a bus when it was really hot, because the bus had no air conditioning. Of course, when it rained . . .

The one day, and one play, that stands out in my memory is when the Clowns played in Royal Oak, Michigan. I was playing first base, and everything seemed to go right for me that day at the plate and in the field. A right-handed pull hitter came to the plate, but my instincts told me to move closer to the base line, and he hit a line drive right to me. Had I positioned myself over more, it would have been a double. Playing semi-pro ball, I remember a game when I pitched for the Plainsmen, throwing a five-hitter against a team of ex-Major Leaguers and bonus babies.

There were a lot of great players on that team. I played with several who went on to sign with Major League teams, and a few made it to the majors. Joe Cherry played with the San Diego Padres when they were a AAA team. Van Rushing was sold to the Red Sox. Paul Casanova played with the Washington Senators, with one all-star selection. Others, who played for the Clowns before I did, made it to the majors, including Choo Choo Coleman, with the expansion Mets, and of course the great Henry Aaron.

I am not bitter that I didn't have a fair chance to play in the majors. I had a good life in baseball, playing into my fifties. I coached for Syracuse University's club team. Still, how can I not reflect on missed opportunities and wonder? How can I not think about the injustice then, and still, today?

—Russell Patterson
Sumter, South Carolina

***

My father was an outstanding athlete, honored as one of the top one hundred in the first one hundred years at Mechanic Arts High School, and inducted into several halls of fame. He was all-conference in baseball, basketball, and football. As a senior, he set a City Conference batting average of .600, a record that stands today. I asked Dad why he didn't play college ball, and his reply to me was, "During that time, the Big Ten didn't offer scholarships to Black athletes." Not surprising, but tremendously sad, that has stayed in my mind.

Baseball became my favorite sport as a young boy, playing pick-up ball whenever I could. Even better, I got to watch my dad, even travel with him sometimes, when he played for an all-Black team, the Twin City Colored Giants. I loved watching him play, and he taught me the game. My father threw a certain way, and I threw that way. He had his batting stance, and I mimicked it. Although he was primarily a catcher, I learned that he played many positions, whatever the team needed at the time.

In 1998, I accompanied Dad to an event at the Minnesota Historical Society of Black Baseball. I listened to the stories of so many gentlemen talking about their connection to Black baseball; all of them mentioned my father. I found out for the first time, when a friend, Jim Robinson, told me, that when the great Negro League teams barnstormed, they had asked my dad to come out and play. When I drove Dad home that night, I told him what Jim had said, and asked him why he had never said anything. His response: "It wasn't important." What? Being recruited to play on those teams wasn't important?

—Frank White, author of *They Played for the Love of the Game, Untold Stories of Black Baseball in Minnesota*
Minneapolis, Minnesota

***

I met Buck for the first time when his team came to my hometown, Saint Paul, Minnesota, in 1946. Buck's team, the Monarchs, was there to play our local team at Lexington Ballpark. I don't recall many of the events, as it was so long ago. I was eighteen, and had just graduated high school. I was a proud ballplayer; I don't like to brag, but I was all-conference in baseball, football, and basketball. I had just set a city conference record by batting .600 for the entire season.

Buck had come up to my coach, after looking at me and saying, "Why are you having that little skinny old boy leading off?" My coach replied,

"You have to see him." My first time up, I dropped down a bunt and beat the throw to first.

Buck's Monarchs tried to recruit me, but my mom refused to let me go. Perhaps, as Buck speculated, she was concerned about the lifestyle of ballplayers, and didn't want her young son to live that life. What is clear is that Buck had enormous respect for me, which fills me with pride. In this interview, Buck reflected on the great pitcher Double Duty Radcliff, saying that if "DD had to pitch to Lou White", he would knock him down. He said that DD was nasty, and would knock White down, because, in Buck's words, "Lou White could hit, man," and that pitchers had to spot their fastballs, because Lou would simply wear out the curve.

—Lou White_

(This story comes from an interview with Lou White and Buck O'Neil. Lou's son, Frank, was the camera man for this. It is a combination of comments by O'Neil and White, told from White's perspective, as well as information from Frank, combined into a single story)

***

I am often asked about my greatest game or day. That is an easy one for me. It took place on opening day in 1943, Memphis, on Easter Sunday. In my first at bat, I hit a double, and followed that with a single. On my third time up, I hit the ball over the left field fence. On my next at bat, I hit the ball to deep left center; it looked like it was going out, but I kept thinking, "Hit the fence." The ball did bounce off the fence, and between the left and center fielders. As I pulled into third base, the coach was waving me home for an inside-the-park home run, but I stopped. I wanted to hit for the cycle!

That night, relaxing in my room, the team's publicist called me down to the restaurant to meet some folks. The owner's daughter was a school teacher. I walked up to her said, "Hello, my name is Buck O'Neil." We were married fifty-one years. That is my favorite day, hitting for the cycle, and meeting my wife."

—Buck O'Neil, as told in a (slightly revised) televised interview with Kwame McDonald and Frank White

KWAME MCDONALD, BUCK O'NEIL AND LOU WHITE

(In this interview, Buck talked about many of his memories. He recalled one time when Satchel Paige was being timed with the radar gun, something that he hadn't experienced before. Paige didn't know the gun was on and was later told he had thrown one hundred miles per hour; his comment was "I didn't know they were timing me. If I knew, I would have thrown harder." Perhaps more significantly, Buck said he was often asked if he felt cheated because he wasn't allowed to play Major League Baseball. He said he never felt that way. He enjoyed his career, and felt that he was in the league playing perhaps the best baseball in the nation. He said that had he been born later, he would

not have had the chance to see Satchel Paige pitch, or Jackie Robinson run, or Josh Gibson bat. He wouldn't have had the chance to watch Ty Cobb, or play against the Babe Ruth or Dizzy Dean All-Stars (games which Buck's teams won more often than not). He never felt cheated. He wrote a book called Born at the Right Time. He also talked about how a very small percentage of the white players he played against were college graduates, while 40 percent of the "Negro" players had a college education. I, of course, did not meet him, but he seemed to be a man of great integrity, humor, perspective, and inner peace.)

BASEBALL:
THE INTERNATIONAL GAME

Baseball is fast taking its place, along with soccer, basketball, and hockey, as a true international sport. There have been Major League Baseball players for over sixty years from a few countries, such as the Dominican Republic, but the last thirty years has seen an explosion of players from Asia, South and Central America, and Europe. This chapter is composed of stories with an international flavor. Some involve baseball played in other countries, perhaps differences in play, or fan behavior. Some are from folks who became interested in American baseball and describe how that occurred. So, whether you say, "Batter up, mate," or "jugar ala pelota," or "shiai kaishi", or "daqiu" ... .. (google translations), it's all "Play Ball".

***

Greece 2004, a warm summer, long before the Greek Crisis, the Olympic Games were coming back to their home after almost a hundred years. Sports fans would visit the mythical country from around the world to experience a variety of sports events and unforgettable moments. At eleven years old, I was starting to explore new sports to see which I might be good at. How would baseball fit into the picture in this European country where, if you say baseball, you need Google translate for people to understand? It started one warm August afternoon in a game between Australia and Greece. The sport new to the country, the Greek national team was founded by Peter Angelos, owner of Baltimore Orioles; since 1997, there had been a national baseball league to prepare Greek players to compete in the Olympic Games. Most of the players of the national team were Greek-American, such as Oriole Nick Markakis.

I don't know why, but I felt that I liked baseball before I even knew what it was; maybe the baseball films I had seen fascinated me, and made me more than eager to learn and play the sport. There was no team in my home town of Larissa in Central Greece, so the Olympic Games were a great opportunity for me to really help determine my interest level. I learned the rules, and then I would go to Athens. A brand new stadium was built for the tournament; never having been in a baseball stadium before, walking into the park and seeing the diamond gave me chills. I sat behind base one, ready to see what the game would mean to me. The first pitch was thrown, and I couldn't believe how quickly the game ended, two hours later. It was one of the best sports events of my life. Every pitch, hit, home run, or stolen base gave me the urge to see more. Greece lost, but it didn't matter. I won a lot that night. Out of nowhere, suddenly I loved a sport.

With the games over, there was once again little opportunity to play or watch baseball, still not well known in Greece. I went to study in the UK, and luckily found my way back to the game, step by step, starting with supporting a Major League Baseball team (Let's go Mets!). I started playing, having the experience that I had craved for so long. One summer I returned to Greece and brought a bat and a couple of balls to play with friends. I wanted them to try this game and have a bit of fun. Most of my friends loved it, and we started playing every afternoon, improving as we learned bat technique and the official rules. No longer was I the only one from home who enjoyed the game. Then I started to wonder why we weren't taught this sport as kids. Though soccer is clearly the biggest and most well-known sport, I thought that if young Greek kids were introduced to baseball at a young age, given the opportunity to play, maybe some could make careers out of it. Hopefully, with the explosion of the internet, people in Europe will have additional chances to learn and follow the game, develop their talents, and continue making baseball an international sport.

It is easy to get hooked on baseball; it is different from other sports, with a magic of its own. The ball park, the movements, the reflexes, the vibe of the diamond, can create an amazing experience, whether you are watching or playing. I feel fortunate that I discovered it at a young age, and had a chance to see a game firsthand and up close to test my interest. It was perfect timing for Greeks to experience a little known, not popular and even mocked sport. I am not the only one who felt that passion, and I am sure it will continue to grow in Greece. The opportunity to just hold and swing a bat, and watch a game in a ballpark provided me with extraordinary enjoyment and inspiration. What I want to share is that although I will experience more great moments with baseball, it is that game in 2004, the memory of the small child in me, that keeps the flame of baseball alive in me today. Always listen to your inner child . . . it is you, without the adult problems, and with a clean mind.

—Cris Harris
Leeds, England

***

When I was twenty-nine and a feature sportswriter at the *Los Angeles Times*, I talked the boss into sending me to Mexico for two weeks to do stories on the Mexican League. My first stop, at Cuidad Juarez, was a doubleheader. In the first game, seven innings, Juarez turned three (three) triple plays. I watched from the radio broadcast booth, understanding only a few of the announcers' words, but caught up in the magic of what I was seeing.

Next stop, Tampico, was a grimy industrial town on the steamy Yucatan peninsula. The old ballpark was in the middle of an industrial area with a lot of railroad tracks. During the game, a switch engine pulled up outside the first base side field fence, and the engineer tooted the whistle. The game was stopped, a gate was opened, the train chugged across the field on tracks that ran across the middle of the diamond just behind second base, and chugged out the left field gate. There's nothing more romantic than ancient ballparks and trains, but who woulda thought to combine the two?

That trip, I also discovered Fernando Valenzuela and dwarf batboys. Que beísbol!

—Scott Ostler, sports columnist, *San Francisco Chronicle*, and author, including an upcoming novel of a wheel chair basketball team
Orinda, California

***

I was a naïve little kid from Chicago, soaking it all in at a Montreal Expos game on a family vacation. The announcers were announcing in French. The signs were in French. The fans were cheering in French. Everything was in French, and I was marveling at my first exposure to a foreign culture, the existence of an entire world beyond the one I knew so well. That is, until the outfielder dropped the ball with the bases loaded, and everyone around me started dropping F-bombs. In English. That's the only thing I remember about that baseball game, that family trip, and my first geo-political wake-up call.

—Dana Rhodes
Skokie, Illinois

***

It had been only a couple of months earlier that my brother Doug and I had the idea of taking the Baltimore Orioles to Nicaragua to play its national team to help build a relationship between the US government and Nicaragua's fledgling Sandinista revolutionary regime.

But there we were, in the colonial town of Granada, fielding throws from the Orioles' outfielders in pre-game practice. The country was at a standstill, with virtually everyone in the ballpark or in front of a TV. It was March 1980, some eight months after the popular revolutionary triumph, and people were finally taking a weekend off from the rebuilding of Nicaragua's devastated cities. Not only was the arrival of the Orioles the first-ever visit by a Major League team to this baseball-crazy country, but the reigning American League champions were led by their outstanding pitcher and Nicaragua's favorite son, Denis Martinez.

This labor of our love for baseball and Nicaragua had not come out of the blue. I had crisscrossed the country a decade earlier playing baseball while a Peace Corps volunteer, and had maintained my baseball friendships during my several visits since. We had contacts with officials in both governments, which, along with the Orioles, gave their blessings and support to the endeavor.

Still, it was a surreal experience to sit in the Orioles' dugout and watch Martinez mow down his compatriots in this context of historic change and intensifying clashes of ideologies. It was equally astounding to witness the Nicaraguan pitchers hold the likes of John Lowenstein, Rich Dauer, Benny Ayala, Terry Crowley, and Len Sakata in check, as the Nicas battled the O's to a 1-1 draw before a boisterous crowd in Martinez's hometown.

The next day, in the northern city of Leon, which had been badly bombed and battered by the tyrant Somoza as he was losing his grip on the country, the wonders did not cease. When thousands of fans, misunderstanding the PA announcer, flooded the field in the seventh inning to embrace the Orioles, it took but one round fired in the air by a fifteen-year-old soldier to stop them in their tracks and coax them back into the stands. Yet this spectacle was soon surpassed when the game resumed, and the Nicaraguan Davids defeated the American Goliaths 4-2.

I know, while there is the occasional miracle on the field (e.g., 1914 and 1951), there are no ties or crying in baseball. But this was the Orioles' pitch-limited spring training, and the celebration of the nexus of baseball, and the overthrow of a brutal, near fifty-year dictatorship. How could one possibly keep a dry eye? This was a revolutionary experience.

—Steve Hellinger
New York, New York

***

When I was growing up, my dad was in the US Navy, and was posted to London in 1974. I had watched a little baseball before we moved there, but mostly what I knew was that Pete Rose was a star, and that he wore number fourteen, so I did, too. My two older brothers had played Little League in the States, but I was the one to play after we moved overseas. In the Bicentennial year of 1976, I decided I wanted to play baseball. There were baseball diamonds on every base in the area. The diamond at High Wycombe (so named because it was on top of a mountain) was a regulation-sized field deemed too large for us, so a high school kid pitched to both teams, maybe to protect our young arms, but the "pitcher" on each team had to field the position. Otherwise, it was name-brand Little League, so the rules were the same. We practiced at fields normally used for cricket matches, and people often walked by and stared. Why were we not play-ing cricket on a cricket pitch? There is a game pretty close to baseball in England called rounders, but it is a girls-only game. The rules are mostly the same, but they use a one-handed bat to hit the ball.

I had just turned nine, the youngest and possibly shortest kid in the league. My uniform pants were way too big. I made huge knots on either side of my waist to make them stay up. My Pirates shirt fit fairly well, but I was pretty comical looking. The uni didn't have many pockets; since I couldn't carry much of anything, my dad would buy my train ticket in the morning when he left for work, and leave it for me at the station. He tried to describe me once to the ticket agent (short kid, white hair, uniform) and the guy stopped him and said, "Oh yes, the Irish kid who wears his pajamas? Yes, I know him." Every time I see a kid in a too-big uniform I think of this.

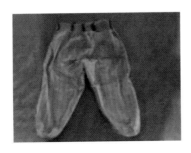

Unfortunately, what I remember most about my playing days is a couple of major "errors," ironically, mental of very different kinds. I was mostly a left- and right fielder, and I experienced every Little Leaguer's nightmare when I did not see or hear a ball hit over my head. The second baseman was screaming at me, and I turned and ran after it. My throw into the cut-off man was right on, but the batter circled the bases and was able to slide in ahead of the tag. We won the game, but I had to run laps for quite a while after that. I made another big blunder while working as the third base coach. Our runner missed third, and I shouted at him to come back and tag it. Everyone in three counties must have heard me. After the play at home was over, the opposing catcher walked the ball up to third and tagged the base. The umpire had not seen the runner miss the base, but I took care of that! The coach was very nice about it, but told me next time keep it to myself.

I was able to keep the uniform at the end of the season because the league was replacing the old ones, and the team that won the championship got them for free. I still have that uniform; my patch from that season is one of my most prized possessions. Two crossed flags, the US and the Union Jack over a baseball diamond. Unfortunately, I don't have a single picture of me in my uniform, or any other pictures of my time in Little League but the summer of '76 lives on in my heart.

—Martin Dunlap
Morgantown, West Virginia

***

I spent a couple of months in Cuba in 2004 during my last year of medical school doing an elective at a hospital in Santa Clara. I needed a break from things, so I took off to Havana for a few days of R&R by myself. I hadn't met any real baseball fans while there, so I (happily) went solo to the ballpark. The Havana Industriales were playing host to a team whose name I can't remember. The Industriales are essentially the Yankees of the Cuban league, with their only serious rivals being a team from Santiago de Cuba (the Red Sox of the league).

There was no Jumbotron, no frenetic music, no animatronic messages imploring fans to "make some noise." Instead, young boys beyond the outfield fence manned the scoreboard, turning number cards with long wooden poles. Jubilant fans, armed with trumpets and snare drums, laid down the game's soundtrack. The field, stands, and fences were entirely unsullied by advertising. Cheers erupted for all stellar plays, regardless of which team turned them. Beer was a buck. And whenever a fan caught a foul ball, he'd throw it back to the players on the field, earning loud applause from the appreciative crowd. Say what you might about the country's struggles to modernize, baseball is alive and well in Cuba.

It will be interesting to see how lifting the embargo affects the free-flow of baseball talent off the island.

—Kevin McKechnie
Nelson, British Columbia, Canada

***

The most annoying thing for me about watching baseball—*basuboru*, here in Japan— (except for games ending in a tie after twelve innings), is the constant noise. Home team players have their intro music for their stroll to the plate; players from *both* teams have their own personal songs performed with horns, whistles, and drums (and sometimes with certain body movements or banner waving) throughout their entire plate appearance.

It's always the *same* song, played the *same* way for absolutely any situation, whether it's a bases-loaded, two-out appearance in the ninth inning of a 2-1 game, or a no-out, nobody on situation of a 10-to-0 shellacking. It wouldn't be so bad if you could get a break when the visitors are up, but there are usually several thousand, well-organized fans with their own horns, whistles, and drums. There's no ebb and flow with what's happening on the diamond; it's a tsunami of sound that's only broken for a couple of minutes when the teams switch sides. Some years ago, one of the twelve teams tried a few games in the "American" style (less noise, more focus on what was actually happening on the field), but the supporters' group protested, and they dropped it.

My advice: If you visit Japan and take in a game, just enjoy the difference; more than that, you might want to bring some earplugs.

—John Revelli
Nagoya, Japan

***

In '72 or '73, I attended a winter league game between a team from Santo Domingo (SD), managed by Tommy Lasorda, and the Santiago team managed by former Major Leaguer Ozzie Virgil. It was played at the Aguilas (Eagles) stadium in Santiago, Dominican Republic. As usual, electrical power had been shut off to the poorer section of the city so the ballpark lights could shine brightly. Cattle trucks with attached racks parked behind the outfield fences, and fans paid five or ten cents to hang on and view the game. After the second inning, a meringue band entered, blaring their crowd-pleasing music. El Presidente, arguably the world's finest beer, flowed freely. A unicyclist performed on top of the Aguila dugout. Team rosters consisted of at least 50 percent Dominicans, with the balance foreigners, mostly Americans from the minors, or aspiring first-year players in the Majors. The Alous were regulars in the league, joined by players such as Tony LaRussa, Rollie Fingers, Gene Clines, and many future Major Leaguers. The umpiring crew consisted of one Domincan and two

American Minor League umps. In one of the middle innings of a closely contested game, an SD batter hit a ball over the right field fence. The first base umpire, an American, called the ball foul. There was no foul pole on the outfield fence, but there was a yellow line painted on the wall. Lasorda immediately confronted the umpire in a face-to-face debate; the ump didn't relent. Lasorda threw his cap on the ground, then removed his shoes and threw them down. The fans cheered wildly. At this point, the umpire threw Lasorda out of the game. But Tommy continued. He removed his shirt and undershirt, and unbuckled his belt, at the same time making a threatening gesture to indicate he might remove his pants. Two security officers and a policeman rushed on to the field and escorted him to an area under the stadium. Fans were in a frenzy, enjoying every minute of the action. What happened the rest of the evening, is unclear. The local newspaper reported that Lasorda was taken to the police station and released later that night. The next day, newspapers reported how this foreigner had insulted the Dominican culture and mores. It was front page news. The sports sections were less accusatory, but highly critical of this American's actions. The story seemed to fade away rather rapidly. Three weeks later, the fans chose Lasorda as the manager of the league all-star team.

—Donald Christians
San Francisco, California

***

In March of 2017, Team Israel competed in the World Baseball Classic (WBC). I was the first base coach.

After winning the qualifying round of the WBC in Brooklyn in September 2016, a small group of coaches and scouts started putting together what could be the Jewish Dream Team of every Jewish baseball fans' fantasy. We could sign Ryan Braun, Joc Pederson, and Kevin Pillar to play outfield, with Ian Kinsler and Alex Bregman playing middle infield. In the end, we did not have a single player currently on a Major League (ML) roster on the team. We were a collection of mostly forgotten guys with something to prove.

Jason Marquis, a ML veteran still looking for a contract after retiring two years earlier, was our ace. Ike Davis, of past New York Mets fame, platooned at first with Big Nate Freiman, who had spent a full year in the majors with Oakland in 2013 before bouncing around the minors for the next three. Sammy Fuld played center field, but couldn't throw, fresh off a shoulder surgery. Ryan Lavarnway, also trying to find his way onto an ML roster, left spring training (ST) with the A's to catch for us. Josh Zeid, another guy who had a cup of coffee, as they say, was our closer. This was our identity. It was going to be the old guys versus the kids. Power versus speed.

In our pre-game coaches' meetings, after looking long and hard at the data, we believed we were better than people thought. And we were right. We started the tournament by beating the host, Korea. The next day, we beat Tawain. We were 2-0, before most teams in the tournament played a single game, and had nearly guaranteed ourselves a spot in the next round in the Tokyo Dome. We had a final game against Kingdom, of the Netherlands, which had a roster stacked with six bona fide ML superstars. We beat them, improving to 3-0. We went shopping for another ten days' worth of clothes, and boarded a flight to Tokyo, winners of the first round of the tournament.

In Japan, we opened against international powerhouse Cuba, and won. We started to think we were going to the finals in Dodger Stadium the next week, but we had to win two more games to get there. The next game was against the Netherlands, again, and they beat us 12-2, their superstars looking more like themselves than in our previous meeting. This set up a must-win game against Japan, the two-time WBC champs, and number-one-ranked team in the world on their home field.

The Dome was packed for the game, with fifty-five thousand fans. It was tied 0-0 in the fifth inning when they scored two runs; we could never recover. We lost the game, and flew home the next day, back to our various jobs and spring training camps, to resume our regular lives. But something special had happened that we didn't realize at the time. We had practiced and played and prepared in our own little world, but after the tournament, the outpouring of support from fans around the world was overwhelming. Major media dubbed us a "miracle team," the Cinderella story of the tournament. Entering the tournament, our international ranking was thirty-seven; we beat the third-, fourth-, and ninth-ranked teams, and won a million dollars in prize money. Fans posted pictures of themselves holding Team Israel signs and wearing our hats. Our team of wanna-bes and has-beens shocked the world, and we'll remember it forever.

—Nate Fish
Brooklyn, New York

A decade or so ago, we hosted a terrific young man from Israel, Elad Shore, for a week. He is a great musician, and good soccer player, and he and David jammed and dribbled together. When he tried to teach him to play baseball, specifically hitting, well, let's just say that Nate will not likely not be coaching Elad for Team Israel in the next WBC. We love you, Elad.

***

Some months back, I was contacted by Harry Grumet, the general manager for MVP baseball, a youth baseball team based in California. Even though we live in New Jersey, they were aware of my son Craig's skills, and wanted him to play on a team that would take a plane trip to, and a road trip through, Cuba. This was arranged through the Cuban National Baseball Association and approved by the US Government (lots of paperwork!). This even preceded President Obama's trip to begin to normalize relations between the nations.

Fifteen boys, ages fifteen through twenty, went on the trip, accompanied by coaches and a few parents. We played four games with different teams at four beautiful ballparks throughout the country. We were nervous at the beginning of the trip, as there were so many unknowns, but people were so welcoming and gracious. Baseball is a nationwide passion in Cuba. One thing we noticed is that there are one-room classrooms near the dugouts at each of the fields; kids attend school three hours a day and practice baseball for six. In a way, it is the reverse of how high school athletics are done in the US, where kids go to school and play sports there, while in Cuba, there are baseball academies at which kids also go to school.

The Cuban teams consisted of kids about the same ages as ours, perhaps a bit on the older side of that age range. We didn't win any games but played a couple of close ones. Of course, seeing the sights of the country, and how people lived, was a wonderful part of the trip. We visited Old Havana, went to cigar factories, saw the culture, and ate some amazing food. We went to the field where President Obama watched the Cuban team play the Tampa Bay Rays. The way we were received by the local people at the games was so heartwarming. Although we could rarely communicate verbally, they would sit with us in the stands, seemingly pulling equally for both teams. While the players from the two countries couldn't really speak with each other, they showed the respect that they each, and the game, deserved. They communicated through the language of baseball.

The Cuban teams were under-equipped, sometimes not even having matching uniforms. We gave them a lot of equipment. Craig gave away all of his bats, but also got a lot of hugs in return. A highlight for him, simple as it might sound, was giving a baseball to a seven year old. Baseballs are like gold there, and we weren't permitted to give them away early in the trip. But when we had played our last game, Craig gave one to that boy. It is hard to imagine saying this so early in someone's life, but this trip for Craig, and for me, was the experience of a lifetime.

—Tracy Matta
Tuckerton, New Jersey

***

On June 25, 2014, at AT&T Park, Tim Lincecum stepped up to pitch for the Giants in the ninth inning. There were no hits yet for the Padres, and the whole stadium was on its collective feet, cheering for the Freak. Something big was happening; my wife stopped responding to my questions. Why? "It's superstition," she said. "We don't want to jinx our team."

I'm French, married to an American, Nathalie, adopted by a baseball family trying to convert me to a sport completely new to me. On vacation in San Francisco at the second game I've ever watched from the stands, I was just as captivated by the stunning view of the Bay as by the game, which, given my level of baseball comprehension and minimal offensive action, seems lacking in excitement. I didn't fully grasp what drove the good-natured enthusiasm of the crowd, mostly families, on this Wednesday afternoon. I was happy to be there, but aware there was a part of Lincecum's feat that was completely over my head. Sure, I sensed the tension in the stadium when the pitcher wound up for his last pitch, his 113th, which would cement his name in the annals of Giants' history. If the Freak closed out this game, he would become the first player to pitch a second no-hitter game against the same team.

He released the ball, and Padres outfielder Will Venable put his all into his swing, desperately clinging to any chance of a fight. He missed, batter out, game over. Forty-one thousand, five hundred people went wild; Giants players exploded from the dugout, running towards their pitcher to celebrate the achievement. Mascot Lou Seal ran an energetic loop around the stadium, showing off his hand-written poster declaring "No Hitter!" Nathalie was beside herself. "Do you realize how lucky you are to be at this game?! This is the first time I've seen anything like this!" she exclaimed. I responded earnestly, "Yeah, it was cool! But I'm kind of disappointed that it wasn't a perfect game." Her cutting response, totally unexpected: "Whaat?! Are you f-ing kidding me?!"

The worst part is, I wasn't joking. I come from a country that is still uncharted territory for baseball. The only visible trace of it exists in headwear; 90 percent of the baseball caps you see on the streets display Yankees or Red Sox logos, with most French people completely unaware of that rivalry, or that "NY" and "B" symbolize actual sports teams. In France, baseball is played rarely, with about twelve thousand players in a population of sixty-five million, a minimal number, compared to those who play soccer and basketball. There's no infrastructure, no Little League, no professional players. I've never seen a game between two French teams on TV, though I've seen many for bocce, curling, snooker, or darts. The World

Series (WS) has only been shown on TV for the past two years, although we've watched the Super Bowl, NBA Finals, and the Stanley Cup on the small screen for three decades. This explains in large part why the French image of baseball is crafted by Hollywood, and no doubt why no one, except a few rare specialists, knows the rules, masters the fundamental techniques, or understands the subtle strategies of the game.

After the no-hitter, we went to Elixir, an historic Mission District bar, to celebrate, and I discussed the game with the other patrons, shoulder to shoulder at the crowded counter. Seeing my enthusiasm, Shay, the bartender, offered me his favorite bourbon, a private selection made especially for the bar. The precious liquid barely hit my lips when, suddenly, a revelation: I finally understood what had escaped me thus far, what distinguished baseball from other sports. It is the only sport where the defense has the ball and initiates action. In all others, having the ball, or puck, or birdie, is synonymous with the attack—a distinct difference for a very different game!

As if I've spent hours driving in the UK and finally realize I'm sitting on the right side of the car, this new perspective, this paradigm shift, allows me to relive Lincecum's exploit in a completely different way. Indeed, I just witnessed something huge, a fantastic introduction to the sport, the equivalent of a football game where the opposing team only gains two yards, a basketball game where the opponent only gets two shot attempts without scoring. I turned to Nathalie to share my discovery. "Everyone is happy about today's game," she responds, "but Lincecum isn't even the best pitcher on the team. The Giants have an incredible roster; they're going all the way this year." History would prove her right. On October 29 that year, Madison Bumgarner's epic performance would close out game seven to give the Giants their third World Series title in five years. It was seven in the morning in Paris, and we watched the game live in the middle of the night (obligatory, with the nine-hour time difference). I'll never forget it. The sun came up, and we headed out to celebrate the new champions.

How better than with a full basket of croissants, a truly giant breakfast? Vive le baseball. Vive Les Geants.

—Geoffroy Fauquier
Paris, France

(I was at that game too, Geoffroy, my first no-hitter)

***

Riding the metro to a baseball game felt very familiar, having disembarked from the N Judah prior to Giants games hundreds of times, but walking out of the station at Jamsil Baseball Stadium in Seoul, Korea on game day was unlike any of my previous baseball experiences. For the previous week, we had noticed ads for baseball all over town. On the subways, people were watching highlights, of both the Korean Baseball League (KBO), and of their heroes in Major League Baseball (MLB), on their phones on the way to work. At dinner one night, a group of young guys came over to our table and started asking who our favorite teams and players were; after a lot of soju and minimal understanding through a thick language barrier, we had bonded over America's pastime. We were just starting to realize how baseball-crazy Korea really was.

Outside the stadium, street vendors were hawking fried pancakes, fried chicken, and soju—the ubiquitous rice wine Koreans seem to drink like water. Following the example of the hometown LG Twin fans headed towards the stadium, my friend and I purchased our bottles of soju, which conveniently came with an empty two-liter bottle for transport through the stadium gates (no glass allowed!), a box of fried chicken, and some mystery street food, and headed in for this midweek tilt between the Twins and the visiting Samsung Lions. After walking through the gates, there was a line to our right for fans to inflate their thunder sticks, and the equivalent of a 7-Eleven on the left to pick up your bottles of Cass beer. The Cass is sold in forty-ounce bottles. Did I mention Koreans like to drink?

I have been to my fair share of midweek "sellouts" at AT&T park, where the loudest cheers of the night are to scare away seagulls, but this night, where the stadium was maybe a quarter full, was the most energetic stadium I have ever experienced (save the eighth and ninth innings of game five of the 2014 National League Championship Series).

In Korea, the fans sit behind their team's respective dugout; the visitors had nearly as many supporters as did the Twins. After the national anthem, we settled into our seats, expecting the standard buzz of the crowd. To our surprise, the energy in the stadium was ratcheted up to eleven as the leadoff hitter approached the plate in the top of the first. Visiting fans serenaded him with a choreographed song, set to the tune of a K-pop song, and everyone on the visiting side was standing, singing, dancing, and cheering on their batter. Leading the cheers were six scantily clad cheerleaders, and one energizer bunny-esque emcee, who didn't stop dancing for the entire game. The cheers, specific to each player, echoed back and forth depending on who was up; everyone in attendance knew every word. Strike out? There was a song for that. Walk? Had a song. Home run? You bet. There were times when both sets of fans were singing their choreographed songs in a cacophonous roar that echoed around the stadium.

After the fifth, the benches emptied, both teams heading to center field to converse and stretch. It looked like a pre-game catch-up between old teammates, commonplace at MLB games, but this was the fifth inning. Had we had too much soju? Had they had too much soju? Seeing the looks of confusion on our faces, the fan sitting next to us explained through hand-motions and limited English that this was the Korean version of the seventh inning stretch. Maybe a stretch in the middle of the game does make more sense. At least it served as an opportunity for fans in attendance to replenish their supply of Cass.

The beer and soju flowed generously through the stands; everyone was in high spirits, happy to be at the game, and enjoying this national obsession. No one left early and no one was glued to their phone. People were there to enjoy baseball. As the night wore on, we started to pick up the songs and hand motions, and tried to sing along. We were hooked; on our way out at the end of the night, we were already making plans to catch another KBO game during our trip.

—Josh Rushakoff
San Francisco, California

***

José Pérez Colmenares Stadium is the home of the Tigres de Aragua, one of the eight teams that currently form the Venezuelan "Winter League." David (aka Dave) Concepción, Cincinnati Reds all-star shortstop always came to Venezuela and played with the Tigres. One game, a ball was hit to Ron (former Rangers' manager) Washington at third base, and he was caught off guard. He barely put some glove on the ball, fumbling it into the air for a clear error and a man on base. Except that it wasn't. Concepción, as if he predicted what was going to happen, was right where the baseball was supposed to land, caught it barehanded, and threw a strike to first base to get an impossible out. Miggy Cabrera started as a teenager with the Tigres as a shortstop, but quickly moved to third base as his young body started to fill up with muscles, and he lost the "grace" a shortstop should have. I saw teenage Miggy smash balls literally out of the stadium. The sound the ball produced when he hit it was a different sound, louder than everybody else.

I also remember a game I attended with a group of friends, mostly teenagers, to see our beloved Tigres, where the weird events in the crowd, typical of the crazy things that happened at a 1980s Venezuelan baseball game, are hard to forget. Adults requested their "buckets of beer"; yes, in Venezuelan stadiums, beer sellers carry the beer in eighteen-liter plastic buckets. Vendors cover a wide space in the stands and may not be available right when you want a beer. So, in those times, you could pay a nice extra tip to the bucket carrier to simply leave the bucket with plenty of beer cans and ice to keep it cold. As you can guess, people drink heavily in those games. (It's very hot in Venezuela all year long.) That day, I remember seeing a very big guy miss a step up in the stands and roll all the way down the concrete steps. We thought he badly hurt himself, but, totally wasted, he just started to snore in the spot where he landed.

What happened later, when Oscar, one of the adults in my group, took my brother to buy a hot dog, and they both wound up in the police truck along with other drunks and badly-behaved fans, is another story. We never really did find out if Oscar paid for those hot dogs . . .

—Javier Ferro
Baden, Ontario, Canada

***

In the early 1920s, Pio Anca arrived in Havana, Cuba, on a ship that sailed from La Coruña, Spain, seeking a new life and an opportunity. He started a business and became successful. At a dance, he met a tiny young beauty, Anuncia Rodriguez, recently arrived from Galicia. They married, and a few years later, their only child, a daughter, Clara Maria, was born.

In Cuba, Pio also discovered a new passion, a sport he came to love. Baseball did not exist in Spain at that time; it barely makes a ripple in the collective consciousness even today. But in Cuba, then as now, it was the national sport of choice. Raised in soccer-crazy Spain, he played competitive soccer in Havana, but gradually learned about, and became captivated by, the favorite athletic pastime of his new homeland. He became an enthusiastic fan of the sport in general, and of the Havana Club in the Cuban Professional League, attending games to cheer on his favorite team. He saw American players during winter ball in Cuba, but the opportunity to experience and fall in love with Major League Baseball, and his future favorite ball club, would have to wait until after World War II.

Pio flew products from US factories to Cuban showrooms; during business trips to St. Louis, his contacts took him to games at Sportsman's Park, and he became a diehard fan of the Redbirds and their star player Stan "The Man" Musial. In Havana, Pio always had time for baseball, and took Clara to games, along with her "big brother" Pucho, the son of family friends. Always a rebel, Clara became a fan of the Almendares, while Pio and Pucho were Havana fans. She wanted to be different, and argue about which team was better. Now seventy-nine, Clara still fondly recalls those games, and enjoys a hot dog at the ballpark with her kids and grandkids as she used to do with her dad and Pucho.

With the Cuban revolution, Pio lost his business and returned to Spain, leaving Clara and her husband behind, but taking his infant grandson back to his homeland. He would never return to Cuba. Baseball was still unknown in Spain; with no internet or cable TV, Pio would not see a game, or even a score for over five years. Sometimes life throws baseball fans a high and tight fastball; "chin music." In a twist of irony, his young friend Pucho remained in Cuba, and became famous as Liborio Noval Barbara, the longest-serving official photographer of a once aspiring young pitching prospect, who the world came to know in a very different capacity: Fidel Castro, the leader of the Cuban Revolution.

In Spain, Pio introduced his young grandson to baseball, continuing this connection after immigrating to the US in 1965. Though they lived in Chicago, he made sure the first baseball team name the boy learned was the Cardinals, and the first player name he could recall was Stan Musial. The two played catch in the yard, and enjoyed the heyday of Cardinals baseball in the late 1960s, from the thrill of victory in 1967 to the agony of Bob Gibson's shocking defeat by Mickey Lolich and the Tigers in game seven of the 1968 World Series. They moved to Pennsylvania, and Pio encouraged his grandson's Little League participation. Both became fans of Pittsburgh Pirates star and fellow Hispanic Roberto Clemente, or "Bob" Clemente, as he was often referred to in those politically incorrect days.

I, of course, am Pio's grandson. Years later, I met a young woman, Kit, from Wisconsin, a Packers fan with no interest in baseball or my new team, the Brewers. Our marriage changed that completely and irrevocably. We regularly attend games, and our "bucket list" includes seeing every Major League Baseball park. An American girl became a fan of America's Pastime because of a Spanish-Cuban immigrant who learned to love baseball in the parks of Havana and St. Louis. My son was a good Little Leaguer but became more interested in soccer; my daughter Kayann, Pio's great-grand-daughter, carries on our baseball lineage. She still treasures the baseball tossed to her by Brewers bullpen catcher Marcus Hanel during the last game at County Stadium in 2000, when she was a cute little girl in pigtails. Years later, she and her fellow fan-fiancé celebrated their engagement at a Brewers game in Miller Park. Her daughter, Clara, is destined to be a fan as well. Baseball frowns on gambling, but what are the odds that Pio, the man from Spain who became a lifelong fan of baseball, would have great-great grandkids who carry on his baseball fandom? To paraphrase Yogi Berra, "It will be like déjà vu all over again."

—Joseph Botana
Kiel, Wisconsin

***

Winter baseball in Melbourne, Australia, is a fun time. My dad got me playing at a young age. There were enough people to field a few teams, but boys usually played Australian-rules football, as I did after a couple of seasons of U-9 baseball. Still, baseball was the game I couldn't step away from. U-16 was a great time; we would play early Saturday morning, and if we were good enough, we would join the older guys, who were known as the firsts and seconds. The "firsts" were the best players from your club, known as "the ones"; the "seconds" were the second nine. We'd leave home Saturday morning to play, have a shower at end of play, go out that night with baseball friends, and come home Sunday afternoon. Baseball in Australia is pretty much the same as in the US, with the exceptions being that wooden bats are used at all levels of play, and in Little League, even coach-pitch, after four balls a tee is brought out for kids to hit off, rather than taking a walk.

My love for US baseball started during the Braves versus Twins World Series in 1991. I was fifteen, and I'd stay up and watch the games in the late hours of the night into morning. I was, of course, tired at school the next day, but all I could think about was the next game. Mum let me sleep one morning; I woke up at midday with a note next to my bed saying, "I left you sleeping so you could get ya rest. Don't want to miss tonight's game."

I became a White Sox fan when Bo Jackson, my favorite player, signed; when the Sox became his team, they became my team, as well. I watched, over and over, the VHS recording I had purchased, a Sox versus Blue Jays game. I still remember asking Mum if she reckoned I'd ever go to a game at Comiskey Park. She smirked and said, "Maybe one day." In 1999, on holiday, I stepped foot inside Comiskey—my dream realized.

—Jason Hosking
Solon, Iowa

***

I can't recall where I was going, or the month or year, but I happened to pass by a football (soccer) field one fine day as I was heading to work. To my surprise, a few guys, around seven to nine in number, were on the field throwing and catching a ball, with others holding long metal and wooden bats. I stopped and looked for a while, and continued to my workplace. Some time passed, and one day during lunch, a man walked into our wood factory, located close to that football field, and inquired whether we could curve a bat for his team, and how much it would cost. This led me to ask if the bat was what I saw on the field being used to hit the ball. Suddenly I became interested in the game, due to the way the man explained the use of the bat and other equipment used for the game, and what it was about.

A week later, I met this man on the same field, and started practicing and learning how to play baseball. I automatically joined his junior team, by then called the St. Nickels Ants, as an outfielder, but also at times playing second base. I played on the team for two years, and then moved up to join the senior team as an outfielder. I played for a while, and saw the need to develop and spread the game in my community. This led to one week of educating the local kids already playing football, about a fantastic game called baseball, that could make them super heroes, and take them abroad in the future if they took it seriously. I was amazed at the number of kids waiting for me on the football field when I got there, and little by little, they became interested in the game, which became accepted by their parents. I formed the Top Royals 13U community team; at first it was all boys under thirteen, which then grew into the 15U Top Raiders community team, and then 18U and above, the Tema Royals community team. Most of them have now finished high school and college, and are now working.

Another intriguing fact is that some of those kids I trained informed their sports tutors and friends in school about their experiences in the game, and that lead me to two schools, St. Paul Methodist School, and then the Celestial School Complex, which I now handle as the coach of the baseball team. I have remained at the school after those lovely first kids left. I also formed softball teams in those same schools, but I had issues with tutors and a few parents for introducing such a game to the girls, not leaving it for the boys alone. I had to halt the girl's part of the game and continue with only the boys.

It was the same story in my community as parents were unwilling to release their girl children to play softball. But the younger sister of a boy who plays baseball, by the name of Clara Baiden, told me one day that she would like to play with the boys. I objected to her request, but she kept nagging me until I gave in one day. I made her stand by me and catch balls thrown to me by the players. Wahooooo! She did that with ease, though I had never taught her how to catch ground balls. Clara was on the field the next time we met for practice, and I had no other choice but to go to her parents and ask permission for her to join the team. Believe me, the parents proved difficult, but I opted to take full responsibility for her safety during and after practice. Clara has been a main pillar of my team since she joined with her brother, playing catcher and second base. I can confidently say that she has been the force that has attracted all the other girls to my team since then. I now have seven girls who can play actively in a baseball game in my community. Clara is now the assistant captain of the 13U Top Royals community team. Since last year, I managed to convince the school authorities to allow a few determined girls to join the school baseball team so that girls' baseball can be developed.

—Victor A. Buxton
Tema, Accra-Ghana

***

On January 19, 1986, at twenty-three years old, I witnessed the best base-ball game I had, and have, ever seen in Cuba, where I grew up. It was at a level close to the famous 2003 American League Championship Series game, when Yankee Aaron Boone hit his home run against Boston.

The game involved the best two teams on the island, Industriales versus Vegueros. The Vegueros had on the mound Cuba's best pitcher at the moment, Rogelio Garcia, sort of a Roger Clemens at the top of his game. The batter was Agustin Marquetti, my childhood hero, first baseman from the Industriales team, a legend of Cuban baseball. He had hit a home run against the US in the XVIII World Amateur Tournament in 1970 in Colombia against Burt Hooton; in Cuba, that was like Bobby Thompson's "shot heard around the world" for the Giants in '51.

On this day, it was the bottom of the fourteenth or fifteenth inning when Marquetti stepped to the plate, with the score tied. On a 0-1 count, Marquetti hit the ball into the right field stands, and kaboom! People went crazy.

It was the best game I have ever witnessed. I still get chills every time I see something about that game. There was an explosion of joy in the whole city that I have never witnessed so far. I guess it's like the one Cubs fans must have felt this year after so many years in the waiting.

—Waldo Espinosa
Burcht, Belgium

***

I am a second-generation American citizen, born in Manhattan in 1954, and raised in the Bronx. My father was born to Greek immigrant parents in Manhattan in 1921, and for whatever reason, loved baseball. All these years later, I still vividly remember the day Dad came home with my first baseball mitt and ball. I was only five, but recall playing catch with him for the first time. He was a passionate New York Giants fan; although very disappointed when they moved to San Francisco in 1958, he never stopped being a big fan, and took my brother and me to Mets games only when the Giants came to town. Secretly, I really liked the Yankees; players like Mantle, Ford, Maris, Stottlemyre, Bouton, and Richardson, were my baseball heroes. I watched their games on local WPIX Channel 11 and listened on the radio.

I played all sports, but baseball was by far my favorite. Like many young American boys, my dream was to play on a big-league team, preferably the Yankees, but that dream was demolished one lazy spring afternoon in 1970, when I got home from school and found Dad home from work early, on the phone booking a flight to Athens. Confused, I asked what was going on, and he said, "Your mother will explain." He'd gotten a new job that would take our family to Athens. That was well and good, but as far as I was concerned, Greece had one major fault at that time: there was no baseball there.

The move was traumatic for me, but I learned to accept this major life change. In hindsight, I must admit my chances of playing baseball professionally, my primary goal, were not very good. With that perspective, moving to Greece wasn't the terrible catastrophe I thought it would be. I obtained a master's degree in management at American universities, and went into business with my younger brother. My involvement with baseball was limited to checking three- or four-day-old box scores of my favorite teams in a local English newspaper, the *Athens News*. However, I was to get another chance to be involved with organized baseball as a player and coach. Baseball actually came to the country where I, and just about everyone else, never dreamed it would ever appear! To do so, something extraordinary had to happen, and it did: the Olympic Games.

On September 6, 1997, the International Olympic Committee chose Athens to host the 2004 games, a decision met with great jubilation throughout Greece. The Greek general secretariat of sports immediately set about evaluating and organizing every summer Olympic sport played in Greece, with great emphasis on track and field events. As the host country, the political leadership wanted to field athletes in every event. Greece had world-class athletes in track and field, weight lifting, swimming, gymnastics, and team sports, including soccer, volleyball, and basketball. However, upon reviewing the list of Greek athletes and teams in each sport, the deputy minister of sports, Mr. Andreas Fouras, quickly recognized that Greece did not have three Olympic-ready teams: field hockey, softball, and baseball. He ordered his staff to set about the task of fielding teams to represent Greece in these sports. Individual sports federations were created overnight for each. While establishing the federations was not difficult from a bureaucratic perspective, establishing teams, finding Olympic-caliber athletes and coaches, was extremely hard. The simple fact was that none of those sports were cultivated, even played, in Greece. Without athletes or coaches, you can't assemble competitive teams.

By 2000, with significant help from Major League Baseball International, the Hellenic Amateur Baseball Federation had organized the first Greek Baseball Championship, with six participating men's teams. By 2001, the Hellenic Amateur Softball Federation organized the first Greek Softball Championship, with six women's teams. It didn't take long for the federations to recognize that the only way to field Olympic-caliber teams would be to identify Greeks of the diaspora who could claim citizenship and compete for Greece. Fortunately, there was a plethora of outstanding athletes of Greek heritage in each sport who were born and raised in North America. Almost all the baseball players were current or former players, with Major or Minor League experience. Identified and recruited by Peter Angelos and the Baltimore Orioles organization, they included Clayton Bellinger, Erik Pappas, Nick Markakis, George Kottaras, Clint Zavaras, and Mike Tonis.

I harbored no foolish pipedream of playing on the team; I would be forty-nine years old at the time of the games. But I did hope to be involved as a coach, or in some other capacity, as I suspected few people in Greece knew the game as well as I did. I volunteered to help with the preparations to field a national team, starting by coaching one of the first teams, Spartakos Glyfadas, comprised mostly of high school students from in and around the Athens suburb of Glyfadas. The dream of participating in the Athens Olympics as a player on the Greek baseball team was on the mind of every player on my team, and in the new league. From the initial six teams, and approximately 120 registered baseball players in 2000, by 2004, it had grown to nineteen teams, and over 1,200 registered baseball players, all with Olympic aspirations.

When I started coaching in late 2000, few of the players understood many rules regarding less common plays, such as the infield fly, dropped third strike, interference versus. obstruction, tagging up, balk, and intentionally dropping a line drive or fly ball. By 2004, my guys knew the rules better than any other players in Greece. I taught them the specific skills every baseball player should have, such as bunting, stealing bases, use of signs, sliding, and how to pick up a breaking ball. Because of those years of training and practice, we won the first Greek Baseball League Championship in 2004. That first championship was greatly celebrated by our team, and surely was the highlight of my managerial and coaching career. I lead my team to five consecutive championships, but that first was surely the most satisfying and memorable baseball moment for me.

—Tom Mazarakis
Athens, Greece

***

It has long been a wish of mine to travel across to the other side of the globe (10,201 miles, to be exact) to Baltimore, the home of two sporting passions of mine, the Orioles and the Ravens. After procrastinating for a few years, I decided it was finally time to bite the bullet and head to America. I planned the trip of a lifetime, coast to coast, Los Angeles to Baltimore, in order to finally see the Orioles live, the team I have long followed and covered on my blog (TBLDaily.com) I planned the entire trip to coincide with Opening Day, 2015. After some fun on the West Coast, I caught my first glimpse of Baltimore as the plane flew overhead. The excitement was growing, but so were my concerns. I had heard issues about safety; more importantly, how would I feel if my baseball expectations weren't met, if the Orioles lost the two games I'd plan to see or worse—if the predicted thunderstorms wiped out both? Would these three days be as good as I'd imagined?

My experiences are too numerous to describe in a short baseball memory. Brian, Megan, and Chris from BMORE Around Town; beers and burgers with seven hundred Orioles fans at Nobles Pub for a pre-game party; an interview with Brett Hollander of WBAL radio, who has shown such interest in someone from Australia covering the Orioles with such passion; watching the game with new friends. Due to the excessive alcohol consumed, the next few hours were a bit of a blur, but Toronto lit up Bud Norris, and the scoreboard was as ugly as the weather. The next morning, very hungover, I wondered how I'd get through another busy day. Plans to tour the MASNSports studio with my friend Pete derailed when I received a Twitter message from center fielder Adam Jones inviting me to the Orioles warm up and take batting practice (BP)—on the field! We had communicated online; I think he's a great player for how he plays the game, and a better man for the charitable work he does for the less fortunate.

At four o'clock, Orioles staff took me onto the field as the O's commenced pre-game warm ups and BP. I stayed for an hour as many of the players and coaches I have come to admire and respect passed by. It was surreal watching Manny Machado's cannon of an arm from a meter away, or Chris Davis launch bomb after bomb from behind the batting cage. Adam came over to chat while he waited his turn. The vibe noticeably changed during warm-up when "Jonesy" appeared; suddenly, everyone was relaxed. When the Blue Jays began warming up, Adam went inside the locker room, and I was ready to head to my seat. Suddenly, "PT," the well-known Orioles equipment manager, invited me into the locker room to chat with Adam. Was this really happening? What an opportunity!

PT showed me around the entire facility. Having seen most areas of MCG, Melbourne's one hundred thousand-plus seat stadium, I was shocked at how different things were. Everything here was bigger; the gym, the equipment, video and medical rooms. We weaved our way to the players' locker room where Adam and a few other O's wandered around. I spoke with Adam at his locker for twenty minutes. I knew I would never have such an opportunity again. Inside the locker room was a putting green, table tennis and pool tables, and many television screens. Davis wandered over, and Adam introduced us. I introduced myself as "Dan Clark, from Australia." Jokingly, he responded, "Chris Davis, from Texas." I was used to watching this man hit balls four hundred-plus feet, with what appeared to be super-human strength, so it was a fun moment as he showed his human side and fun personality.

Adam and I talked until he needed to get ready for the game. After thanking him and starting to leave, I heard Chris' voice from across the room yell, "See ya, Dan Clark, from Australia!" Immediately, I quipped back, "See ya, Chris Davis, from Texas." A round of laughter followed this small moment I will remember forever. Professional athletes are often shown in a negative light as a brutal media focuses on bad behavior. Those few hours had shown me the good in abundance, confirming my view of professional athletes, that most are just ordinary people like you and me. They share common interests and enjoy laughter. I was fortunate to witness this first hand, and wish the media would focus more on this. Journalists have a responsibility to portray athletes in their true form, not simply produce attention-grabbing headlines to sell papers. It's a privilege to speak with these athletes on a frequent basis; it's important their true personalities are highlighted to the public, so people form a fair opinion.

I returned to the field and finished watching the Blue Jays warm up. I thanked PT for the opportunity, and headed to my seat. The game commenced, and it was immediately clear Ubaldo Jimenez was "on," as were the O's hitters. Jonathan Schoop hit his first career grand slam; a late innings 7-0 lead erased my fear of watching the O's lose both games I would attend. I enjoyed the atmosphere of a full stadium watching their beloved O's waltz to a big win. Highlights included seeing fellow Australian Liam

Hendriks pitch (well) for the Blue Jays, and Machado do freakish things at third base. As nine thirty arrived, Zach Britton induced the final out, and the stadium went nuts. There I was, enjoying my first Orioles win unfold right in front of me. It beat watching it ten thousand-plus miles away on my iPhone screen.

So many people, including writers, had come to say hello to me, a humbling experience. I'm just like any other fan, one who happens to share his thoughts from the other side of the world. It was enjoyable, but I don't handle attention well, and couldn't understand what the fuss was about. The one consistent thing at the events was how friendly and warm everyone was, welcoming me to their city, one of which they are rightly proud. Everyone asked about my trip and wished me well for the rest of my journey. I cannot stress enough how nice the people of Baltimore were to me; if you are reading this, please accept my most sincere appreciation, and if you ever come to Melbourne, Australia, please let me know so the favor can be returned. Pay it forward, huh?!

After the Saturday night game, I headed straight to the hotel, exhausted after an amazing few days. Before I set off for New York the next morning, I needed to speak with Nick from Baltimore Media Blog, my final interview in Baltimore. My one regret from Charm City was not meeting with him after the Friday game; my drunken ways prevented that, and I am sorry. I boarded my bus and departed Baltimore some seventy-one hours after arriving. It had been an absolute blast, and I will be back—I just need to save up a lot of money!

Those three days have come and gone; as I sit on my eleven-hour flight from New York to Honolulu, I smile to myself, re-living what was without doubt the most enjoyable seventy-one hours of my life. To say my time in Baltimore was perfect, is an understatement, and doesn't give justice to the people of the city, who, in my honest opinion, are the nicest people I came across on the whole trip, and the most welcoming, friendly, and generous people I have ever met. Anywhere. (Follow my MLB coverage on Twitter: @DanClarkSports)

—Dan Clark
Melbourne, Australia

***

NOT QUITE THE MAJOR LEAGUES

Earlier, I mentioned how the scope of this book has changed significantly since its inception. Originally focused on Major League games, a few stories started rolling in about Minor League games, and college and high school games, then Little League and softball games, and finally games that kind of defy categorization. Baseball is the game, whether played by men with $20 million per year contracts, or five-year-old girls. Differences in the games have been noted and respected in an earlier chapter, but for purpose of this book, and this chapter, it doesn't matter whether it's with a hard ball thrown at ninety-eight miles per hour, or a really large, Chicago-style softball arced high in the air. The common denominators are a ball, a glove, a bat, and four bases to run around. You will get the entire gamut in this chapter of people's experiences with baseball of all levels.

***

Many years ago, I played for a softball team named the Outlaws. Sometime in the 1980s, our shortstop, who was the athletic director for San Quentin Prison, arranged for us to play against the inmates. We were told not to wear blue jeans so that while we were in the prison we could be distinguished from the inmates. I remember driving up to San Quentin village, parking, walking through the gate, and being told by prison security that if we were taken hostage, they would do everything in their power to get us out, but they would not negotiate for our release. This was not very comforting to hear, but we moved along through halls to the big field in the center of the prison complex, where many big, strong men were pumping iron. As we got to the softball field, I noticed plenty of inmates on the grounds, but very few guards. There were a few up in the towers overlooking the field, but if there was any trouble on field, we were going to be out of luck. I did not feel very assured about our physical safety.

As I walked around and talked with some of the inmates, I started to feel more comfortable. I realized that the prisoners really enjoyed having outsiders come and play ball. I am sure it helped ease, if just a little, the monotony of prison life. Our teammate who worked at San Quentin said there had been a lot of talk and betting going on the week before the game, with a lot of trash-talking the following week. We played two games that summer day.

Betting evidently was a very important part of this game. I remember being told that three of the four umpires had money on the inmates. At a critical play at second base, the one umpire who did not bet on the inmates made a crucial call in favor of our team. I'm not sure he had money on us; maybe he was just an honest ump. The other three ganged up on him, getting him to change his call, which ultimately caused our team to lose the game. The second game was called on account of blood, or so we were told. Sometime during the game, what was thought to be blood was noticed in the cell block, and our team was escorted off the field and into the cafeteria for lunch. The game was cancelled, the prison went into lock down, and we walked out of the prison. We never were told the real story.

As I get older, the details of this great experience grow fuzzy in my mind. I remember the apprehension I had about playing there, but I also remember enjoying the experience and feeling more secure on the playing field as we talked with the inmates. One told me he had just arrived at San Quentin from within Marin County, where the prison is located. I didn't know him, but it struck me that we lived in the same county, but in vastly different worlds. It seemed all the inmates, players, and spectators really enjoyed themselves. This experience is something I will always remember from my twenty-five years of playing softball.

—Joe Reilly
Mill Valley, California

***

Our son, David, was in Little League, and never mentioned to us, or displayed any indication that he was not enthusiastic about playing baseball. He was, however, far more interested in nature than the game. There came a play when he was on third base, and had to run home after the batter hit the ball. Everyone yelled at him to slide into home plate, but he didn't, and was tagged out. Afterwards, he was asked why he didn't slide. He reached into his pocket and said, after pulling something out and displaying it in his hand, "I didn't want to hurt this worm." How can you argue with that?

Years later, when my son was twenty-one, I told him about this book and my story, and I asked why he wouldn't swing at the ball when he was up to bat. His response: I really was never interested in baseball, I was more interested in the different bugs and flowers in the outfield."

That more or less confirmed what we already knew.

—Fran Gingery
Roseburg, Oregon

***

It was a crisp, clean, sunny Sunday in the spring of 1988. The grass in the yard immediately outside our home was just shy of ankle deep. My wife Betsy and I, with our young kids, Tedd, three and a half, and Emily, one and a half, were enjoying the beautiful weather, while sharing with our son the game of baseball using a whiffle ball, bat, and sticks for bases.

Betsy was pitching—underhand, of course—to Tedd and me. Standing behind Tedd, together, he and I held the light plastic bat, and together we would swing at the lobbed plastic ball. Our at-bat resulted in a feeble grounder toward first base. As we ran to first, Betsy and I announced "Safe!" in unison.

Tedd was instructed to stay on first, and I took my turn up at the plate. Betsy once again served up a pitch I was able to hit into our imagined outfield. Tedd stayed fixed on first, saw our excitement, and waited for his instructions. "Run, Tedd, run!" He began to run somewhat in the direction of the second base stick, but as our direction was simply to "run," he did; reaching second was a minor detail. Then I yelled, "Tedd, run home! Run home!" Following his dad's instructions, he made a sharp left turn and headed straight for the front door of our house, ran through the open door, and directly into the living room, where he waited for his next instruction.

—Nick Rama
Stone Ridge, New York

***

Every year on the summer solstice, the Midnight Sun Game is played in Fairbanks, Alaska. It's the longest day of the year, and the sun only goes below the horizon for about ninety minutes. The game starts at ten thirty; since it doesn't get dark, no artificial lights are used. This game has been played every year for the last 110 years. I planned and saved for two years, and in 2015, my son Jonathan and I made the trip.

The Alaskan Baseball League (ABL) has six teams, operating out of five cities, comprised of college players from across the country who have played at least one year of college ball, yet have at least one year of eligibility remaining. The Fairbanks team, the Alaska Goldpanners, was playing a semi-pro team from Seattle, the Studs. We spent a week prior to the solstice exploring Alaska and watching other ABL teams. On the day of the solstice, downtown Fairbanks turned into a giant party. Several blocks closed down, with live music, dancing, and food and crafts for sale. This went on all day. At eight o'clock, people started making their way over to Growden Park to arrive when the gates opened. By the time the game started at ten thirty, the stands were completely full, with about five thousand fans in attendance.

At first pitch, the sun was still shining brightly, although it was approaching eleven o'clock at night.

My son and I sat in the top row of the bleachers overlooking third base, giving us the best view of the ballpark, plus the sun setting behind us. I talked to quite a few locals sitting around me who said they'd been coming to the game for many years. One man said he'd seen Tom Seaver play in the Midnight Sun Game in the 1960s, and Dave Winfield in the '70s. It made we wonder if any of the current players would be household names someday. At midnight, the game was stopped, and a woman came onto the field to sing the Alaska state song. The crowd slowly started to shrink after midnight; maybe half of the fans were still there at the end. With one out in the ninth, a batter hit a high pop foul into the stands. The man next to me caught it. He said that since we'd come all the way from Michigan, my son should have it. It's now proudly displayed in his case at home.

The game finished at 1:10 a.m. As advertised, the lights never turned on. The Goldpanners won 7-4. In fact, since 1960, when the Goldpanners started hosting the event, they have only lost the Midnight Sun Game one time, in 1974. Immediately following the game, Jonathan and I had to make an overnight (but still not dark) drive to Anchorage so we could fly down for another ten days of baseball in Washington and Oregon.

—Bart Wilhelm
Traverse City, Michigan

***

On Saturday night, September 3, 1983, the Albany-Colonie Athletics, the Double A affiliate of the Oakland Athletics, played their final game of the season in their first year in the area against the Nashua Angels. In the game, Athletic player Mike Ashman did something never before done by a professional ball player: Ashman played all *ten* positions on the team. He started the game as the designated hitter. From the second inning on, he played a different position in each inning. During the second inning while playing in left field, his manager brought him in to pitch to one batter, putting the starting pitcher into left so he could continue to pitch after Ashman's pitching.

There have been occasions when a player saw time at all nine field positions during one game, but this was the first time that, being the designated hitter, someone played all ten. The Capital District made national news on this night, and it was an enjoyable way for the team and over eight thousand fans to end the first season of pro baseball in the area in almost two decades. Several of the players went on to have solid Major League careers, with Mike Gallegos and Steve Ontiveros being the most notable.

—Dave Hubbard
Ballston Lake, New York

***

I grew up in Portland, Oregon, so it's not surprising that many of my most cherished professional baseball memories are centered on the legendary Portland Mavericks, a Class A team that called the city home for five memorable seasons, 1973 to 1977. A great Netflix documentary, *The Battered Bastards of Baseball*, introduced the Mavericks to a whole new generation, but for me, it was a refresher course.

The Mavericks were born when the AAA Portland Beavers of the Pacific Coast League fled to Spokane following the 1972 season, leaving the Northwest's second-largest city without pro ball. Veteran actor Bing Russell, who had hung around Yankee spring training camps as a child, and never lost his love for the game, stepped in to acquire a single-A Northwest League franchise and move it to the Rose City. But this wasn't going to be just any Minor League team—not by a long shot.

The Mavs were the first minor league team in decades to operate without a Major League Baseball affiliation. Instead of serving as a farm club, they would invite cast-offs of professional baseball to try out for the team, and they came from all corners of the US, and beyond. I went to a lot of games during those five seasons.

In 1973, I saw future Hall-of-Famer Jim Bunning, manager of the AAA Eugene Emeralds, and two seasons removed from his last Major League pitch, take the mound against the Mavs in an exhibition game (at forty-three, he didn't have much on the ball, and lasted two innings). I watched Jim Bouton's first professional pitch in five years when he flew out from New York for a one-game shot with the Mavs. He won, and that was the beginning of the journey that took him back to the majors in 1978. I saw the Mavericks on top of the dugout armed with brooms, celebrating the sweep of a home series. It's been imitated countless times in the decades since, but the Mavs were the first to use the broom.

Perhaps most important of all, I spent those warm summer nights with my dad, Carl Hall. RIP, Dad.

—Claire Hall
Newport, Oregon

***

My dad made me a promise in 1945, when I was eight. He was my baseball rabbi/guru. Along with a baseball mitt came a crash course in Baseball 101 and Cubs history, with special chapters on Hank Greenberg and how to keep a scorecard, followed by my first game at beautiful Wrigley Field. When the Cubs clinched the pennant, I asked Dad if he would take me to the World Series. He felt I was too young, but made a *promise*: He would take me the next time! For the next six years, I cleaned the grandstands for free game passes; at the end of the first year, the kid next to me looked at the National League Championship 1945 pennant flying from the left field foul pole, and said something I heard for the first time, and every season since: *"Wait until next year!"* In '47, I went to two special games: Greenberg was with the Pirates, playing in his first National League game in the Cubs season opener, and I had mixed emotions when his two out double in the sixth drove in the only run to beat my Cubs 1-0; and Jackie Robinson's Chicago debut for the Brooklyn Dodgers before forty-seven thousand fans. What I remember most about that historic day was so many fans brought binoculars to get a closer look at the future member of the Baseball Hall of Fame.

I moved to San Francisco in the early sixties, and became a freelance photographer. I saw the end of the beatnik era, and the beginning of the flower power summer of love era. I became involved in the early gay rights movement, counted soon-to-be Supervisor Harvey Milk and Mayor George Moscone as friends, and helped on Moscone's Save the Giants campaign. I was the publicist on the play Bleacher Bums, a nine-inning comedy about a group of loyal Cubs fans who always sit together in the bleachers in Wrigley. That would change my life. Active in Cubs activities, local media tabbed me the Bay Area's resident Cubs fan. I convinced the Giants organization to honor retiring Cubs announcer Jack Brickhouse, creating the Hey! Hey! Award (his signature home run call), handling the microphone in giving awards to Brickhouse and former Cub great, and then Giants batting instructor, Hank Sauer. I had gone from calling myself "Bleacher Creature" to "Bleacher Preacher." In 1987, Harry Caray tabbed me the team's number one fan. I moved back to Chicago in 1988.

JERRY AND HARRY CARAY

My best playing moment came as a thirty-eight-year-old rookie in America's first gay-sponsored softball league. I became a pitcher, throwing a knuckle ball that danced in the Bay winds. In 1978, Moscone accepted my invitation to throw out the first pitch of the season before two thousand fans at Lang Field. Our team, sponsored by Oil Can Harry's, won the league championship, and the chance to represent San Francisco in New York for the Gay World Series. Before going, we played the annual Gay-Cops game before eight thousand, and I pitched shut-out ball, retiring nine cops in a row, including seven on seven pitches. We arrived in New York, and our team was disqualified from the tournament for having too many "straights" on a roster that included city firemen, a doctor, two Vietnam vets, and a banker! Moscone gave our team a proclamation for diversity, which truly represented San Francisco. In 1979, I played on the first gay seniors' team; one of my teammates was Dr. Tom Waddell, the former US Olympian (and later the creator of the Gay Games). In 1980, I pitched in the play-offs, and struck out former Major Leaguer (and friend) Glenn Burke on one of my knucklers.

All Cubs fans know there have been times when that Promised Land was near, but something always got in the way; Padres, Giants, and Bartman, to name a few. Still, I wait to fulfill Dad's promise from 1945.

—Jerry Pritikin
Chicago, Illinois

(Jerry's experiences were varied and fascinating. Instead of focusing on one, I gave bits of a few. I saw Bleacher Bums, evidently when he was involved with it, a great play. I played softball at Lang Field. I met Jerry in Chicago, and he now has that World Series Championship.)

***

The greatest game of my life did not lead to a fairy-tale ending, but that didn't—and still doesn't—matter. In 2010, my Fairfield, Connecticut Little League team was comprised of a group of kids who had been together since we were nine or ten years old. We knew we could be a good team, and began a winter strength conditioning program, ending every session with the cheer "One, two, three, Williamsport!" Our goal was to get to the World Series. What made this team special is that no one cared about their own home run, or perfect game, or any individual goals. It was all about what we would accomplish together as a team. We were not the best team even in our town, but we knew what we were capable of doing. We knew we were special.

We went through the district and state tournaments fairly easily, but in the last game of pool play in the regionals, we faced a tough opponent.

Down late in the game, one of our best hitters, Jack Quinn, came up with two outs and one on. He had not had a single hit throughout the tournament, but he never got down on himself during this slump, and we cheered him on. He hit a game-tying home run, and we were so happy for him. We won in extra innings, the seventh, when I hit a two-run homer.

Then came the most memorable game of my life, when I pitched against Rhode Island in the regional championship. We were the underdogs against the number one seed, the team that had earlier given us our first loss of the season. I'd pitched that game, too, and I was up all night, so amped up, thinking about this game. Controversy was to mark this game. First, questions about my residential eligibility to be on the team were quickly resolved. It was the most nervous I have ever been, and I was facing their ace. We mostly traded zeros, with few hits and lots of strikeouts, the only run coming on a third-inning home run by our shortstop, Tim Ryan. I had given up a hit to lead off the game, and not allowed any others. Our center fielder, Chris Howell, made a leaping catch in the fifth inning. In the sixth, I threw a curve in the dirt; the batter claimed he was hit by the pitch. With the game broadcast on ESPN, tournament officials inappropriately decided to use replay, not allowed at this stage of play. The batter was awarded first base. The next batter hit a comebacker, and I threw him out at first—but he was called safe. For some reason, replay was not permitted for this play. At eighty-three pitches, two from removal from the game, I walked the next batter to load the bases with two out.

Our number three pitcher came in, and I moved to shortstop. He was new to this kind of pressure situation, and was facing the number five hitter with the bases loaded. Our team never doubted him; we were prepared with a strong bond and trust of our teammates. On our team, the subs, who only played the required two innings and one at bat, knew and accepted their roles. We knew he'd finish the job. On a 3-2 count, in front of eight thousand fans in Bristol, Connecticut, he threw a chin-high pitch. The batter swung and missed. Our pitcher, like everyone else, had done his job.

Our team was the smallest, and probably least talented, in the sixteen-team tournament in Williamsport. We beat Washington in the opener, and then were crushed by Texas and lost to Washington. We all smiled and hugged each other. Our goal was to get to the Little League World Series, and that we did—as a team.

I never went to school with any of my teammates, and we rarely hung out. We do now. I am still friends with a number of them. Some of us play college ball. This was a very special time in our lives, and none of us will ever forget the trust, camaraderie, support, and team that we built and sustained.

—Nicholas Nardone
Fairfield, Connecticut

***

In the late fall/early winter of 1993, rumors began about Michael Jordan's retirement from basketball as perhaps the best to ever play in the NBA. Soon after the announcement, B-roll TV montages of Jordan appeared wearing a Chicago White Sox uniform, taking cuts in a batting cage, looking like he was lobbying for a shot at playing professional baseball. Many pundits thought such a notion was pie-in-the-sky nonsense. I called a guy I knew in the Sox organization. Their Triple-A affiliate was in Nashville then, and I often covered the Sounds, Nashville's team. My source kept my fax machine filled with the latest on Jordan; when the news came down that His Airness had agreed to a AAA contract, I was proud to say that my twice-weekly, five-thousand-circulation paper had that news on the same day as the *Chicago Tribune*.

Jordan was assigned to the Double-A Birmingham Barons; due to the genius of Sounds' owner Larry Schmittou, Nashville agreed to harbor Charlotte, North Carolina's Double-A team, naming them the Nashville Xpress. When the Xpress hosted the Barons at Hershel Greer Stadium, nearly seventeen thousand fans buckled the rails as Jordan took the field for batting practice. Terry Francona was the Barons' manager; several players quietly mused, some with slight derision, that the fans were there to see Jordan. One Baron coach said, "Give these fans a reason to see you play."

Jordan got his first official extra-base hit in that series and made a circus catch in right field, holding on to the ball after taking a spill. My impression was that he had some baseball skills. His arm was above average, although he was a bit awkward in the field. As a hitter, he could zero in on the fast ball. He admitted, in his post-game presser, that the curve ball was menacing him. Jordan wasn't as well versed as a base runner, with a propensity for error on the base path.

He said after the game that he was really enjoying his baseball experiment. He seemed to be the kind of guy who, if he could, would sign every autograph. Fans before the game actually bent the rails of Greer Stadium, cramming to get close to him. He was ushered away by state troopers and Barons' media relations personnel, reluctantly. Sadly, many of the fans weren't interested in the baseball, just Jordan. Under the circumstances, that was understandable, but many wandered the stands, as if in a crowded night club, until he came to the plate, which many others found annoying. But it was a lot of fun watching Jordan making a run at a baseball career.

—Jim Steele
McKenzie, Tennessee

***

It was Cooperstown, New York, home of the Major League Baseball Hall of Fame, and my son, Easton, was playing in an under-twelve tournament. Easton was one of the better players on the team, and with short fields, around 250 feet deep, I thought he was capable of hitting a home run or two.

All the parents, of course, were cheering on their kids as they came to bat. When Easton was in the on-deck circle, I, for some reason, started calling out, "If you hit a home run, I'll buy you a Corvette!"—a ridiculous, and what I assumed everyone knew was a joking comment. Well, on a 3-2-two count, Easton hit what proved to be the go-ahead and game-winning home run. Of course, knowing what I had "committed" to, I kept up the chant in subsequent at-bats, hoping to come even on a double or nothing.

He's only fifteen now, so I still haven't had to come to a reckoning with this promise.

—Drew Lish
Tremonton, Utah

I'm still only fifteen, so I haven't had to make Dad fulfill his promise. He did get me a little three-inch mini-Corvette car. He thinks that will fulfill his obligation.

—Easton Lish
Tremonton, Utah

***

I was a mediocre softball player, playing into my sixties on a coed softball team. It was the lowest level in the league, but still competent and competitive. I was really not a good hitter, with far less power than you would think from my size. In a good year, I would bat .700 if my usual ground balls found holes between third base and shortstop; if they went right to the fielders, well, chop that batting average in half. I was a fairly good infielder, at short and third, quick, though not fast, and a pretty accurate infield arm. These are two stories about the power and limitations of adrenalin—and the need to recognize the latter.

Ground ball double plays are not common in softball, with short bases and balls often not hit hard enough. One game, on a grounder hit up the middle, I glided over to field it, stepped on second, and threw to first for the double play. Well, I was pumped! The very next play the batter hit a pop fly into short center field. Still high from the previous play, I yelled, "I got it!" and immediately recognized that I had no idea where it was. I fell on my ass, rolled over, and tried not to look at my laughing teammates.

As I mentioned, I was a singles hitter, always pulling to the left side. One at-bat, I hit a line drive into right center, how, I am not sure. It was a legitimate double—maybe the outfielder misplayed it a bit—but there was no error. I was now chugging my way into third, already an unchartered sprint for me. And then I realized there was never going to be, ever again, an opportunity for me to score on the power of my own hit. I figured, what the heck, I was the manager of the team, so ignoring the hold sign being given by my third base coach, Neal, I went steaming (or gasping) towards home plate. Of course, I was out by about forty feet, which I pretty well expected. I tried not to look at my laughing teammates.

—Eric Gray
San Francisco, California

***

I was in a softball game in which I got to play with both of my sons. This took place near where we live in a small town in northern Alabama, Anderson. A friend got a mostly church team together for a weekend charity tournament, and was a few players short, so he asked us to play. I was pushing fifty, and Jason and Michael were twenty-five and twenty-one. We played a couple of games; I played some third base and first base, while the boys played in the outfield. The last game I was in left field, with Jason in center and Michael in right. I knew it would be my last game when, in the top of the last inning, a line drive was hit straight at me, and I froze! The ball hit a few feet in front of me, and I was lucky to stop it. After I threw it to second, I stayed bent over with my hands on my knees. My son jogged over and asked if I was okay. I said, "Yeah, I just can't play this game anymore." There was a time I would have caught that ball while sliding down, maybe behind my back if it was just practice. Now I watch my grandson play, travel to Minor League games when I can, and read about the good ol' days.

—Johnny Phillips
Killen, Alabama

***

One of my oldest memories of baseball is from when I was seven or eight years old, and begged my parents to let me join our church Little League team. I was very excited to play a team sport with my friends and to meet new ones. I had loved playing Tee-ball, but this league was different—no more tee to hit off! I had a difficult time making contact, and struck out often. I was terrified of getting hit by the ball in the field, and didn't make many plays. Overall, I was terrible, and didn't help the team. It really upset me, so much so, that after one really bad game, I came home crying, telling my parents that I was done. I'm pretty sure I said a few things that weren't true, like how much I hated the game. My parents refused to allow me to quit, insisting I stick with the team I had begged to play on, and not give up so easily. I went back and continued to struggle, but there were little signs of improvement here and there, thanks to all the extra practice and games of catch with my dad.

During this horrific first season, it became known throughout the league how I was an automatic out. At our August church fair, all the teams played in a tournament. Lots of folks took a break from the rides, games, and food to just sit back and watch the kids play baseball. I was a nervous wreck, and pretty sure I didn't want to play in any of these games, terrified I would humiliate myself. Late in the game, I came to bat, trembling with fear. To make matters worse, all the fielders for the opposing team decided to take a break and sit down at each of their positions, knowing I wouldn't make contact! This had quite a few people upset and yelling at these kids to get up in case I did connect, but they continued to sit. It also lit a fire inside of me—or at least, I like to believe it did—because I drove the ball deep into center field, well over everyone's heads, and past one of the dumpsters in the parking lot. I ran the bases for a home run (there was no outfield fence), but probably could have just walked. I caught everyone off guard with this hit, including myself, and it is a memory I will never forget. To this day, it is another reason I am proud to say I listened to my parents and didn't give up on this great game—and this lesson stands for life in general, not just the game of baseball.

—David Rigelhof
Warren, Michigan

***

I have been playing baseball, in one form or another, since I was seven years old. Being one of the only (or sometimes the only) girl on the team was a source of both pride and frustration for me. When I was nine, I was on the "Reds." My coach was not keen on letting me—a girl—try all the different positions on the field. In fact, he often excluded me from drills, saying they would be too dangerous for a girl. Needless to say, I didn't play much, or have much fun on the field that year.

The following year, I was on the "Twins." There were several girls on our team, one of them the coach's own daughter. He watched me at batting practice, pulling me aside to show me a few things. Within ten minutes, I was whacking hard line drives over the second baseman's head. Then it was game time.

I got up to bat, shaking in my helmet; I could hear my breath. I saw the pitcher announce to the team, "It's a girl," who was up to bat. All the fielders moved forward, figuring I couldn't hit, because I was a girl. Wouldn't you know it? I whacked it hard—straight up the middle. I was on base, and later in the inning, I scored! I was so happy! I was always a hitter after that!

—Aimee Golant
San Francisco, California

(Aimee has been on my co-ed softball team for years. She still can hit, and plays a good outfield and second base.)

***

My teammate, Dick "Wolfie" Wolff, despite being the recipient of a purple heart in Viet Nam, was not much of a power hitter. Standing about 6' tall and 240 pounds, by looking at him one would expect that he could mash the ball; however, in his years of playing semi-pro/amateur baseball, he had never reached the stands for a home run.

Almost every town in Wisconsin has a local team, with leagues throughout the state, including the 3 oldest in America (Home Talent League, near Madison, Land o' Lakes League, around Milwaukee, and Rock River League, between and north of those 2 cities.) We were playing at Hustisford, where the fence in left-center was 315', one of the shortest anywhere I have played. The solid wooden fence was covered with advertising from the local businesses to raise money to sponsor the town team. Wolfie came to bat late in the game and lofted a fly ball toward that short fence; when the outfielders realized they couldn't reach the fence to rob his hit, they stopped to watch. Amazingly, the ball hit the top of the fence and instead of going over, it bounced back onto the field of play. Wolfie pulled in to second base with a double, while his teammates on the bench just roared with laughter at his unlucky bounce.

The following week, we played in Rubicon with the deepest left-center fence, but a short right field AND a terrace about four feet high, running from center to the right field line. Picture this as similar to the CF terrace in Houston's Minute Maid Park, not as deep but steeper. I was on second when Wolfie launched a fly ball toward right center. I watched as the centerfielder got a bead on the ball; just as he was about to catch it, he hit the terrace, causing him to stumble. This loss of balance caused him to drop his head and lower his glove to re-gain his balance, allowing the ball to bounce off of his head and over the fence for Wolfie's first, and only, career HOME RUN! I've never disclosed the name of the unlucky center fielder.

—Lynn Held
Stevens Point, Wisconsin

***

I wasn't exactly a tomboy. In fact, I was a downright prissy little girl, with lace-edged socks and barrettes to match my dress. My favorite activities were reading, drawing, and making outfits for my dolls. Once the weather warmed, during school recess, we were all chased outside. My friends and I would walk around and talk, or play jump rope, but in fourth grade, when spring came, most of the kids headed for the "big field" to play baseball. Not wanting to be un-cool, we went, too; before I realized what was happening, I was in left field, playing "work-up."

I had no idea what to do. Being in the outfield wasn't so bad; as I began to move up, it was obvious that soon I was going to have to do something. Third base wasn't so hard, and then I was shortstop, whatever that was, and my worst fear came true. Someone hit the ball straight at me; I tried to get out of the way, but moved in the wrong direction, and it hit the straight skirt of my Girl Scout uniform and fell at my feet. In a panic, I grabbed it and threw as hard as I could (like a girl, of course) to the nearest boy, who happened to be the second baseman. He threw it to first, and two players were out. I heard them talking, "Did you see that? She almost caught a fly!" "Wow! A double play!"

Now I was confused. A fly? I looked at my skirt to see if there was an icky squashed insect there. Double play? Was that like "double dutch"? I knew I was really in trouble. Fortunately, the bell rang, recess was over, and my secret was safe, at least for the time being.

It didn't take the other kids long to discover that I didn't know anything about playing baseball. They were nice about it, especially since I was usually glad to let someone else take my place at bat, or as the pitcher. Those were the opportunities for total embarrassment that I avoided whenever I could. We played baseball every recess for the rest of the year, and for years afterward, but I never had another play as impressive as that very first game.

—Marcia Roberts
Seattle, Washington

WHAT BASEBALL MEANS TO ME

It seems that this chapter is really the heart of the book, and in a way, what many of the stories touch on, even if not directly. As such, I have debated where to place this chapter. I could have had it be lead-off, starting the book with some truly sentimental stories. I could have placed it last, as if from the bottom of the order, it comes from behind to knock in a few runs and win the game walk-off style. I decided to put it in the middle, right in the heart of the order, so to speak.

Baseball has long been known as America's Pastime. Does it hang on to that moniker because of tradition, or longevity, or simply the continued love of this unique American game? One could argue that these days, basketball and football are more popular, and command larger television and attendance audiences. Is it because there are fewer games, more difficult to take them for granted, and each game means more than in a long baseball season? Is it because they're more action-packed, more visceral, more explosive? Everyone has their own criteria and reasons for why they're passionate about their sports. It seems to me, though, that there's so much more literature about baseball, handing down of traditions about baseball, endless discussion about the history of the game, the players, the statistics, the records about baseball, than in any other major American sport. The following folks provide a few examples about why baseball provides such an anchor, a legacy, an insight into self, whether it is the game itself or their favorite team.

***

I have a passion for baseball. The game cuts to the core; like life, it can be beautiful, sweet, lucky, cruel, and unfair. My love for the game was passed down generationally from my grandfather, who remained passionate about baseball his entire life.

Frank Bertram was born in Paterson, New Jersey in the 1920s, when the New York Giants were at the top of the National League and Babe Ruth was crushing home runs for the Yankees. He remained an avid fan of the Giants until his move to San Francisco at a young age, so his father could work the docks. His love for the game shifted to the Pacific Coast league and the San Francisco Seals. He was a great story teller, and had a remarkable memory. One great story from his childhood involved him and his best friend, Dutch, whose parents ran a bakery in the Mission District; they would sneak on the bread delivery truck and into Seals Stadium to watch Vince and Joe DiMaggio, as well as Frank Crosetti, play ball before they were household names. It is widely assumed he and Dutch took advantage of that bread truck a lot.

The baseball story veers from here. This is not about a moment in the park, or listening to a shot heard around the world, but took place in a little town in Germany, Bad Hersfeld, and the power of an image related directly to baseball, involving my grandfather on September 28, 1944. Frank was a navigator in a B-24 Liberator during the World War II. On September 27, his plane (among a slew of others) was shot down during the Kassel Mission. This was, and still is, the greatest casualty loss in the history of the American Air Force. Frank was able to bail out of a burning plane and parachute into enemy territory. On his person, he carried a miniaturized leather baseball glove that his wife gave him before heading off to war. It was his lucky charm, and proved so during the dozens of bombing runs he did over Germany.

After crash landing, sustaining significant injuries to his lower body and hiding throughout the night, he was discovered by a young boy, Walter Hassenpflug. Walter immediately alerted the local authorities, and helped my grandfather, walking him to a makeshift jail in the small town of Bad Hersfeld. After receiving medical attention, he was taken and questioned quite roughly by two German officers. All his personal belongings were taken from him: his small prayer book, his identification, and the baseball glove. During this interrogation, there was a young woman in the room, possibly a secretary, observing this. After the interrogation, he was led into a jail cell for the night before his transfer to Stalag Luft 1, a POW Camp on the Polish coast.

That night, there was a loud knock; shortly thereafter, the door to his cell flew open. Frank thought in that moment he was a dead man, as a significant number of US Servicemen, especially ones involved in the bombing raids, were killed late in the war. Instead, it was the woman who'd been in the room during his interrogation. Very quietly and quickly, she threw something at him, and it hit his chest. It was the baseball glove. All of the stuffing was ripped out, and it was turned inside out (probably searched for intel), but this young woman must have known that it was a lucky charm, and wanted to make certain that he had it back before being sent away to the POW Camp.

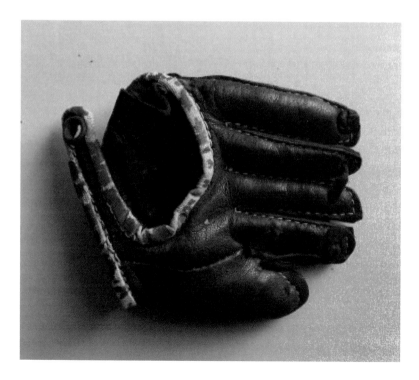

Frank made it back to the States a little over a year later, after being liberated by the Russian Army and sent to camp Lucky Strike. He moved with his wife to the Central Valley, started an amazing family, and remained a huge fan of the game. He was grateful that his childhood team had relocated to the West Coast, and even more so that he got an opportunity to experience a few World Series championships before passing away in April 2014. To tie back into the power of baseball, for the last six years of his life, he was completely blind, but the games as called on the radio kept him going.

The young boy, Walter, literally saved my grandfather's life. As a Hitler youth (forced), with an option to shoot any enemy combatant on sight, he chose to get him help; this is even more amazing since he had just lost his entire family a few weeks before due to an American bomber dropping a wayward bomb in an effort to save on fuel heading back to England. Walter and my grandfather became best friends after a letter addressed to Frank arrived at his home in 1980. These men worked together to build a joint memorial on the site of the lead American plane crash, little more than two miles from where my grandfather was found. I've met Walter, and he is the most compassionate man I'll ever meet; he shows what forgiveness and sheer human decency means.

That's my baseball story. The power of an image, the power of kindness in the midst of devastation and suffering. That glove represented home to my grandfather, his wife, the country he fought for, his love for baseball; and to the young woman who gave it back, it was hope, compassion, and solidarity. One of our most coveted and prized family heirlooms is that small baseball glove that he had during his time overseas. It's hanging on my father's wall.

—Dan Kindelberger
Chicago, Illinois

***

My dad was Harry Oscar Kent, a Cubs fan, from Lucas, Iowa. He grew up on a farm in Iowa with four other brothers, all farmers, and always lived within a five-mile radius of where was born. He played stick ball as a kid, and coached a men's slow pitch softball team he called "Harry's Boys." Almost everyone on the team had the last name Kent. He pitched when they had "unlimited arc," and could put the ball so high in the air no one could hit it. He stopped playing only when his health did not permit it, in his sixties. A Des Moines television station did a feature on him called "Doda's People."

Dad was a Cubs' fan all his life. I remember him listening to games on WGN Radio. The static was so bad, I had no idea how he could hear what was being said, but he could. On the rare occasions when a Cubs game was televised, we were all glued to the TV. If he was in the field, and he usually was in the summer, he would have his transistor radio up to his ear while baling hay and doing other farm work. The *only* thing he would quit working early for was a Cubs game, or his Harry's Boys games. One event shows his dedication to baseball/softball. I was moving away from home, to Arizona, after graduating college. *No one* in our family of two girls and five sons, with me the youngest, lived more than fifty miles away. My car was packed full of stuff. Dad had left early that morning, as Harry's Boys had a softball tournament; Mom was upset that he was not there to tell me goodbye, but I understood. That's how Dad was. All of us are Cubs fans. It's our common denominator. It's our bond, what holds us together. My nieces and nephews are all Cubs fans. It's how we carry on the Kent tradition, and how we honor Harry Oscar Kent. And is it not a coincidence that the famous Cubs announcer shared the name Harry, and the first song Dad taught me was "Take Me Out to the Ballgame"?

—Sherri Kent-Roberts
Largo, Florida

***

Being a Yankees fan is not as easy as one expects. You would think twenty-seven world championships would make it a little easier, but this only brings attention and hatred to those who wear the pinstripes proudly. The success of the Yankees, and the history associated with the legends of Yankee Stadium, continue to be a focal point for any other teams' fans to scream, "The Yankees just buy their players and championships!" However, I'm not a Yankees fan because of their success; I bleed pinstripes, because watching them play reminds me of a time in life where I felt loved, safe, and secure, and all I cared about in life was the pitch count, who was on base, and how many outs were left in the inning. Although, I must admit watching my beloved Yankees win six World Series in my short lifetime of thirty-seven years has been pretty awesome to watch.

I was born in Yonkers, New York, about eight miles north of the old Yankee Stadium. My childhood was challenging, as I learned to survive in a dysfunctional home littered with drugs and alcohol. My parents were good parents, but continued to work through their challenges. Living under these dynamics, there was an atmosphere of hostility and lack of safety for a child. However, I had one escape: When my great grandfather, Lawrence (Larry), and uncle would ask me if I wanted to go see the Yankees play during the dog days of summer, I was ecstatic to know that the only sounds I was going to hear were those of Yankees baseball. The first sound to always help set the stage was the voice of the one and only Mr. Bob Shepard, the longtime Yankees announcer. When he would recite the lineups for the game, I knew that I had nothing to worry about. During these moments, I felt at peace.

As we watched the games, Larry shared stories of all the former Yankees he watched as a kid. He, too, was born in Yonkers, in 1904, and started going to games during the Babe Ruth days. He was a book of knowledge, and could tell you stories of games he attended between the twenties and fifties, talking about all the greats, including Gehrig, DiMaggio, Berra, Mantle, and Ford. Larry believed in keeping score, and ensured I knew how to do so as well. We would work together throughout the game, and he would make sure that I was scoring the game correctly.

As I watch the Yankees today as an adult, I am able to escape from all the daily responsibilities that we all endure; work, personal, and family life demands. I am able to disappear into the innings of a game and take the time to soak in the sounds, and follow my team throughout the spring, summer, and hopefully October baseball. Watching my Yankees reminds me of the time I was able to spend with Larry, and I thank him for giving me these experiences, and helping me feel like a child who shouldn't have to worry about adult things associated with a dysfunctional home. I am reminded that life is like baseball: We all have strikes against us; we all get out from time to time; but the important thing is to always get up and swing the bat the next time you are at the plate. Play ball, and let's go, Yankees!

—Chris Allen
San Jose, California

***

I was born in 1950 in a hospital near Wrigley Field and I was raised on the North Side of Chicago, Cubs territory, but my father was from a southwest suburb, Cicero, a White Sox fan, so they became my team, too, my inheritance. My dad was an intelligent, hardworking man who worked long hours, and when he came home from work, he was exhausted. I wish I had more memories of us playing catch, but we would watch games together on television, and go to the occasional Sox game. I wanted to be close to him, but even as I got older, I never felt I got the attention or respect I craved from him. About the time I turned seventeen, in the spring of 1967, I felt that starting to change a bit; in any case, we sent away for tickets to a couple of Sox games for the summer.

On the first day of his summer vacation, he spent the morning doing errands. In retrospect, I knew something was wrong, as he parked the car at a very extreme angle. He couldn't navigate the steps up to the house, so he just lay down in the shade under the stairs. Mom told me to call an ambulance, and as we all sped to the hospital, I, wanting to help but not interfere, asked the EMT if there was anything I could do to help. He gave me a nothing task, handing me some tongue depressors to hold, and I figured it was to make me feel like I was doing something. Then we were all inside the ER; the doctors tried to revive my dad, but the electric clappers just didn't work. I held my mother, turning her so she faced away from the table. Eventually, the EMT put his arm around my shoulder, pulled me a few feet outside the door and out of sight, and I'll never forget what he said, "Well, son, it looks like you're the man of the family now." I didn't cry until the day of the funeral but even then, the funeral director told me not to cry because "you will upset everyone." I may not have understood then what I do now—that was one of the most astonishingly horrible things he could have said to me at a time like that.

The first pair of tickets we had ordered in the spring were for a game just five days after the funeral. I went by myself; the other seat was for my dad. I sat in my seat and cried throughout the game. My whole life I had wanted a closer relationship with my dad, to be treated like an adult, and now, suddenly, as that was just beginning to happen, he was gone. This whole day was so symbolic for me, the way that baseball helps people connect. It is a game that I relate to more in a visceral, than any logical way. It was the bond between me and my dad.

I have told this story many times over the years. Rarely, if ever, have I cried. I did today telling it.

—Richard Shapiro
Evanston, Illinois

***

I'm looking out the French doors of my wife's home office onto a backyard covered in four inches of wet snow. The skies are gray, and it is thirty-three degrees. The birds aren't chirping, and the squirrels that were out last week are gone. The only sound is the faint slush from the nearby highway. The only green I can see is a weathered plastic Adirondack chair. Sprawling fields of Kentucky Bluegrass and Beam Clay are a distant memory in

Boise, but on Saturday, I got my first indication that things are changing. As I made the loop between home and my barber shop, a parking lot full of cars at the local high school caught my eye: Little League tryouts; fifty-plus kids, ankle-deep in snow, undoubtedly miserable, but wholeheartedly devoted, getting their first cuts of the season. That was the moment for me this year. Baseball was back.

I moved from Southern California to Boise four years ago, chasing love and a quick-start on an adult life. An "a-ha baseball moment" never existed to me until I came here. This was my first ever taste of a proper winter, and so began my crash course in the relationship between baseball and the seasons. It happens every year now. Sometimes it's triggered by something as simple as the first lawn mow; sometimes it's an emotional breakdown. After my first Boise winter, one early March day when it topped 50 degrees for the first time all year, I pulled into the parking lot of Squeezers Burgers on my lunch break. "Centerfield," by John Fogerty, came on the radio. I couldn't help but finish the song, head down on the steering wheel, smiling, fighting back tears. For some reason, that is my favorite baseball memory ever. I've been a conscious observer of pro ball since 1995. I had a somewhat decorated youth baseball career, yet the humanity of that moment rings clear as the one.

It's an added wrinkle to the complex relationship between human emotion and baseball. The narrative of the game goes so well with the changing of the seasons, that living in a tropical or arid climate dilutes the natural course of it all. The line that stuck out to me the most in all of Ken Burns' *Baseball*, is this: "It follows the seasons, beginning each year with the fond expectancy of springtime, and ending with the hard facts of autumn."

My favorite part of seeing those kids play catch in the snow was knowing that nine hundred miles south, pitchers and catchers from the Dodgers and Diamondbacks organizations were doing the same exact thing. Despite the cold and the snow here, Major League Baseball is back in operation; in seventeen short days, we can watch sleepy players hit home runs at eleven in the morning, as they groggily work their way back to season form.

Outside the doors of this office, it still looks bleak. Drips of melting snow look extra uncomfortable after seeing at the first footage out of Glendale and Scottsdale. The snow, however, will melt. The grass will turn green. The birds will chirp soon. Soon enough, the Dodgers and the D-Backs will throw their shrimp on the proverbial barbie and play real baseball games in a cricket stadium in Australia. Soon enough, I'll be neck deep in MLB.tv, living vicariously through the beautiful monotony of the season. Soon enough, I'll be in the backyard, teaching my two-year-old how to hit off a tee. Soon enough, the kids of Northwest Ada Little League will be spitting sunflower seeds and picking dandelions. These are all facts. Baseball isn't just a game—just like the clockwork of the seasons, it is simply a fact.

—Timothy Moore
Meridian, Idaho

***

I opened my eyes to the sound of birds outside our motel room window; my phone showed me it was seven in the morning. I shook the cobwebs from my head, trying to remember where I was. It was another day of baseball travel for the six of us, my son Ryan, and our friends Rob, Tony, Nick, and Shawn, in the midst of another baseball tour. Today was an "off day," but we were going to visit one of the places I had dreamed of seeing my whole life: The *Field of Dreams* movie site, in Dyersville, Iowa. Most of the group was still sacked out, but Ryan was ready to hit the road. By eight thirty, we were ready to make one of the ultimate baseball pilgrimages . . . to a cornfield in Iowa.

Most baseball fans know the story of the movie, my favorite of all time, which touches on everything I hold dear: love of family, baseball, and magic. Miraculously, just before our trip, I found that it would be playing on a big screen in a town near us, so the six of us had a *Field of Dreams* night out. When the iconic last line was spoken, Ryan put his head on my shoulder and patted my leg. "He gets it," I thought, as I wiped away a tear from "something in my eye."

The thirty-five-minute drive to Dyersville seemed like an eternity; I was antsy to get there, and wanted sufficient time when we arrived. As we pulled into the parking lot, I refused to look at the field; I didn't want my first view of "Baseball Movie Nirvana" to be through the windshield of a rental van. I closed my eyes, opened the door, got out, and looked around. It was as if I'd stepped onto the movie set, twenty-five years ago. To the right, the white, clapboard farmhouse that Kevin Costner and Amy Madigan called home; surrounding it, the white picket-fence. I turned and walked towards the field, which actually did rise out of the corn. I was momentarily overcome, and took a deep breath, trying not to let my emotions overwhelm me. Some folks have their moment staring at a beautiful sunrise, or waves crashing on the beach; perhaps it is seeing the Eiffel Tower, or the ruins of ancient Greece. This was it for me; I'd always sworn I would visit this place, and there I was, with my own son. It was almost too much to digest.

Ryan and I stood behind the backstop, staring out at one of the most beautiful fields I had ever seen, sun-splashed, perfectly manicured and green. We gazed towards the outfield, and finally our eyes stopped at what should have been an outfield wall, but instead was just what we were hoping to find: a tall, lush field of fully ripened corn. Honestly, everything was perfect, just like the movie. "Is this Heaven?" Ryan asked, laughingly stealing a line from the movie. "I do believe it is," I replied, altering the script. "It's everything I hoped it would be," he said. "Me, too," I answered in a soft, hushed, tone. "Race you to the center-field corn fence." He laughed, taking off as if he were seven again, joyful and care-free. We were at one of our favorite places, a baseball field—*this* field—and it was magical.

JIM AND RYAN

"Hey, Dad, wanna have a catch?" Ryan asked. I always get a catch in my throat when I see that scene; having my own son say it to me, here, made it even more poignant. "I've been waiting for this my whole life," I told him, grabbing my glove. The six of us ran the bases and stood on the mound. We played catch in different combinations. We took photos walking into and coming out of the corn, as the "ghosts" do in the movie. I kicked off my sneakers as "Shoeless" Joe Jackson would have done. A lady offered to take a group photo of us, which now hangs in my office. Rob took a video of Ryan and I having a catch, ending it by "melting" into the cornfield.

As we headed to the infield, I noticed Ryan running back towards us with some corn. "What are you doing?" I asked him. "I was grabbing some of the corn for our scrapbooks," he told me. "But you grabbed three fronds," I said, looking puzzled. "One's for Grandpa," he replied. "He should be here, but since he couldn't come, I thought we should bring some of the field back to him." Once again, my son had showed me what kind of a person he was becoming. Knowing how important it was for me to be there with my son, he extrapolated that it would be even better were

I with my dad, as well. I was so proud of him; I grabbed him, gave him a big hug, and told him so.

Then it was time to go. We bought some souvenirs to commemorate our time there. It was hot, we were all tired, but it was time to hit the road for our next destinations, the sites of Buddy Holly's last gig and his plane crash. We'd done all we could at the "Field of Dreams," so we climbed in the van and headed north to Clear Lake, Iowa. It was a magical, memorable day.

—Jim Kulhawy
Ramsey, New Jersey

(This is a shortened version of Jim's wonderful recount of this memorable, emotional trip. Please look at the full post, and his others, at Jimkulhawy. blogspot.com.)

***

Baseball is a big part of my life. There is no me, or life as I know it, without it. My dad played semi-pro ball in the sixties. I was born in April of 1966, so there was a whole season of games ahead of me. I was six weeks old when I saw my first game, and I played from the time I could walk. I was three when I sat on Dad's lap and watched the Mets win the World Series; to this day, my mom can't believe that I don't remember when she sat me on *her* lap in July of '69, when a man walked on the moon, but I remember those Mets. My first Major League game was in 1972 at Shea Stadium, as the Mets took on the Pirates. In my thirties, I met my future husband, Tim, on a softball field; he told me he loved me for the first time as the scoreboard clock in Yankee Stadium read 2:53, and former Yankee David Cone was on the mound for the arch-rival Red Sox. Tim proposed in Cooperstown at the Hall of Fame by the plaque of my namesake, Robin Roberts, and we were married at 2:53 p.m., in that very town where baseball was born. I became a Cubs fan along the way; every time I'm at Wrigley, I'm a little kid experiencing baseball for the first time . . . all over again. It's true what they say: "Baseball has always been there." It's just part of who I am.

copyright 2003 C. Pettograsso

ROBIN AND TIM

—Robin Tefft
Ewing, New Jersey

***

Love affairs don't often begin at the tender age of six, but this one does. In truth, the seeds for this romance were planted long before the day that stands out as one of my earliest baseball memories. My dad grew up in the neighborhood surrounding Wrigley Field. My grandfather, a part-time lawyer and a postal worker who worked the mail car on trains running between Detroit and Chicago, would pick up my dad and his younger brother after school and take them to afternoon games, which often started at three o'clock in those days. My grandmother had been a teacher, and school was the boys' top priority, but baseball came in a very close second.

My grandparents retired to a farm in Michigan but eventually relocated to the milder climate of South Carolina. With no Major League Baseball teams anywhere near where they were going, before they left, they visited friends and family in Chicago, including one special farewell: seeing the Cubs play at Wrigley. I got to come along.

School was also the priority in our house, so missing it was not taken lightly. But then, neither was baseball. My folks knew how to arrange my early departure with school and my first-grade teacher, Mrs. Smith. The catch: I couldn't tell my friends why I was leaving early that day. Keeping a secret isn't easy for most six-year-old girls; it wasn't for me, as I still remember when my parents arrived at the classroom door to summon me mid-morning. I had to leave without telling anyone where I was going. After all, you couldn't allow all the kids to take off a day to go to a ballgame (even when their daddies took off a day from work). My classmates were so curious: Was something wrong? Where was I going? I knew I had to keep it quiet, have a somber face, but it was terribly hard because there was so much joy, the treat of doing something special, on a school day, with my family. Best of all: going to a Cubs game!

I'm not sure if this was my first game; frankly, it seems likely. I don't remember the game at all, or anything beyond my stoic, secretive exit from the classroom. But if the message that baseball was special hadn't been imprinted on my young mind before then, it surely was fixed indelibly on my brain that day. I've been to many Cubs games since then, including official school field trips a few years later (ah, those were the days!). Ernie Banks was my first crush, and he could still make my heart skip to his dying day, more than fifty years later.

I, too, left the chilly Midwest not long after college, eventually settling in San Francisco, near my sister (Hank Sauer was her favorite Cub, before he came to the Giants). After many years as a Cub fan, I've embraced a second team, the Giants, who broke my heart a few times but also rewarded me with three World Series championships in five years. I'm still waiting for the Cubs . . . but I know it will be worth the wait (perhaps not too long now). That's how love works.

—Dee Amaden
Richmond, California

***

It was the seventh inning, but I didn't know what an "inning" was. It was a Dodgers game in 2002, but I don't remember who they were playing. I was thirty-two years old, didn't know baseball, and didn't know where my life was going. It was a year of being a misfit. As an Asian-American Christian with a master's in business administration, I was supposed to be married, have a corporate career, and be a leader in the church. Instead, I wasn't dating, was working at a low civil servant job, and experiencing minimal spiritual community. I learned to forget all expectations.

But somehow, I felt different at the game. There were no expectations from my friends sitting next to me, Neil to my left, and Joe to my right. Between fervent cheers and bites of peanuts, we talked and laughed. We shared our lives. For a brief moment, in 2002, I felt connected, accepted, and respected.

The Dodgers have moved on, or I guess I have, to San Francisco. Neil and Joe are in different places. I am now married and middle-aged. I am still clueless about baseball, but I know about being human. For that brief moment in time, in 2002, maybe for one of the first times in my life, I *felt human.*

—John Chang
San Bruno, California

***

I have been a New York Yankees fan for as long as I can remember. Reading and watching everything I can about the history of the greatest team in baseball is what I care about most, except, of course, my kids. I have gone to Yankee games since 1969 at the original Yankee Stadium, and my interest continues to grow stronger. My first baseball memory was a game with my dad at Yankee Stadium. I was struck by its enormity and the deep green of the grass. It was Old Timer's Day, and I saw Mrs. Ruth, Mrs. Gehrig, and many other greats from the past. Whitey Ford "pitched," and Mickey Mantle hit a tremendous drive towards us in left field. I knew it was coming near; the guy right in front of us grabbed the ball just out of my reach. After the game, we walked across the field past the monuments, then in center field, of Gehrig, Ruth, and Miller Huggins.

I took my son Steven to his first game, about the same age as when my dad took me to mine. His reaction was the same: awe and joy. We saw Bernie Williams get his two thousandth hit as a Yankee. I took my daughter Ashley to the game when the Yankees paid tribute to Mariano Rivera, with highlights seeing Mrs. Jackie Robinson and watching Metallica perform live Rivera's entrance song, "Enter the Sandman." The Stadium truly rocked that day.

Fifteen or so years ago I began to frequent sports bars around the "House that Ruth Built." One day, in an article about Gehrig, I learned that he and Ruth used to go for a beer after the ballgames at a place called the Yankee Tavern. That museum of Yankee history is located just off the Grand Concourse; I knew I had to visit it, so a couple of friends and I went in after a game. It was like stepping back in time, with all the pictures and newspaper articles adorning the walls. Luckily, it was not crowded, and I decided to do something to drink in the history. I proceeded to sit in every seat in the establishment. The Iron Horse and the Bambino would have sat in some of those seats, or at least those locations and I wanted to feel a part of history. It certainly was heaven on earth, and my life felt complete. As a side bar, my father had passed away, and in going through his things, I found an old coffee can that my mom had said he wanted me to have. I opened it, and to my surprise, I found two baseballs that his uncle had given him. To a baseball fan, it was like finding a buried treasure. The signatures adorning the balls included some of baseball's all-time greats, names like Walter Johnson, Connie Mack, Ruth, and Gehrig. My eyes welled up with tears, as this was the greatest gift my father could have ever given me.

Babe Ruth said, shortly before he passed away, that "Baseball is the best game I know." Having written a book about my idol, Gehrig, I understand his comment about being the "luckiest man alive." Baseball has gotten me through some rough personal times. Because of baseball, I also feel quite lucky.

—Kevin Larkin, author of *Gehrig: Game by Game*
Great Barrington, Massachusetts

***

I was born in 1947 and moved to Ashland in 1970. When I first arrived at the height of the hippie movement, new friends would ask me, "What's your sign?" I would answer "Jackie Robinson, with Israel rising." You see, my birthday is December 23, 1947, almost in the exact middle of when Jackie Robinson became the first Black baseball player to play in the Major Leagues on April 15, 1947, and when Israel was reborn as a nation on May 14, 1948. These two events, as distinct as they are from each other, shaped my childhood, and influenced our nation as well.

I'm not alone in the belief that April 15, 1947, marks the beginning of the civil rights movement. How can a sport like baseball, and a team like the Brooklyn Dodgers, affectionately known as the Bums, be credited with having sparked what soon would be called the civil rights movement? It's simple, really. Social change does not begin in the ivory tower of academia. It does not occur because of postulates, theories, and suppositions made in doctoral dissertations. Rather, good doctoral dissertations and academic studies are reflections and analyses of what is going on in the lives of everyday people. Sometimes entertainment is a reflection of the current situation in society, but sometimes entertainment is at the cutting edge of social change.

So, what is it with me and baseball, beyond being born between these two dates? Truth be told, it's a pretty personal thing to me, as it was to so many kids who were born in the wake of World War II and grew up in one of the boroughs besides the Bronx. Brooklyn hosted a huge immigrant population, a population of Irish, Italian, Jewish, Gypsy, Puerto Rican, and Black families who identified with the seemingly hopeless struggle of the Dodgers to defeat the Yankees. In a way, identifying the Dodgers as "Dem Bums" was to identify yourself with the struggle to make it in America.

In 1947, my brother Jerry Stern was twelve years older than I was. His new baby brother was like his little parrot, his ten pounds of clay that he could shape at will. My first words of English—and this is no family legend—were the names of the Brooklyn Dodgers. Jerry would bring me to his teenage friends and show me off like we would a new iPad today. He'd say, "Pee-wee," and I would respond, "Reese." He'd say, "Duke," and I would respond, "Snyder". Carl and Erskine, Jackie and Robinson. By the summer of 1950, rumor had it he could do this forward or backward with me. Furillo and Carl, Hodges and Gil. He took me to my first games at Ebbett's Field, and ingrained in me the ethos of civil rights. It sounds so naïve today, but in the early 1960s, white Americans asked each other, "Do you believe in integration?" We asked the question as if there really could be two possible legitimate answers. I was one of those kids who asked that question, and one of the ones who answered in the affirmative when asked.

Is it a coincidence that when my daughter graduated from college she moved back to Brooklyn after having grown up breathing the rarefied air of Oregon? In 2016, she gave birth to my granddaughter, Amaya Zahar, who has a Jewish mom and African-American dad. How cool is that? My granddaughter born in Brooklyn, in the wake of the civil rights movement, just one mile from Israel Zion Hospital where I was born, and one mile in the other direction from Ebbets Field, where my conscience concerning civil rights was born and shaped.

The Mets' new stadium is a veritable tribute in stone to number forty-two, Jackie Robinson, the Brooklyn Dodgers, and Ebbets Field. I haven't seen it yet. I'm going back to see my granddaughter soon; maybe I'll teach her some new words in English. I'll say, "Pee-wee," and she'll say,

"Reese." Or Roy and Campanella. Definitely, I'll say, "Jackie," and she'll say "Robinson."

—Rabbi David Zaslow
Ashland, Oregon

***

Being originally from England, baseball wasn't a sport I knew anything about. I grew up on football (soccer), rugby, and cricket, so when I moved to Canada at the age of twenty-one, I had to learn many new things. In 1992, I was living in a very French town, Quebec, on the outskirts of Ontario; it was a very difficult time in my life. I'd experienced some very horrific things in my teen years, and hadn't dealt with them in healthy and progressive ways. I was at the lowest point in my life, with self-destructive behavior, and even contemplated suicide. I knew no one, felt I had nowhere to go, or anyone to talk to. There were only two channels on my TV that were English-language, with the rest in French (Quebec is predominantly French-speaking). With limited options, I started watching the Blue Jays. At first, I wasn't interested, as I didn't understand the rules or the strategy of play, but I soon found myself becoming intrigued with both the play and the players. I began to closely watch, and started to understand the rules and statistics. This gave me focus, which turned into somewhat of an obsession. It took my mind off all the issues I had and gave me something to look forward to. I couldn't get enough baseball, and started to also follow the Mariners and the Orioles, so I could watch as many games as possible.

As the season progressed, the Jays became more and more exciting, and my focus became stronger. I went to the Sky Dome in Toronto to see live games; it was as if a new fire had ignited, and was burning out of control. I loved this feeling, and didn't want it to end. The Jays won the World Series that year, but I found myself wondering how I would make it through the winter until the new season started. My depression came back as the nights got colder, but I knew that spring would soon be here, and I could reignite that fire. I wasn't disappointed; the Jays were on fire, and so was I. I didn't miss a game on TV, and went to more games at the Sky Dome. The Jays again won the Series, with a three run, walk off home run on a 2-2 count against Phillies pitcher Mitch Williams to win 6-5 after trailing in the ninth. I remember it like it was yesterday, and will always cherish the feeling as it became the big turning point in my life. I realized I was capable of positive emotions and started healing for good. It took another five years to fully deal with my demons but, I believe that baseball was the starting point of my recovery and actually saved my life.

—Lisa McIsaac
Aldergrove, British Columbia, Canada

***

I have always loved baseball, from the first days playing catch on the side of the house, tossing a ball back and forth, listening for the rhythmic "thwack" in my glove. We'd stay out after it was too dark to see the ball. I just didn't want to give up that peace; it was as close to meditation as a kid could get. My father started taking me to Yankee Stadium in the early sixties during the Mantle/Maris days. The Yankees won every time, and every game, Mickey hit a home run. I assumed that's how it always was. The first time I experienced a loss was to the Tigers, and it felt like the universe had shifted.

The first moment I walked onto a Little League field at eight, I felt at home. Even though I was short and skinny, I was pretty good. I learned how to throw a curve at twelve, and pitched a no-hitter to kids who had no idea what was happening. There was no greater feeling than putting on my scratchy wool uniform, getting on my bike, and riding to a game. I usually did pretty well; in fact, so well, that when I was fourteen, I got to try out for the all-star team. So, I did. And something happened.

I don't know how, or why. There was no conscious effort to change anything, but for some odd reason, I got into the zone. As I stood in the box, I simply watched the pitcher's wind-up. I saw the ball come out of his hand. I could see if it was a fastball or curve. I knew where it was headed. It was like I could slow it down in my mind. And I could hit it. I went twenty for twenty-one in the tryouts. Why, almost fifty years later, I remember the stat, I don't know. But, I remember.

In our second game, I was at short, made a play or two, and maybe booted one. I walked a couple times. Then it was the bottom of the ninth, two out, and the bases loaded. We were down by a run, and I came up. The pitcher was a tall guy, much taller than me, and he threw faster than I was used to. Unfortunately, for some reason, the zone was gone. I was shaky, unsure; the confidence and ease I had just weren't there. All I needed was a single or walk to tie the game. I ran the count to 3 and 2. I remember praying for a ball. He threw a fastball strike. I swung. I whiffed. It wasn't close; the game was over. I returned to the dugout and cried.

I play softball now. I'm still pretty good, a solid hitter, and decent at short. And I still love it. Grabbing my bag and driving to the field, I get the same rush I did when I was twelve, pedaling on my bike. Every once in a while, I get a taste of that zone feeling, where things slow down. And it's quiet, meditative. But the few times I've gotten up with bases loaded, two out, I've flashed back to that moment, as if I've been given a chance to avenge the strikeout, a chance for redemption. So far, no strikeouts, maybe a hit or two. But I'm still waiting for that grand slam to finally get that fifty-year-old monkey off my back. Maybe next Sunday.

—Ian Gurvitz author of *Freak-Out, the 2016 Election and the Dawn of the American Democalypse*
Los Angeles, California

***

What does baseball mean to me? Well, a lot of feelings that are very important to me. Memories. Friends. Family. Tears. Travel. Connection. Home. I was born in Mexico and came to the US at the age of eight. Of course, soccer is life there, so I didn't really know about baseball until I moved here. We lived in many different cities throughout Southern California, and while we never lived in Orange County, my parents would take my sister and me to Angels games. I still have one of those magazine photos you can take at the fair where my sis, Stefany, and I were the cover for *Angels Magazine*. I'm sure many of my friends would like to use it as ammo now! Stefany and I both played softball, and that's when we discovered Ken Griffey Jr., who became her favorite player. He became my favorite player, too, as I fell in love with the best swing in baseball. At any rate, my entire family strayed from the Angels. Mom is a Padres fan, and Dad follows the A's. Stefany is a Red Sox fan, and I am a die-hard, blue-bleeding Dodgers fan, with a tattoo to prove it. I also am the most knowledgeable when it comes to baseball.

My best friend David and I have the same main item on our bucket list: visit all Major League Baseball stadiums! He moved from California to Florida almost twenty years ago, and for the past few years, we have made it a point to meet up at a new stadium every year with his sister and her fiancée. Together we witnessed Vin's last game at AT&T park, and David Ortiz' number thirty-four retirement ceremony at Fenway. I was also at the Vin Scully tribute game at Dodger Stadium. In addition, I travel with my large Pantone 294 (the specific shade of Dodger Blue) "family," a Dodgers' fan club that "takes over stadiums." I attended the first takeover of the Rancho Cucamonga Quakes' stadium, and participated in the home invasion versus the Cubs. This year? Busch Stadium, the Coliseum, and Safeco Field, and a photo of me with the Griffey statue!

So, that's my life with baseball, and it runs through the family. My oldest daughter participated in the first softball camp at Dodger Stadium, and I helped coach her team. I play second base in a coed softball team, and am the only female administrator of the Facebook group MLB Flock. And, of course, I spend countless hours watching my team at Dodger Stadium, or on TV. Instagram: karlablue23. Memories. Friends. Family. Connection. Home.

—Karla Olmos
Riverside, California

BUNTS

As I said earlier, the original concept of this book was a compilation of short anecdotes, with emphasis on the word "short." Well, stories started pouring in, often ignoring this expressed thought. No complaints here—the book is infinitely better because of it, but there are a number of short ones that I want to include, so I'm calling this chapter "Bunts"; the hits may not go far, but they sure get on base.

***

I have been to a couple of games that have been particularly interesting for me. I recall attending a game in which Jim Bouton was the starting pitcher in his rookie season. I took my son Jeremy to the first night gave ever played at Camden Yards in Baltimore, the second game of the season. However, the most significant game for me was during the 1986 World Series. I am not a diehard Mets fan, as the Yankees are my team, but I certainly preferred them to the Red Sox. It was my first ever visit to Fenway Park, and it was great to see leadoff batter Mookie Wilson blast Dennis "Oil Can" Boyd's off-speed pitch into the right field seats leading off game number three. I cheered wildly, and had a beer thrown in my face by the typical Red Sox fans seated behind me. It tasted great.

—Barry Glovitch
Lutherville-Timonium, Maryland

***

I recall being the leadoff batter in Little League when I was twelve. It was Opening Day, the first game of the season for everyone, and we were visitors. They always announced the players, but when they called my name to come to the plate to open the game, I wasn't there. Instead, I was running out of the bathroom from behind center field as I heard my name over the PA system (I was just a little nervous!). I jumped into the batter's box with no practice swings; the first pitch I saw was at my eyes, and I whacked a home run over the center field fence. I remember the feeling still with so much joy and elation.

—Bill Mitchell
Auburn, California

***

In the early 1960s, when the Dodgers first moved to Los Angeles from Brooklyn, they played in a stadium not intended for baseball, with some very bizarre dimensions and features. I don't recall who they were playing, but when Duke Snider came up to the plate, the other team decided to walk him. Even though it was to be an intentional pass, the fielders shaded to the right side toward first base, although not like the complete shift we have come to see in recent years. Instead of taking ball four, and the walk, Duke bunted the pitch down the third base line all the way to the short left field fence, completely fooling the defense. I will never forget old man Duke getting a double, driving in two runs on a planned walk.

—Bill Staples Sr.
Hesperia, California

(A bunt double—which could happen if lefties knew how to bunt down the 3B line against a shift. If this story doesn't belong in this chapter, I can't imagine what would.)

***

I was on a baseball bus trip a few years ago. One of the stops was the Field of Dreams in Dwyersville, Iowa. Of course, I wanted to go into the cornfield. I asked one of the owners if I could. She said yes, and then thanked me for asking as she said not many people have done that. Well, I stood in front of the cornfield and held up a sign saying "Help! Shoeless Joe is after me."

—Anne Chamberlain
Ontario, Canada

***

On August 24, 1983, I attended a game at Memorial Stadium in Baltimore, the Orioles versus the Blue Jays. Without going into all the details easily found on line, in extra innings, with benches depleted and players at all kinds of positions with which they were unfamiliar, Oriole reliever Tippy Martinez came in with Barry Bonnell at first base. Bonnell was immediately picked off, although it was credited as caught stealing. Dave Collins walked and just as quickly was picked off as well. Willie Upshaw hit an infield single and, well, you can guess the outcome. Cal Ripken homered in the bottom of the inning, and the Orioles won the ballgame. Martinez retired no batters, but pitched an inning, and got a win.

—Becker Drane
San Francisco, California

***

In 1951, my Uncle Charlie took me and my cousin to see the Giants play at the Polo Grounds in New York. Bobbie and I were teenagers, and ardent Giant fans, eager to see this new "phenom" the Giants had just brought up from the minors, a kid by the name of Willie Mays. The kid wasn't doing too well. He was hitting about .120 (twelve hits out of hundred at bats) at the time, but manager Leo Durocher stuck with him. That day, he was facing Hall of Famer Warren Spahn. Willie hit his very first home run that day, a majestic shot over the roof in left field, and out of the ballpark. Spahn was later jokingly quoted as saying, "If only I had struck him out, maybe I wouldn't have had to face him again." I will never forget seeing the Say Hey Kid hit his first round-tripper.

—Alan Wollman
Los Angeles, California

***

My son Kyle played in the Mel Ott Little League for many years. My pop was born in the thirties, and grew up playing the only game they played in those days: baseball. I was an average player, at best. Kyle started playing, and he could really pitch; Pop was overjoyed that we had a hurler in the house. Kyle wrote an essay for a church contest on why he wanted to go to baseball camp, saying his grandpa came to watch every game and practice, and had showed him how to bat and catch while his mother and I were at work. He won that trip at the University of Buffalo Baseball Camp, and was chosen to throw out the first pitch at Pilot Field. Kyle stepped up on the hill, reared back, and threw a perfect strike. As I videotaped this, I peeked over at Pop; he was all choked up, and couldn't speak as tears of joy came down his face. I got choked up seeing this. It was a *Great* day for our family. Kyle, now twenty-three, coaches his own Little League team, and lets me hang around. Pop is gone now, but he never misses a game, looking down on the hill from above.

—Gregg Pfeiffer
Tonawanda, New York

***

I was watching my niece Tayah's softball game. My brother, Alex, was the coach. At one point, I got really excited as she rounded the bases, and

I blurted out something to the effect of, "She got to fourth base!" Okay, I realize it's "home plate," but that fact escaped me for a moment. Who cared? She scored!

—Lia Kantor
San Francisco, California

***

I loved old Tiger Stadium, and saw tons of games there. I would get there early for batting practice, and stay late, hanging around outside the visitors' clubhouse for autographs. The most unusual thing I have seen occurred on July 15, 1973. I witnessed Nolan Ryan's second no-hitter from the upper deck, first base side. In the ninth inning, Norm Cash, who had struck out three times, came to the plate with a table leg as a bat, having gone into the locker room and broken it off in hopes of getting a hit with it. The home plate umpire told him he couldn't use it, and Cash's response was "Why not? I won't hit him anyway." Ryan's reaction was more "What the heck are you trying to do"? Cash popped up to end the game.

—Ron Gdaniec
Hamburg, Michigan

***

My band was playing at a nightclub on Second Avenue in New York called O'Lunney's. Sometimes people got up to play with the band. The bassist and drummer weren't baseball fans; the female lead singer didn't know who he was when she announced, "Stan Musial is going to play a couple of songs" I was flabbergasted! He was quite nice, and a very passible harmonica player. Nobody else knew who he was until I told them. The bartenders and waitresses were all from Ireland, and it was late, with few people in the bar. I was the only person in the club who was aware that Stan the Man was playing harp.

—Kenny Davis
Manlius, New York

***

I went to a White Sox game when I was about twelve. It was Hoyt Wilhelm's birthday, maybe number forty-six? They gave out cupcakes to commemorate the day. I relished mine, and saved the wrapper for years.

—Neil Haglund
Marion, Indiana

***

I loved going to games in Kansas City when the Yankees were in town on Casey Stengel's birthday. Originally, from Kansas City, he was, of course, the Yankees manager; if the Yankees played the Athletics on or near his birthday, huge cakes were baked, and fans were given a piece as they entered the ballpark. I even met legendary announcer Mel Allen on the concourse one time, as he stopped to shake hands.

—Bruce Haag
Kissimmee, Florida

(Casey's birthday: July 30—just like mine, but a few years earlier.)

***

I came to Chicago to apply for a job with the Chicago Transit Authority, dressed in a sport jacket, casual shirt and spit-shined shoes. The mental aspect of a test qualified me as an "L" engineer; having to hang around the

Wrigley Building for two and a half hours for a physical, I started thinking how good I had it at the post office, so I left and ended up at Wrigley field in time to see the Cubs blow a five-run lead and lose to the Giants 9-7. A bit despondent as I left the park, I headed for the Addison bus. A few kids were standing around with their scorecards in hand; I don't know why I did this, but on impulse, I grabbed one kid's card and signed my autograph. After all, I was dressed like a ball player after a game. I handed it back to him, and four more were shoved at me. I signed each one, but beat a hasty retreat when one kid yelled, "Who the hell is Dave Graf?" Another said, "Yeah! Never heard of him!" Today there may be some older guys in the Windy City saying, "Ya know, I never did figure out who that %#% was!"

—David Graf
Port St. Lucie, Florida

***

In 1961, the Indians hosted Cleveland Hebrew Schools Day. It was a Sunday afternoon, and ironically the Indians only Jewish player, Barry Latman, was pitching. Our rabbi summoned Latman over and blessed him. He still lost. It was also the only game where I actually got my hands on a ball hit into the stands. And it was mine until a big jerk kicked the ball while I was picking it up, and he just reached down and took it away from me. I learned then that catching a ball is a competitive sport!

—Sheldon Green
Cleveland, Ohio

***

We lived a couple of towns over from Jim Rice, and since he was on the disabled list, my son decided to invite him to his birthday party. My son really thought he would come, but was both a little disappointed and delighted when Rice returned to the lineup that very same day. The next day we received an unmarked large manila envelope in the mail. Inside was an autographed glossy of Jim with his apologies for missing the party. Good man!

—David Gordon
Boxford, Massachusetts

***

I was at a spring training game, Royals versus Rangers, on Saint Patty's night. At the end of the game, a group of Kansas City players was leaving the field. One of them was Alex Gordon. As he passed a row of fans on the third base side, he put his game bat in the glove of an eight or nine-year-old kid and walked on. You can imagine the look on the kid's face—he lit up like the stadium lights coming on! Someone asked the kid, "Is he your favorite player now?" The kid replied, "He already was."

It was great to see as a fan; really helps remind me that even with the amount of ink spent on issues with performance-enhancing drugs, there's still a great heartbeat to the game, thanks to players like Alex Gordon and his kind.

—Sam DeSiato
Aurora, Colorado

***

I was at a doubleheader at Yankee Stadium during the great 1961 baseball season when Maris and Mantle were chasing Babe Ruth's home run record. During a late inning of the second game, Yogi Berra was inserted in the game in left field; soon, the opposition had loaded the bases with one out. A long fly ball was hit right to Yogi, easily long enough to score the runner on third. Yogi had to really run for the ball; he made the catch but fell down, so not only did the runner on third score, but the runner from second did as well! Yogi Berra was the iconic Yankee catcher for so many years, and the idea of him playing left field was, to me, bizarre! As was this play.

—Hari Huberman
San Francisco, California

***

A brother-in-law of mine, one I wasn't particularly fond of, invited me to the fourth game of the 2001 World Series. Just getting into the stadium was an ordeal, with 9/11 having just occurred. I had been there the night before, when George Bush, of whom I was never a big fan, threw out the first pitch; I cheered for him that night like I had never cheered for anyone. In this game, Tino Martinez hit a two-out homer to tie the game in the ninth, and Derek Jeter hit one to win it in the tenth. I remember hugging and jumping with my brother-in-law and feeling the stadium sway twice. River Road, the street behind the stadium, was a sea of people yelling and screaming. It was such a release of all the pent-up anger of September 11.

—Bob Cohen
New York, New York

SINGLES

As stories have come to me, I naturally think about others I have received, in terms of organizing chapters. I have done this over a thousand times, and it doesn't get old. Some easily fit with others: catching a ball, first games, meeting the stars. Some are just terrifically unique, weird, funny, or tragic. Here are some stories that are just one of a kind; they don't fit with others, but they need to be told.

***

Whether by alphabetical order or height, I always ended up in the last seat of the last row throughout elementary school. Every year, when it came time to test everyone's eyesight with the eye chart situated squarely in the front of the room, I had a decided advantage: I would go last. One after another, my fellow students would get up, go to the back of the room, and read the eye chart as best they could. By the time it was my turn, I had memorized the entire chart based on their repeated verbal readings. This was certainly serendipitous, since when it was finally my turn, and I stood in the back reading the chart, I couldn't see anything very clearly. So, I simply recited the chart from memory, and did perfectly well with the test. And that was the point. As everything else that took place in school, I looked at this as a test I had to pass. So, year after year, my eyesight got worse, as my answers got better. This might have gone on for years more, but fate finally intervened when I was nine. My dad had purchased tickets to take my younger brother, Randy, and me to a ballgame. Growing up in the Bronx, not far from Yankee Stadium, I was already a big Yankees fan, as my father was before me. I had been to a number of games over the years, but I was particularly excited to go to this one. It was the Summer of '61, and Mantle and Maris were battling it out for the home run crown. It was a perfect day for a ballgame, and nothing quite ever matched the feeling I would get as I ascended through the tunnel to the stands and got a glimpse of the field. We settled into our seats on the first base side with our scorecards, crackerjacks, hot dogs, and soda. The game was about to begin when my father and brother started laughing. I asked them what was so funny, and they pointed to the left field stands and a banner they said was hysterical. I looked, but all I saw was a blank sheet. Turning to them, I said I didn't see what was so funny about a banner with nothing written on it. They looked at me like I was crazy. My father said, "You can't see the writing on there?" "No," I said. Then he said he'd better make an appointment for me right away with the eye doctor. So, he did. And I've been wearing glasses ever since.

—Alan Zapakin
Los Angeles, California

***

One minute I was a five-year-old Dodgers fan, cheering my dad's favorite team, the Men in Blue. The next, I was a Giants fan. My mom, dad, sister, and I were at my grandmother's house celebrating a family holiday, along with my aunt, uncle, and cousins, who decided that it was time, as a San Franciscan, that I become a Giants fan—their team. Having a young and malleable mind, my extended family, Lynn and Eric, Rachel and David, saw the perfect opportunity to convert me. Not much was required for this conversion to take place. They told me a couple of times "Giants rule! Dodgers suck!"; gave me T-shirts and hats, and that was good enough for me. I have been a die-hard Giants fan since then, and I have never looked back.

Years later, my friends and I arrived at AT&T Park one night with one goal in mind: We were going to piss off the opposing team's batboy. Why? Because we could; we were high school boys, and *why not?* Our seats were in prime batboy heckling position: two rows up between the visiting team's dugout and home plate. We spotted our target as soon as we got to our seats. He was similar in age to us, but he walked around with a little swagger we did not find befitting for him, further fueling our efforts.

Between the first and last pitches of the game, every time he emerged from the dugout, we acknowledged his presence. Our constant heckling was neither clever nor funny; the key is that it was *constant*. "Hey, batboy, run faster!" "There he is." My favorite was a simple standing ovation by the four of us showing our "approval" for the job our friend on the field was doing. Around the sixth inning, we got what we had been waiting for: the illustrious middle finger! Mr. Batboy was headed out for one of his many trips to the on-deck circle, and he'd had enough of our heckling, so he turned and erected his middle finger at us. We rejoiced as if the Giants had just won the World Series (which they did soon after, many times). The fans around us were greatly amused, and applauded our hard work. Whether he was fired for his response, we of course don't know, but for us it will go down as one of the great moments in baseball history.

—Josh Gray
Santa Clara, California

(I completely disavow any involvement in telling five-year-old Josh that the Dodgers killed Bambi's mother. I'm only grateful that my brother didn't beat the daylights out of me.)

***

If only he spoke English, Francisco Cabrera could have been elected mayor of Atlanta, maybe even governor of Georgia. In the final inning of the final game of the 1992 National League Championship Series, playing for the Atlanta Braves against the Pittsburgh Pirates, he delivered the Hit Heard Round the South.

I was there to see it—only I had to watch it on a tiny television monitor carried by a fetching young woman covering the game for Atlanta station

WSB, the local CBS outlet. She and I had never met, but we both had a rooting interest in the Braves. We put our heads together—literally—and watched the bottom-of-the-ninth action outside the home clubhouse, deep in the bowels of Atlanta Fulton County Stadium.

Just a few minutes earlier, it looked like that clubhouse would be a morgue. Trays of champagne bottles were brought into the Pittsburgh clubhouse, and workers nailed up sheets of plastic to protect personal belongings of Pirates players. But that was before the unthinkable happened in Atlanta's last at-bat.

I had been upstairs, in the press box, covering the game for United Press International, then the wire service rival of the Associated Press. With Pittsburgh leading 2-0, and staff ace Doug Drabek coasting through eight and a third innings, UPI sports editor Fred McMane told me to take the elevator to the Braves clubhouse, where I encountered the WSB girl. Huddled together, we watched Terry Pendleton blast his second double of the game to deep right field. David Justice, representing the tying run, hit a routine grounder to Jose Lind, a sure-handed second baseman—except at that very moment. His error put runners on the corners with nobody out. Sid Bream walked, ending the night for Drabek, who had lost two earlier games in the best-of-seven match. Stan Belinda then threw a pitch that Ron Gant almost converted into his second grand-slam of the series. Caught by Barry Bonds in left, Pendleton waltzed home from third. Damon Berryhill walked, reloading the bases, and Brian Hunter pinch-hit for weak-hitting infielder Rafael Belliard. Another fly ball would tie the game but Hunter, hoping to win it, over swung and popped it up.

With two down, manager Bobby Cox called on Cabrera, no better than a third-string catcher who had spent most of the season in the Minor Leagues, to bat for pitcher Jeff Reardon. Cox knew the lanky Dominican could hit, and counted on him to connect. With a 2-1 count, Belinda had to throw a strike. He did, and Cabrera didn't miss it. His liner to left scored Justice easily, tying the game, but Bream looked like a dead duck at home plate. The slowest man in the majors, he was playing on notoriously gimpy knees, but Cox left him in because he had no other first baseman available. Bonds, whose one weakness was a weak throwing arm, was playing too deep to make a great throw. Moreover, he didn't heed the warning of center fielder Andy Van Slyke to move in. On top of that, catcher Mike (Spanky) LaValliere stood at only five eight and couldn't stretch to reach the sliding Bream when the throw from Bonds was up the line. Bream, a former Pirate, scored the pennant-winning run, giving the Braves their second straight National League flag, while the Pittsburgh outfielders, stunned, sat on their gloves and watched the home team cavort at the plate. The final score was 3-2.

I got to cavort a little too, hugging the cute WSB girl for what seemed like many minutes before proceeding into the clubhouse. There I encountered a single solitary figure—and what a figure it was!!

Jane Fonda, who had married Braves owner Ted Turner less than a year earlier, was standing alone, waiting for the on-field celebration to end.

"What are you doing here?" I asked her. She said she didn't want to wind up at the bottom of the pile, and was waiting inside for Ted. It sounded like a pre-planned arrangement, but it gave me a chance to have a private conversation with a celebrated Hollywood star. Too bad there were no cell phones then, or I would've taken a picture—maybe even a selfie—with my head next to hers, and my hand around her tiny waist. Jane seemed excited, far from the sleepy image she and Ted inadvertently projected during televised games that ended past their bedtime (and everyone else's). But she couldn't have been as excited as I was, standing in the home clubhouse of my favorite team seconds after clinching its second straight pennant, and standing with a star.

That game, which took place on October 14, 1992, is still remembered in Atlanta as "the Francisco Cabrera Game." Had it not happened, he certainly would have been forgotten long ago.

—Dan Schlossberg, author of The New Baseball Bible: Notes, Nuggets, Lists & Legends From Our National Pastime
Fair Lawn, New Jersey

***

My first remembrance with baseball was on October 1, 1932, when I was eight years old. Our large extended family had all moved to Brooklyn from the Bronx, where Yankee Stadium was located, and the Polo Grounds, home of the New York Giants, was a few hundred yards away across the Harlem River. My cousins were all avid Giant fans, now surrounded by ardent Brooklyn Dodger supporters. The Yankees were not loved or hated the way they were today; they were, after all in the American League. However, everyone admired the home run prowess of Babe Ruth and Lou Gehrig.

Our neighborhood was lower middle class, second generation Jewish, dotted with small synagogues. My grandfather belonged to an Orthodox shul on Williams Avenue; that's where I was on October 1, Yom Kippur, the highest Jewish holiday, requiring a full day of devotion. It was also the third game of the Yankees-Cubs World Series. Though neither the Giants nor lowly Dodgers were involved, there was a lot of interest in the series by many of the young men in the congregation. There were no radio broadcasts of the games; even if there were, we wouldn't have been allowed to listen to them. But at about four o'clock in the afternoon, something unique happened, which is etched in my memory. We—the under-thirteen males—were given a break of about an hour, while prayers were suspended and some of the elders read from the Torah. By some coincidence, most of the other synagogues also went on break.

If one were in an airplane at that time passing over East New York, one would have seen streaks of blue emerging from various buildings, heading north to a wide avenue, where they merged into a large blue mass. On the ground, it was several hundred youths dressed in blue gabardine suits, heading for Pitkin Avenue, the area's main drag, and camping in an area across the street from a poolroom. On the second floor of the poolroom, on the picture windows was pasted a box score of the game (it was tied 4-4 in the top of the fifth inning) and a large diamond with a home plate and bases. The batter and base runners were represented by ping pong balls, and they moved accordingly. The poolroom reported the play by play, receiving the information by telegraph. It was expensive, but it was a poolroom, after all.

In the Yankees fifth, the first batter was retired, with a pause before the second batter made any movement. Then the white ping pong ball was moved around the bases. Home Run! A few moments later, another homer! Yankees went ahead, 6-4. Moments later, murmurs spread from across the street through the crowd. The first homer was hit by Ruth (the famous pointing to the stands homer, we learned later). The second one was stroked by Gehrig. This was news we would not have gotten until evening. The game was still in doubt as the blue streaks began returning to the buildings they had left, but there still remained a handful of young men in blue suits and knickers, Yankee fans, perhaps, who claimed they would stay for the rest of the game, risking severe rebuke, if not damnation.

—Robert Rusting
Great Neck, New York

***

In a Mustang Division Little League game, I was stung by a bee on my left middle finger while I was in the dugout. It swelled so much I could barely bend it. The next inning, I had an at-bat against the second fastest pitcher in the league. I was hit by a fastball squarely on the shoulder, and awarded first base, advancing to second with a stolen base. The next batter hit a well-placed line drive to right field, and the third base coach waved me around, running home as fast as my legs could carry me. I slid into home plate as the catcher received the throw from the right fielder, and in one motion caught the ball and swung both hands, mitt and ball, smashing me in my face. I'm fairly certain I beat the throw, but nonetheless, I was called out. That was the last season I played baseball.

It wasn't until a decade later that it occurred to me that being struck by the pitch—and who knows, maybe the hard tag at home—wasn't a co-incidence. (I don't think the smashing tag was retribution orchestrated by the catcher, more likely just the unfortunate combination of my body on the slide and how he caught the ball and applied the tag). I was young and naïve, and did not for a second think at the time about how my swollen finger, definitely extended because I couldn't grip the bat with a finger that wouldn't bend, might have been misconstrued! Perhaps this was all a streak of unfortunate events.

—Daniel Gorelick
San Francisco, California

***

I have been going to baseball games since 1941, when I saw my home team, the St. Louis Browns, host the Detroit Tigers. The difference between what I expected to see—constant movement, fast pace—was surprisingly very different from what I saw. I can't remember for certain whether they played that day, but there were three future Hall of Fame players on those teams, Charlie Gehringer, Hal Newhouser, and Rick Ferrell. Skipping many decades ahead, I attended the games when Cap Ripken tied, and then broke Lou Gehrig's consecutive game streak. But one game really sticks out in my mind.

I saw Pete Gray, a one-handed outfielder, play for the 1945 St. Louis Browns. While I don't recall any particular game or play, it was fascinating how he would make a catch with his gloved hand, tuck the glove under his stump, and then retrieve the ball and throw it back into the infield. I thought about this years later when Jim Abbott, a one-armed pitcher, made his debut with the Angels, and went on to have a solid major league career.

—Chuck Edson
Chevy Chase, Maryland

***

As the son of a former Major League ballplayer, my "stories" of the major leagues might be from a different perspective. I'm not much of a fan today, and my interest and knowledge are of baseball from my dad's playing era and a little beyond, when he was the third base coach for the "expansion"

Washington Senators (1961 to 1963). I had many wonderful opportunities because of him. I met Jesse Owens in 1961, and we had a nice conversation about my dad's race against the legendary Olympic sprinter in 1946 at Municipal Stadium in Cleveland. I attended game two of the 1950 World Series, Yankees versus Phillies, with Dad at Shibe Park in Philadelphia; I was with him again in 1975, in Cooperstown, for the induction of Bucky Harris into the Hall of Fame, for whom Dad had played. But my most unforgettable story occurred in 1961.

I had worked out with the Washington ball club at Griffith Stadium (that in itself was an amazing experience), taking batting practice and infield practice on the same field where Dad had played. After showering and getting dressed, I was sitting in the dugout next to the presidential box, where President Kennedy was about to open the 1961 season by throwing out the first ball. Suddenly, I was surrounded by Secret Service agents demanding to know my identity and why I was sitting there. One then went to the first base line where the Senators were lined up, and brought my Dad to the dugout to identify me as his son! Needless to say, this was quite an experience.

—George W. Case III
Yardley, Pennsylvania

***

Kitty Dukakis and I collaborated on a book on mental health, and every year since then, the four of us—Michael and Kitty, my wife and I—go to a game at Fenway Park. Michael is a lifelong fan; Kitty loves being out and schmoozing, with Fenway as good a place as any. That night, Michael was teaching late and was going to meet us at the ballpark. Early in the game, someone, I wish I could remember who, hit a screeching line drive towards our seats near the Fenway grounds crew. It came so fast I barely saw it, and my reflexes are sufficiently slow that I couldn't react. The ball whacked Kitty on the arm, ricocheted, and hit her a second time, on the chest.

I was a longtime medical reporter at the *Boston Globe*, and had done scores of stories on the Sox and player injuries. Until that night I'd never seen, or even known about, the area beneath the stands where they treat injured fans. Teams don't advertise that, for fear it'll scare fans and inspire personal injury lawyers. It turns out lots of fans are injured through the season, although they all implicitly accept conditions written onto their tickets saying they are okay with the risk. In Kitty's case, charmer that she is, she interviewed the docs who were treating her, to their huge delight. By the time we got back to our seats the worried fans around her gave her a standing ovation. And Michael, who got there just after that, said, "Leave it to my loving bride to have a target on her back."

Larry Tye, author of *Satchel: The Life and Times of an American Legend*
Boston, Massachusetts

***

As the daughter of baseball executive Gabe Paul, I had many special opportunities to be around the game. Dad had a lot to do with opening the avenue for Cubans to play in the States, starting the Cincinnati Reds' Minor League team, the Havana Sugar Kings. One of those players, Orlando Pena, played for the Reds, and I got to know him when I was a little girl in 1958. By 1967, when dad was with Cleveland, Pena was an Indian. One of his teammates was power-hitting first baseman Tony Horton.

One day that season, the Indians had a scheduled doubleheader. Dad wouldn't let me sit behind the home dugout because I always tried to peek in and say hello to the players, so I sat with the family's long-time housekeeper, Elnora Bridges, by the visiting dugout. Between games, the bat boy came over and said nervously, "Miss, Tony Horton wants to see you right now." I could see into the dugout that he was pacing back and forth. I looked at Elnora, saying I wondered what this was all about. I went over, and he introduced himself, asking what my name was. I told him it was Jennie, and he replied, "Did you see me waving to you the whole game? My friend Orlando said he would give me fifty dollars if I could get a date with you. Would you like to go out with me?" It was a strange way to ask for a date, but I said sure (he was very handsome). He told me to meet him outside the clubhouse door after the second game. Knowing that I would be driving home with my dad, I sent a note to him telling him I couldn't meet him there, and asked if he could come to my house. He obviously didn't know who I was related to. I obviously didn't think about how my dad would react. I was only fifteen years old.

He left to go to the between-games meeting in the clubhouse. My dad had "spies" around the park, and the clubhouse man, Cy, reported what happened. When Horton found out that Pena had "set him up," he got furious, and crumpled the note and threw it to the ground. Pena was in stitches. Cy evidently told Dad, because as soon as the game was over, he told me we were leaving. A man of few words, Dad produced the crumpled note and said, "Jennie, what is this?" I was busted. Nothing more was said.

Tony Horton suffered from depression, which ultimately led to his leaving baseball. I, too, suffered from bouts of depression. Years later, I wrote him a note, telling him that I wished that in those days there was more attention given to helping athletes cope with mental health issues, such as depression. This has become a lifelong passion of mine, provision of mental health assistance to athletes. I never heard back from Tony, but I sure hope he found some peace.

—Jennie Paul
Fort Lauderdale, Florida

***

Baseball is a great game that takes you in different directions, and lets you meet a wide range of people. It took me on a ride I never could have imagined. As a kid, I had always wanted to see and meet the players, who, up to then, only appeared on my baseball cards. Years later, as a scout for the Texas Rangers, I attended a game in Oakland, the A's hosting the Rangers. I sat in the "scout" section, 117. The Rangers pitcher, Kevin Brown, was a tall, rangy right hander, with outstanding stuff, and had the A's eating out of his hand. The scout next to me asked, pitch after pitch, exactly what type of pitch Brown had thrown. I answered politely each time; he was evidently a long-time scout who needed my younger eyes at this time. The only excitement the A's could muster was Rickey Henderson getting on base and doing his Rickey thing, stealing bases.

Brown left the game in the sixth inning. I began talking with this older scout, and we had a great conversation. We marveled at the hitting of young Rangers right fielder Ruben Sierra who was a sensational switch hitter; he hit a bomb off the A's left hander, a name long forgotten. With a small gathering at the yard that evening, you could hear the very loud crack of the bat. The scout on the other side of me was Charlie Silvera, a backup catcher for Yogi Berra, with the Yanks. He made a reference to the gentleman next to me, so I asked his name, and what team he had played for. He replied he was Hank Sauer, had played for the Cubs and Giants, and was the 1952 National League MVP.

Hank became a friend of mine; we watched a lot of baseball for several years after that, and I was always the "eyes" for the older scout who always wanted to sit next to me. This was especially great, as I had his baseball card; I brought it to one game, and Hank personalized it. I still have that card today, and will never sell it. Hank passed a few years ago; he was one of the nicest baseball men I ever met. That day brought baseball cards to life, when I never would have imagined meeting one of those legends.

—Richard Griffin
Oakland, California

***

I was at the final game at Connie Mack Stadium in Philadelphia, October 1, 1970. The Phillies were playing the Montreal Expos. I was ten years old, and went with my dad, a huge, lifelong Phillies fan. It is generally common knowledge that Phillies fans are rowdy—and that's a polite way of putting it. Their jeering and booing of players is legendary, and the target can be either a Phillie or an opponent. Anyway, this night was destined to be about more than just the game. Fans came into the stadium with tool boxes, and proceeded to strip the stadium bare. By the second inning, there was a steady rhythmic pounding in unison, all around the stadium, of fans trying to bang their seat bottoms off of their hinges. We took our seats home (my dad has his in his office to this day). Fans were on the outfield warning track by the seventh inning trying to pull planks from the fences, and the umpires threatened a forfeit if they didn't keep off the field. I remember cars with urinal troughs tied to the roofs after the game. I don't think anyone was even aware, or cared, that there was a ball game going on.

The Phillies won 2-1 in ten innings.

—Chuck Brodsky, singer/songwriter *Baseball Ballads, Volumes I and II* Asheville, North Carolina

(Chuck is an incredible songwriter, with baseball songs to his credit in Cooperstown. I am glad to call him a friend. Listen to his songs.)

***

I grew up in Cincinnati, a baseball fan and Reds fan. Our family was in the meat business, and our sausage floor foreman, Joe Blum, an official of the Knot Hole League (that era's Little League in Cincinnati) gave me tickets to the game against the Boston Braves on June 18, 1947. I was sixteen years old, and excited to go to this game. The starting pitcher for the Reds was Ewell Blackwell, a tall, lankly side-arm thrower, who would finish the year at 22-7. The Reds won 6-0. Babe Young hit two three run homers to account for all the runs. Blackwell actually walked more batters (four) than he struck out (three), but on this day, he achieved baseball history by allowing no hits. All baseball fans dream of going to a game where they catch a ball, see their team win a World Series, or see a no-hitter; some wait decades, hundreds of games, or even their entire lives for events like these to occur. For me, at age sixteen, well, that was as lucky as could be.

What came next is now unclear to me. His next start was four days later against the Brooklyn Dodgers, and he carried a no-hitter into the ninth inning, trying to become just the second pitcher, after Johnny Van der Meer nine years earlier, to hurl consecutive no-hitters. His bid was broken up by Eddie Stanky, and it became a complete game shutout win, 4-0. What's unclear to me is whether I actually went to that game, as planned, or just wanted to go so badly that I have incorporated that into my memory.

—Dr. Mark Oscherwitz
San Francisco, California

***

I attended the final regular season game of the 2010 when the Giants finally beat the Padres to reach the playoffs. As with most games that year, it was "torture" (a term coined by Giants' announcer Duane Kuiper) until the end. Throughout the game, there was so much electricity in the air. It was magical; little did we know, it would be the first of many wins through the post-season. When they won, the players were charged up, and ran around the stadium, high-fiving fans and waving to the whole crowd. Everyone stayed at their seats for a long time. A similar scene occurred at the last game of the 2014 National League Championship Series, the crowd on edge to the end. It was surreal to see Travis Ishikawa hit the home run that returned the Giants to the World Series. It seemed to me that the playoff games hold a lot more excitement, anxiety, and anticipation than the actual Series games. Am I the only one who thinks that?

—Cheryl Wong-Ng
Concord, California

(Yes, Cheryl, you are! Cheryl was at the 2010 game with me, Lynn, and our friend, John Lee. It was a year later, when Cheryl, Lynn and our daughter Rachel, were at a game, when I asked the question—"What was your favorite game?" That's where this book began.)

***

It was the summer of '69, and I was a recent high school graduate from a small town in Minnesota. I was at Midway Airport, flying "student stand-by," returning home from Chicago after visiting my wonderful cousin Lynn. As I waited to get on the plane, I was informed that the Cleveland Indians were on the plane—*really*, the entire baseball team! (Times were so different . . . they flew commercial).

It was a dream come true. Luis Tiant, Ken Harrelson, and Lenny Randle were among the famous Indians stars on that plane. But so was David Earl Nelson. David was a young, handsome man who, from that day, would become my lifelong friend, a friend to me and to my children. Thanks to David, during those forty-five years, I have seen a lot of amazing baseball, and my kids had great opportunities, including my son visiting the clubhouse. Because of David, my cousin's kids were able to get some great autographs, including Doc Gooden. But most importantly, I have a friendship I cherish.

It truly was the best plane ride ever!

—Andi Upin
Saint Paul, Minnesota

(Postscript: David Earl Nelson died on April 22, 2018, at age seventy-three in Milwaukee Wisconsin—and the world misses him.)

(Andi's cousin, "Lynn," would be my wife; of course, those kids are Rachel and David. We briefly met David N. at a game at the Metrodome. A great guy, he was).

***

Like so many people, I have many great baseball memories. My surf/instrumental band, The Ultras, played the National Anthem and "Take Me Out to the Ballgame" during a game at Candlestick Park, Giants against the Dodgers. I went to the longest doubleheader in Major League Baseball history at Shea Stadium, the Mets and the visiting Giants. The second game went twenty-three innings in about seven and a half hours, had a triple play, and Ed Kranepool played all thirty-two innings on the day he was called up from Triple A Buffalo. I was ten, and laughed when I heard my dad order tickets on the phone to see the "New York Metropolitans." Was he the only one to ever call them that? But another unique experience was on June 27, 1967, at Shea. A baseball sequence for the movie *The Odd Couple* was being filmed before a game between the Mets and Pirates. Roberto Clemente was supposed to "hit into a triple play." However, the speedy Pirate kept beating the throw to first base. After several takes, Clemente slowed so much he appeared to be walking, so Bill Mazeroski, a slower runner, although excellent ballplayer, was offered the part instead. It wasn't as exciting as a real game triple play would be, but it was fun to a small part of this filming for a movie.

—Eric Lenchner
Oakland, California

***

In 1951, my twin brother and I were a month shy of our fourteenth birthday, when a family friend, who had come to New York City specifically to see the World Series, took us to games four and five at the Polo Grounds. The most improbable pennant winners in history, the Giants, took on the mighty Yankees. My brother had ruined our seven-inch-screen Motorola a week before, when his beloved Dodgers fell to Bobby Thomson's homer; I screamed with joy as Leo Durocher animated the screen with his jumps just before the shoe brought on the permanent "horizontal." I was the Yankee fan, glad the Dodgers wouldn't make it to the series. I was pretty sure we could beat the Giants.

The Giants were up two games to one when game four rolled around. What great seats (tongue in cheek); we were behind the Yankee bullpen in left-center field, four hundred feet away from the plate. Never mind; what a thrill for two kids from Brooklyn, a World Series and for me, the Yanks to boot! I recall three things to this day: a bullpen catcher with a high-pitched voice joking with the fans, having a high old time just hanging around because, Allie Reynolds, "The Chief", went all the way in victory beating Sal "The Barber" Maglie. That was Ralph Houk, who went on to manage the Yankees. We saw Joe DiMaggio's last ever home run. With one on, it sailed to the right of us in the left field stands. What a thrill to witness that one and only trot, even from far away. He was my idol, and I've never forgotten the ease of his swing and the grace inherent in that trot. Last, I remember thinking the so-called rookie phenom in center for the Giants wouldn't amount to much since he wasn't hitting well. He would not be around long in my young expert opinion. Of course, this kid's name was Willie Mays.

The next day "Easy Eddie" Lopat also went the distance in a one-sided rout featuring Gil McDougald's bases-loaded home run, again to the right of us, hitting the overhang of the upper-deck, which made a 275-foot shot a homer in the Polo Grounds. Not to be out-done by his infield mate, Phil Rizzuto rifled a shot to right, which had to have traveled less than that. The Polo Grounds had foul-lines about 270 feet away, and center field 500 feet away.

I'm seventy-seven years old now, and have never again been to a World Series . . . how could I forget this one?

—Armando Quiroz
Denver, Colorado

***

I grew up a Mets fan in upstate New York. Later in life I moved to St. Petersburg, Florida, and became a Devil Rays fan when they started playing in 1998, living through ten rough years of mostly last place teams.

I opened an art gallery/café and started presenting monthly concerts featuring nationally known musicians. In 2006, I presented our first performer, baseball troubadour Chuck Brodsky, the start of his annual

Craftsman House concert when he comes to town to see Phillies in spring training. Every year, we catch a game together, sometimes the Phillies, other times the Rays. In 2008, we saw them play each other at Al Lang Field in St. Pete. The previous year, the Rays had finished in last place with the worst record in the league; the Phillies had lost their ten thousandth game in franchise history, becoming the first professional sports team in modern history to achieve that milestone.

I don't remember who won that game, but I recall at the end, one of us said, "We won't play each other again until October." We both laughed. Later that year, the Rays shocked everyone, finishing a season that rivaled the 1969 Amazin' Mets. They faced the Phillies in the World Series!

Unfortunately, the Rays lost to the Phils (and the snow), but it was a season to remember!

—Jeff Schorr
St. Petersburg, Florida

***

The last time I played baseball was May 1979, the year I graduated high school. I played fast and slow pitch softball for many years afterwards. In 2007, my brother-in-law, Mike, started a baseball team in his town. He asked me to help coach and I agreed, with the understanding that I also intended to play a few games. We were in a league against college kids and players in their twenties. At forty-six years old, I was facing guys chucking in the mid to high eighties. One day, my son Alex, twenty-one years old, took the mound, and I went behind the plate. We were a battery for three-plus innings, and I even had a couple of plays at the plate. One kid bowled me over, but I held onto the ball! Getting to catch my son in a real baseball game is one of the highlights of my life! I forgot to mention that I'd had back surgery six months prior to that game. I took two game balls, one for me (it will go to Alex later), and I sent one to my surgeon.

In 2011, I started having back issues again. I went back to the surgeon so he could do tests to determine if there had been a problem with the surgery. When I went into his office, he still had my ball on desk!

—Jeff Wyllie
Pottstown, Pennsylvania

DOUBLES

I'd like to be a little more creative or cerebral about describing this chapter, but the title pretty much speaks for itself. These are two stories that have something in common, but don't neatly fit into another chapter. They could be about the same game, or the same player, or just similar or opposite experiences. They are whimsical, or emotional, involve experiences or feelings. They are solid extra base hits.

***

Fans can be merciless sometimes, caring about what their players, their teams, have done for us now. Overpaid and under-performing? Let's boo. You struck out again, or gave up another home run? You suck. But sometimes—not often enough, perhaps—we appreciate the efforts.

The Giants 2013 season was not a happy one for Giants fans. Our team began the season as defending World Series champions, and ended it tied for third place, only one step up from the cellar, with a dismal won-loss record under .500. The year 2013 was dotted with a few high points, such as Tim Lincecum's no-hitter, but after a promising start, the team slid into darkness. Key players were lost to injuries as the season progressed. In May, we lost pitcher Ryan Vogelsong and center fielder Angel Pagan, who went on the disabled list after sliding into home on that spectacular, extra-inning inside the parker (I was at that game, but that, of course, is another story). Pablo Sandoval and Marco Scutaro, keys players in the 2012 championship season, struggled with injuries. Our ace, "the Horse," Matt Cain, was hit in the arm by a line drive in August, and was out for the year. It was just not their year.

But how can a fan complain? Two championships in three years! Two glorious post-seasons. Two magnificent parades down Market Street. Well, complain, fans did. Listening to sports talk radio, you'd think the world was coming to an end. Callers ranted about the lack of offense. After each loss they questioned every management decision. The most common, angry complaints were about Zito and that "damned contract." In 2007, the Giants signed Barry Zito to a seven-year, $126 million contract. Was it outrageous? Of course. Was Zito's performance a disappointment? Absolutely. His pitching was so awful in 2010 that he was left off the post-season twenty-five-man roster. But no one was more disappointed in his pitching than Barry himself. He worked tirelessly. He never blamed anyone other than himself. He was a stand-up guy who did so much for the community, with his various charity projects. He *almost* redeemed himself, at least in the eyes of some of us (myself included) with some masterpiece performances in the 2012 post-season—winning the National League Championship Series elimination game against the Cardinals, and a decisive World Series win against Detroit's ace, Justin Verlander. But then came 2013, the final year of that bloated contract. His dismal, final year was the worst of all. He stunk.

I was at the ballpark for the last game of that season against the San Diego Padres. With the Giants down by one run, Barry Zito took the mound with two outs in the eighth inning for his last time as a Giant. He struck out the Padre batter to end the inning, and started to walk off the mound. The AT&T park crowd rose and gave the man a thunderous standing ovation. As Zito acknowledged the crowd, I felt a tear or two well up in my eyes. I wondered if there were other towns where this would have happened. Maybe. But I also knew that there were places where it certainly would not. At that moment, I was so proud to be a San Franciscan, and a Giants fan.

The Giants scored twice in the bottom of the ninth for a win, ending the season on an up-note (and keeping us from falling behind the Padres in the final standings—a small victory, indeed). But I went home with a feeling of pride that had nothing to do with the team's record that year.

—Lynn Rhodes
San Francisco, California

(I, too, was at that last game. Of course, I'm there virtually every game Lynn is at...),

***

The most amazing baseball moment in my life began with a loss. It wasn't at all your everyday, regular season, we-can-get-'em-tomorrow kind of loss. The Oakland Athletics were up two games in the 2012 American League Division Series (ALDS) going into Detroit, and a couple of days later found themselves back in Oakland for game 5. The Tigers had their star pitcher, the reigning American League MVP *and* Cy Young Award winner, Justin Verlander, on the mound. He silenced the A's bats pitching a complete-game shutout. As the losing home team dejectedly started to walk off the field—they'd lost in the playoffs they worked so hard to reach—the crowd began to chant, "Let's go, Oakland!" Soon everyone in the Coliseum was standing and chanting.

The players on both teams started to realize what was going on, and the A's began acknowledging the crowd. Tigers players even tipped their caps to the A's and their fans out of respect; they showed a lot of class that night, taking their celebration inside so the A's and their fans could experience this special moment. The feelings of solidarity and pride inside the Coliseum that night were incredible and breathtaking, the emotion was palpable. The ovation lasted for a full five minutes (it's on YouTube).

What made the moment even more magical was the back story. The A's were predicted to lose one hundred games, but the team that no one but their fans believed in won ninety-four of those games. On October 3, they faced off with the Texas Rangers in Game 162, tied at ninety-three wins each, in front of the home crowd. The A's defeated them 12-5, taking the American League West crown away from the Rangers. The team was in first place for exactly one day that season, and that day turned out to be the only one that really mattered—the final one. That was actually a pretty incredible day as well. The players circled the field, high-fiving fans and spraying champagne. After all, they'd done what had been deemed impossible. They won the division.

The spontaneous ovation that took place after the final pitch of game five of the 2012 ALDS is my favorite baseball memory. I've seen a perfect game, and witnessed the team win twenty games in a row, but the raw emotion in the Coliseum that day between all the players and the fans cannot truly be described, and will likely never replicated. The A's had lost, but the crowd was so proud of what they had accomplished that a spontaneous ovation broke out, and every single person at the Coliseum was a part of it. It was an amazing experience, and one that I will never forget.

—Jen Rainwater
Pioneer, CA

***

In 1946, Jackie Robinson was playing his only year for the Dodgers' Minor League affiliate based in Montreal, the Royals. I can't recall if they were playing the New York Giants' Jersey City Giants affiliate, or the Yankees' Newark Bears Minor League team. My cousin George Leavy, who had played sandlot ball with Phil Rizzuto (George at shortstop, Rizzuto at second base), and also for the Dodger Rookies, took me to the game. It was a doubleheader, and it started to rain very hard just before the start of the first game.

When the game was postponed, we were able to go into the locker room. George was good friends with teammate Al Campanis, (later the Dodgers' general manager) with whom George had also formed a double play combination at George Washington High School and New York University. Campanis introduced me to Jackie Robinson, and we had a brief conversation. I wished him luck, and said I looked forward to him playing for the Dodgers. Of course, Jackie had not yet broken the color line in the Major Leagues; we could not anticipate how good a ball player he would be in the majors, but I knew I had met someone very special.

I later had the opportunity to meet him twice more. In 1948 or '49, when I was at City College of New York, he spoke to the Sociology Society. I asked him if he could envision a time when it would be common that "Negroes" would develop in the Minor Leagues along with "whites." He responded that he didn't know, but sure hoped it would be in the near future. What a thrill.

—Jules Organ
Boynton Beach, Florida

***

Jackie Robinson was a friend of mine. When I was a kid, my dad wrote Jackie a letter and told him how much I admired him. He wrote back and said he wanted to meet me when the team came to Milwaukee. Thus began a friendship that lasted twenty years with many handwritten letters, lunches and dinners, and phone calls. I was very fortunate.

Once after a game he came out of the locker room in Milwaukee, and the players were getting back on the bus to go back to the hotel. I was walking toward the bus with Jackie, talking to him as he signed other kids' autographs. Along came a priest with a whole parish of kids who wanted autographs; as no surprise, Jackie began signing. The players on the bus started opening the windows, hollering at him to get on as he was holding them up. He went to the driver and said, "Take the guys back to the hotel. I'll take a cab." He stood there and finished signing autographs for every kid. That was the type of person he was. That was the man I was lucky enough to know.

We, of course, gave him a ride back to the hotel.

—Ron Rabinovitz
Minneapolis, Minnesota

Every baseball fan has a player they would like to have met. Some were greater than Jackie Robinson, but few had the impact on the history of the game that he did. How lucky for these two men that they were able to meet him; how lucky for me that I know them both.

***

By 1963, I was a New York Mets fan, and attended a number of games at the Polo Grounds. That June, I watched a game between the Phillies and the Mets. In the middle of the game, Jimmy Piersall (of *Fear Strikes Out* fame) hit his (in)famous one hundredth home run. He was at the end of his career, and wasn't likely to hit many more. What he did could never occur in today's game: He ran around the bases backwards. It was a memorable day for Piersall and the fans.

***

On June 20, 1963, the Mets were playing Yankees at Yankee Stadium in the first of an almost twenty-year annual contest, the Mayor's Trophy game. Duke Snider, back in New York with the Mets at the tail end of his great career, was playing center, and Marvelous Marv Throneberry was in right. One of the Yankees hit a ball to right center; Throneberry called for it and then fell down trying to catch it. Instead of going after the ball, Snider proceeded to put his hands on his knees and started laughing. Needless to say, it was an inside-the-park home run, but the sight of Snider laughing at Throneberry sprawled on the ground was priceless. The Mets were really hapless (but fun to watch) in those years. And they won that game 6-2, providing a measure of revenge for Mets', and former Yankees manager, Casey Stengel.

—Ken Entin
San Jose, California

(I have tried to use only one story per person in this book. I flipped a coin, did eeny meeny meiny mo, but I just couldn't figure out which of these I liked best. Ken, this is your first double in a few years.)

***

The Game that means the most to me would have to be Seattle Mariners versus Oakland Athletics, on September 6, 2009. There was wasn't much to the game, but I remember the long conversations with Joe, about guns, girls, baseball, and his future as a father someday. Between pitches, we would keep score, and I even let him have a drink of my beer. He acted like it was gross, and hated it, but I knew he was putting me on. The Mariners lost 3-2, but it was the last father-and-son time we had before he joined the Marine Corps. I guess in a way baseball is a time where fathers and sons can share a memory and experience to last a life time, regardless of who has to carry on the story. This game is very special to me because it was the last game I ever saw with my son, Joe, who was killed in action in Sangin, Afghanistan on Easter Sunday 2011.

Thank you for the opportunity to give you a little story that means a lot to me, and share my experiences, strength, and hope through baseball.

—Shawn Marceau
Yakima, Washington

(I met Shawn one time. We talked about our jobs, and baseball. Every time someone thanks me for giving them the opportunity to tell their story, to relive memories, I delete it from the story. It isn't that important. This time, it was necessary to leave in Shawn's thanks, so that I could reply. Thank you, Shawn, for letting me tell others your moving story.)

***

The first time I had a beer with my dad was when we went to a Tigers game. It had come home on leave from Iraq where I spent my 20th and 21st birthdays. Dad tried to get tickets for Opening Day but had to settle for the second game of the season. Without thinking, he ordered two beers, one for me and one for him, from the vendor walking up and down the aisles. Dad handed it to me, looked over and smiled and said: "this is the first beer we've ever had together." It is crazy, I know people that died in war before they even turned 21, before they ever got to share that kind of moment. In our country, you can fight for your country, even die, but you cannot have a legal drink.

I could tell my dad was very proud of me. He was never an emotional guy; he never told me loved me until a phone call I made to him when I was in Iraq. But I remember seeing him get emotional that day, with him realizing that I'd had a brush with death. His son was a war veteran before he could even legally buy a beer. Dad had coached me throughout my entire childhood baseball career. We always bonded over baseball. To share that moment with him at a baseball game was a very proud day for him. We had hot dogs and peanuts, and cheered on our Tigers all game and watched them win. It was a great day for both of us. I think for my dad it was one of those moments that you always look forward to spending with your son. The fact that he almost had that chance taken away from him while I was in Iraq was devastating. Sharing that moment over baseball was so important because dad watched me grow up on a baseball diamond. He taught me everything I know about baseball.

—Anonymous
Detroit, Michigan

***

I was born the son of a crazy baseball fan. During the Depression he sold programs at both Wrigley Field and Comiskey Park. He loved both Chicago teams, and taught me to do the same. In July of 1968, I was in my second year in medical school. The lectures were not particularly useful (the books were better), and I had something more important to do than sitting in a lecture: go to see the Cubs, who were looking good, could possibly be in a pennant race, and could finally reach the World Series. The team seemed on the move since the disastrous 1965 season. With Banks and Williams, Santo and Kessinger, Fergie and Holtzman, how could they not finally become the National League representatives in the Fall Classic? What I remember most about that day is that sometime around the sixth inning, sitting in the bleachers, a home run sailed over my head. Turning to watch it, I spied my father two rows behind me. Dad had flexible hours at the post office and had decided to go to the game. So here we were, father and son, Bleacher Bums, both of us, ditching work and school, and meeting at Wrigley Field. I moved up to sit next to Dad, and we shared our love of the Cubs, and also the unspoken agreement that my mom, his wife, was not to know. I don't remember who won that game, or who the Cubs played, but I clearly remember that moment. My father and I made a deal to meet in the bleachers every Friday home game that summer. Mom never found out.

—Jerry Bernstein
Highland Park, Illinois

***

When I was a teenager, I went to a Yankees game with my parents, three younger siblings, and a big group of family friends. The group was made up of moms and dads and kids whose ages ranged from one or two years old to older teenagers. We were sitting in the upper deck, about as high up as you can get. Old Yankee Stadium had an extremely steep upper deck, and my youngest brother, Christopher, three or four at the time, was horsing around like little kids do when they get bored. Mom was a few seats over from us chatting with one of the other moms and dad was supposed to be looking after him. As the game progressed, and Dad got ever more engrossed in it, he looked away from Christopher just long enough for him to do something particularly athletic, lose his balance, and tumble and roll three or four rows down, where he finally landed, wedged between the back of a chair and a startled stranger who had been leaning forward for a better view. In a panic, Dad glanced towards where Mom was sitting. She had her back turned, and one of the other moms intercepted my dad's look, put her finger to her lips, shook her head slowly side to side, and gave Dad a warning look that said plain as day, "Keep your mouth shut, and retrieve that child pronto if you want to live much longer." Dad crept down and retrieved Christopher, thanked the startled stranger, and kept his hand around Christopher's wrist for the rest of the game. And that was a story Mom didn't hear for a looooooong time.

—Leah Prestamo
New York, New York

***

In 1973, I went with my father to an afternoon game at Memorial Stadium in Baltimore to watch the Orioles play the Detroit Tigers. We were sitting in lower reserved seats behind third base. Early in the game, maybe the third inning, Dad, who rarely went to baseball games (he's from London and never liked baseball) left to get me a hot dog. While he was gone, Brooks Robinson began a triple play! Frank Howard hit a smash to "The Human Vacuum Cleaner," who threw to Bobby Grich at second, who in turn threw to Terry Crowly at first. The crowd went crazy; by the time Dad came back, the excitement was over. When I told him what happened, he just shrugged his shoulders! He had no clue, and didn't care.

—Alex Schonfield
Oakland, California

***

My childhood was spent in Brooklyn, but early on, I had no interest, or experience, with baseball. Shortly after the Dodgers and Giants moved west, I recall a kid outside of school asking me which team I liked best, the Yankees, Dodgers, or Giants, and then beating me up when I said, "I don't know baseball." At age eight, shortly after the 1961 season started, I found some baseball cards lying on the street. I asked my dad about the abbreviations on the back of the cards, such as HR (home run) and BB (base on balls), and thus began my love affair with baseball.

It was a great year for baseball, especially in New York, with the Maris and Mantle home run record chase. Through work, my dad got two box seats, in the seventh row off of third base, for a game against the White Sox. The date was August 16, 1961, which was Babe Ruth Day at Yankee Stadium, as it was the thirteenth anniversary of Babe Ruth's death. It was also my parents' twelfth wedding anniversary, and it became the date of my first Major League game. The observation that I clearly remember is how much smaller the field looked than it did on WPIX television. The bases seemed so close to each other, and the mound so close to home plate. On TV, the infield seemed gigantic; in person, it was so much smaller.

It was the bottom of the ninth, with the score tied 4-4. White Sox outfielder Jim Landis had hit two two-run homers, which matched Roger Maris' two two-run homers, with Yankees second baseman Bobby Richardson on base both times. The Yankees loaded the bases, and Bob Cerv, nearing the end of his career, came up to pinch it. On a 2-2- count, he was hit by a pitch, and as he trotted to first, the winning run came in from third. It was a particularly uneventful end to a game, but I remember my dad, who certainly knew the rules of baseball, standing up and shouting out loud to himself, "What? That's it? That's the end of the game? That's all there is?"

It may have been an odd ending to a game, but it began a lifelong love affair with baseball.

—Jerry Ginsberg
Key West, Florida

***

The first real memory that I have is of a baseball game. On August 18, 1967, the Red Sox were playing the California Angels at Fenway Park. I was five and a half years old. Every year my dad would take me to a game with his Knights of Columbus Council in South Weymouth, Massachusetts. We'd get on a chartered bus and head to Fenway for a night game. This was very exciting stuff for a five-year-old and his dad. That year, the Sox were in the middle of their "Impossible Dream" season and Tony Conigliaro was the young right fielder and reigning American League home run champion. At the plate against the Angels' Jack Hamilton, he was hit by a pitch on the left cheek. I have still vivid memories of the "at-bat," mainly the crowd's rising cheers with every pitch. All of a sudden there came a mass groan and stunned silence. I remember the stretcher at home plate, and the cheers as the player and his career were rolled away. I can still recall my line of sight from the grandstand under the roof on the first base side of home plate. I can still picture the dim lighting of the field in the night, and can contrast the memory to games today where modern lighting really has advanced. While some memories of the event are hazy, I still have the extremely vivid recollection of the stretcher and the lighting and the abrupt hush after the cheering.

—Paul Leary
Benicia, California

***

On May 7, 1957, Herb Score, the great Indians pitcher who a few years earlier had set an American League rookie strikeout record, was facing the Yankees. In the first inning, Yankees third baseman Gil McDougald hit a line drive right back at Score, hitting him in the face. McDougald, instead of running to first base as game situations would have "required," ran to the pitcher's mound to help. It was a bloody mess, to say the least. McDougald was heard to have said in the locker after the game that if Score could not play again in the future, he would also retire. Score, because of subsequent arm injuries and change of pitching motions, did pitch continue pitching but never as well as he did in his early years.

—Howard

(I met Howard, just by chance, at the dinner table of the facility where our Aunt Bernice was living. We just coincidentally started talking baseball. I was never able to contact Howard again to get more information, but he gave me some nice stories. He's one of only four people other than myself, who have more than one story in this book. I wish I could show it to him.)

***

I was at the Giants/Marlins game when Buster Posey was seriously and famously injured (resulting in rules changes for plays at home plate). It was my first summer out of college, and my friend Alex and I went to this game together. Alex is a die-hard fan, and knows the entire history of Giants baseball. We were catching the ferry back to Alameda, our home town, and left our bleacher seats early to beat the crowds, but we decided to stand on the Ghirardelli Trolley Car at AT&T Park to watch the final plays of the game that had gone into extra innings. We watched Scott Cousins run down the third base line, and stared in horror as he slammed into Buster. The crowd went silent as Posey was almost motionless on the ground. The entire crowd remained silent until they walked Posey off the field, not yet knowing that it was a devastating injury that would sideline him for the rest of the year. The Giants had a disappointing loss that game, and I remember thinking I was a curse to the Giants as they lost every game I had gone to that summer. This was perhaps the crazy in me thinking, but the horrible end to this game, Posey's injury, further fueled this belief.

—Marlena Nip
New Orleans, Louisiana

***

Fun fact about me: My first word was "baseball." My dad and sister heard me say it. It wasn't "mom," "dad," "sister," or "brother." It was baseball. I think that was a sign that baseball was meant to be a part of my life, right? My story involves my brother, CJ Saylor, as a college player and professional prospect.

When CJ was being recruited by San Diego State University, I went with him to meet the coaches one afternoon. As we walked into the coaches' office, I noticed a man pitching on the field. I thought to myself, "Wow, that looks like . . ." But of course I didn't say anything. If it truly was him, wouldn't my brother or dad have noticed this all-star pitcher? When CJ's meeting ended, this man who I thought I recognized came walking towards us. As he got closer, the coach turned around and said, "Hey, Stephen! I would like to introduce you to our recruit and his family!" Starstruck, all I could do was choke out a hello as he shook every one of our hands. Still shocks me to this day that I met Stephen Strasburg!

I practically grew up on a baseball field. It has been a very important part of my life, and always will be. Even though I can't physically contribute to the game any longer, I hope to be able to find another way to participate and give back.

—Lauren Saylor
West Covina, California
P.S.: My brother is now playing in the St. Louis Cardinals organization

Marlena and Lauren met when they were assigned to be rommates at college. I met them at spring training when they were walking together, Marlena in her Giants jersey, Laren in her Dodgers jersey. Deciding to ignore the fact that it could be construed as a little creepy chasing after two young women a third my age, I asked them how they managed to make this team rivalry/friendship work. The stories have literally nothing in common, but these two young women are forever linked in my mind.

TRIPLES

What can I say? As with doubles, these are groups of stories with connecting themes, but three-of-a-kind. They involve having to get to that game, a throw, the weather and child-like naivete. They are solid, stand-up triples.

***

During the mid-1980s, I was covering the Padres for the *San Diego Tribune*. At one game during spring training in the Phoenix area, the Padres were playing the Giants in Scottsdale Stadium, an old-time, outdated, ballpark. The facilities in general were not great, and there were few amenities. Trailers were set up down the right field line to serve sandwiches for the press. As I left the trailer and headed up to the press box, I ran into Padres' pitcher Eric Show in the stands. It was odd to see him there, dressed in his full uniform. I knew Eric from covering the team, and I asked him where he was going. He answered matter of factly, "I am going to buy a hot dog." I suppose this struck me as even odder than seeing him in the stands, so I suggested that he go to the trailer and grab a sandwich. He said, "Thanks a lot," and headed off. I thought nothing of it.

But this is how it played out. Show went into the trailer and started helping himself to sandwiches. At that point, he was confronted by Giants executive Al Rosen, who became infuriated at his presence. He demanded to know why Show was there. Show responded with "Who are *you*?" and Rosen replied that he was president of the Giants. He looked at Rosen and said, "Barry Bloom sent me here," and then asked Rosen the amazing question: "Whose authority is higher, yours or Barry Bloom's?"

I wasn't there for this conversation, but was told about it by quite a few writers who all had a consistent story. The consensus was that Rosen did not find it amusing. Many of us thought it was, and we have discussed this annually.

—Barry Bloom, author and national columnist for mlb.com
Phoenix, Arizona

***

I have been fortunate to make a career out covering sports on radio, television, and the written media. I spent many years covering the Giants on their flagship radio station, including hosting the pre- and post-game shows. I first became acquainted with Dusty Baker when he was an outfielder for the Dodgers. He was a guy you could always speak with. He was honest, straightforward, and made time for me so I could do my job. When he became the Giants batting coach in 1987, we reconnected, and I found him to still always be available. He became manager in 1993, the year that the Giants had the 103-win season but still did not make the playoffs, getting nosed out by the Braves in the pre-WC years. Dusty was always regarded as a "players' manager"; he wore his heart on his sleeve, just as he wore his orange wrist bands as a way to show his players that he was with them in spirit, not just as their manager. He cared deeply about his players, personally and professionally.

In 2002, during the period of time that I traveled extensively with the team, the Giants entered the playoffs as the National League Wild Card team, ultimately reaching the World Series, only to lose to the Angels. This team had a good rotation and very strong line-up that featured the individually incredible, but dynamically contentious, duo of Barry Bonds and Jeff Kent. On the trip to Atlanta, we checked in to the hotel about one in the morning, and as I headed down the hall to my room, Dusty was in front of me. He turned around and said, "Bruce, come to my room. I want to talk to you." I thought, well, this can't be good.

I went to his room, a huge suite. Essentially, Dusty just wanted to use me as a sounding board, to get things off his chest. We spoke for twenty minutes about all the things that were causing him stress, some on, some off the field. After he was done, I headed to my room and immediately got a phone call from him, as he wanted to continue on. This was an amazing experience for me, knowing that Dusty trusted me enough to confide in me, knowing I would never betray his confidence. I have never spoken about those conversations, and even now I am being vague. The story for me is that he trusted me.

When I stopped working for the Giants in 2006, I got nice, supportive phone calls from many folks, such as the great Giants announcers Mike Krukow and Duane Kuiper. They left me an awesome joint message. But the one that means the most to me was the one left by Dusty Baker.

—Bruce Macgowan, author of *Game of My Life*
Fairfax, California

***

Growing up in Phoenix, Arizona, the most-anticipated events each summer were trips to visit family in Southern California, and the chances to go to Dodger Stadium. As a child in the mid-sixties to mid-seventies, every game seemed to offer a glimpse at some of the greatest players in baseball: Aaron, Clemente, Rose, Mays, Marichal. But for me, it was those legendary Dodger pitchers: Koufax, Drysdale, Sutton.

With older brothers and male cousins, finding someone to accompany me to Chavez Ravine was never difficult. A family friend worked as a concessionaire at the ballpark and offered me two tickets for the July 20, 1970 game as the Dodgers prepared to host the Philadelphia Phillies. One of the occasional "Businessman's Special" weekday afternoon games, this day became a challenge: Four in the afternoon game time on a Monday. As the hours rolled by that morning, I began to panic. Nobody I knew was free, and I was still a few years away from driving. At the last possible moment,

I convinced the one brother with absolutely no interest in baseball to take me. If memory serves, I agreed to clean his room for a week.

I was accustomed to big crowds, noisy night games, lots of energy and excitement in the air. But this day, less than eleven thousand were in attendance. The Phillies were in the midst of an injury-riddled, losing season; the Dodgers' starting pitcher was a twenty-six-year-old right-hander named Bill Singer. He'd had a breakthrough season in 1969, winning twenty games in his second full year in the majors. But this season had been interrupted by a bout with mononucleosis causing him to lose six weeks. This would be only his seventh game; later in the season a broken finger would shut him down after just sixteen starts.

We settled into our third-level seats between home plate and first. The Dodgers scored three early runs, and Singer was retiring the Phillies in seemingly effortless fashion. The pace of the game was quick, with no standout plays or memorable moments that stick in my memory. I was keeping score in my Dodgers' program, and when the Phillies were retired in the top of the sixth, I turned to my brother and said, "Hey, I just noticed, the Phillies don't have a hit yet." For the first time all day, he showed some interest in what was happening on the field. "Are you sure?" He looked over my scoring, and then said, "Well, you're right. Maybe this will be more than the usual boring baseball game."

And so, it was. That afternoon, Bill Singer no-hit the Phillies in a 5-0 win. The game has taken on much more importance to me over the years, because after working in Major League Baseball for the last nineteen seasons, I *still* have not seen another no-hitter. I've often come close, and each time I remember Singer. My brother, who hasn't attended an MLB game since, occasionally brags about attending a no-hitter, implying tongue-in-cheek that it his presence galvanized Bill Singer that day.

A smart move by Dodgers' manager Walt Alston made it happen: When LA took the field in the top of the ninth, he removed error-prone third-baseman Steve Garvey, and replaced him with veteran Maury Wills. And wouldn't you know, the Phillies' leadoff hitter in the ninth slapped a rope down the third base line, and Wills made a diving stop and throw from his knees to get the out.

The game remains the most memorable to me for one more reason. My first partner in the booth during my first year working in baseball was a man named Byron Browne, an eight-year MLB veteran, who played for the Cubs, Phillies, and Cardinals. Where was Byron on July 20, 1970? He heard me telling the story of Singer's dominance one afternoon, and he leaned forward and surprised me when he said, "Oh yeah, I remember Singer's no-hitter. I pinch-hit that day. Went down fast."

Over the years, Byron has become a close friend, and is one more link for me, one more reason I consider myself so fortunate to have been exposed to baseball from my earliest years . . . and so extremely blessed to work in the game.

—Eric Lenaburg
Phoenix, Arizona

***

In 1970, my older brother, Cottrell, was asked to be a pitcher for an all-white baseball league team. I was ten years old, and we lived in the small town of Magnolia, Arkansas. When I heard about this invitation, I became both excited and fearful because the leagues in town were segregated. My father called a family meeting to vote about whether this would be a good thing for Cottrell to pursue. The whole family finally agreed it would be a wonderful opportunity for him, and he began to practice that Monday morning. Once he made it home from the first day of practice, he shared that he'd had a great day. He was striking out his teammates and also hitting home runs. I asked him if he was treated differently from his teammates, and he said he felt that he was treated like a star.

On Saturday, the whole family jumped into the car to see his first game. When we arrived, I felt nervous, unsure if we were permitted to sit with the white people, but we were welcomed by everyone. It was so exciting to see Cottrell take the mound. The crowd was quiet until the first pitch (strike), then the second and third, a strike out. The crowd went crazy. Cottrell allowed no hits, just strikeouts and foul balls throughout the whole game.

The most amazing thing is that he also hit two homers. That day marked one of the greatest moments for my brother and the whole family. This experience made me realize that it wasn't about the color of his skin but the magnitude of his skills. I love my small town.

—Cathy Revels
Rialto, California

***

In 1984, I was living in New York City (NYC) and was, as I am today, a baseball fanatic. I got to know the owner of the Met Food grocery story, Arif, and his son Riyadh. I am Jewish; they were Palestinian. I was a Mets fan, Riyadh was a Yankees fan. I am an attorney, and Riyadh was hoping to go to medical school. Our baseball preferences and cultures did not stand in the way of our friendship, and we felt very free to talk about our differences with respect (well, maybe not so much for me about his beloved Yankees). Of course, there was plenty of trash-talking about our teams' rivalry.

One day we were talking baseball, and the subject of stickball came up. The game involves drawing a box on a wall, the strike zone, a pink rubber ball, and usually, a broom handle, or the rare, specific, stickball bat. Riyadh thought he could destroy me in a game, so the challenge was on. I was thirty-nine; he was nineteen. He did not realize that, unlike in baseball, there is an advantage to batting first, so I convinced him that he should pitch the top of the inning. He was ready to pitch, and despite my encouragement to do so, he did not wish to warm up; that was part of my plan. He started off by continuously throwing above the box, walking the bases loaded. Then, the pitches started coming in lower, and I got hit after hit, not so much power, but the relentless singles right past him. Soon, the score was 13-0, his arm was really tired, and he decided to concede without ever having the chance to bat. I had certainly psyched him out. For some reason, he challenged me to a rematch, and I said that I would bat last. I warmed up and gave up a couple of runs in the first inning. Then, he warmed up as well, but it was obvious that his arm was still spent from the first game, so he gave up a bunch of runs and quit soon after.

Riyadh felt humiliated and begged me to not tell his dad. I was happy to do so, but mentioned something I had read in Leon Uris' book, *The Haj*. In Arab culture, it was noted, when the favor of keeping a secret is agreed to, the person asking the favor is obligated to forever protect the life of the person maintaining the secret. I jokingly reminded him of this, suggesting that if a Palestinian military organization ever attacked NYC, Riyadh would be obligated to hide me and save my life. Relations between these groups has long been a sensitive issue, both in the Middle East and the States; because of the friendship we had developed through our love of baseball, despite our differences, important (religion and nationality) and not important (which team was our favorite, although who is to say choosing between the Yankees and Mets is not important?), we were able to kid about this.

Thirty years later, Riyadh is a successful physician. All these years later, I have kept Riyadh's secret. Well, I guess until now.

—David N. Stein
Towaco, New Jersey

***

I am a Black man and grew up in Huntington, West Virginia, on the Ohio River, 160 miles from Cincinnati. Huntington was a somewhat segregated town, but baseball had a way of bringing people together. When you talked about baseball in general, and the Reds specifically, it did not matter what your skin color was. I spent so much time, and fell in love with baseball, listening to Reds games on the radio, on my front porch, with my father and other people in the community. I didn't know what the ball players looked like; at school I formed friendships with other students who liked the Reds. In June 1970, I rode the train to Cincinnati to see my first professional baseball game at old Crosley Field. Seeing the ball players in person was a complete joy. That day, the Reds beat the defending World Champion

Mets. I bought a program with the players' pictures and profiles; for the rest of the year, whenever I listened to a game, I would look at and read these. I still remember that glorious day I spent at Crosley. From then on, until I left to join the Air Force, I lived and died based on Reds' wins and losses. In 1975, when the Reds won the World Series over the Red Sox, I rejoiced as though it was my birthday, Christmas and New Year's all rolled into one.

I will never forget the starting line-up for the Reds that day in 1970, with Sparky Anderson as the manager: Rose, Tolan, Perez, Bench, May, Carbo, or McRae (guess I forgot a little!), Helms, Woodward, and Simpson. This was the beginning of the era of the Big Red Machine.

—Joe Pearson
Sacramento, California

***

Are you a fan of a team that has exciting, knowledgeable tv/radio broadcasters, or, well, boring ones who flatly just report the action? They can have such a powerful effect on viewers/listeners, in terms of explaining, teaching, and just converting folks to being fans. Kruik and Kuip shaped my daughter's interest in baseball. Man, I loved Hank Greenwald. Here are stories about some of the greats.

I grew up listening to Vin Scully call Dodgers games. I am now sixty-five, and he's still calling the games. He must be 115 years old. I heard him on the radio call all of Koufax's gems, including his perfect game. He is the only sports announcer I ever heard who could improvise a poetic phrase to describe a play as it was happening in the field. "Wills flicks his glove as if he were shooing a fly away from his shoulder, comes up with the bad hop, and nonchalantly throws to Howard at first to beat the runner." "Two gone in the ninth, 3-2 count on Mays. Koufax delivers. It's called strike three, the bar is closed ladies and gentlemen, all patrons must head home." He made calls like that every game. Easily the greatest ever.

—John Raskin
Berkeley, California

***

When Phillies legendary broadcaster, Harry Kalas—the "Voice of Summer" to so many—passed suddenly while prepping in the sound booth for a game against the Nationals, the microphone truly went silent. I heard the news report on television. Watching in shock with the rest of the sports world, I was overcome with emotion as several of his peers broke down during live broadcasts, reporting that Harry had passed only hours earlier. It was clear how much he meant to the Philadelphia fans. Even if you had never met him in person, you felt as though you had. I never had that privilege, yet like so many others, was devastated at the news. Growing up listening to Harry and Richie Ashburn (Whitey), you felt that a piece of your childhood had now been stolen from you. His golden voice earned him a well-deserved entry into the Broadcaster's Hall of Fame in Cooperstown, New York. His sons said that he died doing what he loved, "at his second home." Harry waited an entire career to be able to make the call that the Phillies were 2008 World Champions of baseball. He died in April 2009.

I wrote and recorded a song entitled the "Outta Here Anthem" (in honor of his trademark "That ball is outta here!" every time a Phillie hit a home run). I posted it to YouTube three days after his passing. After going through every channel imaginable, the song reached the desk of Phillies' video man Dan Stephenson. "I think we can do something with your song," Dan said. One of the greatest honors of my life was having the song featured in a Harry Kalas tribute as part of the 2009 Phillies Video Yearbook, entitled "Legends of the Fall." If that wasn't honor enough, my family was invited to the grand opening of the Harry Kalas Memorial Exhibit at Laurel Hill Cemetery, where a plaque, and the story of how the song was created, is displayed for all to see, alongside Harry's infamous blue blazer and white loafers. Harry loved the players, and the players loved him back. He loved to entertain, and loved to sing. His signature song at the end of every game and in the clubhouse was "High Hopes." To this day, and in his honor, it is played after every home game. In our hearts, Harry, you'll never be "outta here." RIP.

—Lisa Ozalis Graham, composer/singer "Outta Here Anthem"
Southampton, New Jersey

***

After my father was killed by a drunk driver, I spent a year in several foster homes. I later moved back home and my grandfather, Jay Rodgers, took me under his wing. Unlike my dad, grandpa loved Tigers baseball and started my interest by listening to Ernie Harwell. I hitchhiked twenty miles to listen to games with him. I never could take him to a Tigers game because it was too difficult for him to be physically comfortable at games, but he was always with me in spirit.

Thirty years later, a close friend, Warren Bradley, who was friends with Ernie, took me to his house. I was in awe of how nice Ernie and his wife Lulu were. After spending a couple hours at their home, I told Ernie about how he and my grandfather got me hooked on the Tigers and helped me turn my life around. Ernie sat there listening with a smile on his face and a tear in his eye. We became close friends, spoke with him on the phone often, and visited his home several times. A great broadcaster, a wonderful man.

It is, of course, a totally different story, but the time my son Tony and I met "The Bird," Mark Fidrych, was amazing. He invited us to his house, offered us beers, and let us stay overnight at his place. A good friendship developed from that. He, too, was a great guy.

—Byron Hatch
Flint, Michigan

***

I am a lifelong Cardinals fan fortunate enough to have seen many great, including post-season, games. My wife and I went to game one of the 2011 World Series to see the Cards win a 3-2 victory over Texas; that was nothing compared to what was to come. When the Cards pulled out a win in game six, I call it the David Freese Game, to tie the series at three games each, I immediately knew I *had* to go to game seven with the people I cared about. This is where it got interesting.

I watched Stubhub ticket prices go up by the minute. I woke up my dad, who lives two hours away, and insisted he go with me the next day; of course, he agreed. I called my sister, who lives in Atlanta, getting her out of bed, convincing her to come to town, not realizing until after she agreed, that she would be with her husband in Boston for a wedding the next day! A huge sports fan, he totally understood, and supported her coming. In the early hours of the morning she had to pack, book the first flight to St. Louis, and get to the airport with little sleep. What a trooper! These commitments secured, I spent a small fortune on three tickets and promptly fell down the stairs after printing them, with fortunately just a sore tailbone. I went to bed after sending my wife a text telling her I was going, knowing she had an all-day management meeting in Springfield and couldn't make the game.

This was mistake number one in a so far easily executed plan. She was asleep when I sent the text and didn't get it until the morning. She was *not happy at all* that I didn't get her a ticket! Wow, was I wrong! I told her I would take care of it, sold the three tickets, and bought four others, actually making a little money and getting better seats, at that. Disaster avoided!

I took the day off, picked up my sister at the airport, and got her clothing to wear; wedding clothes were not suitable for a cold baseball game. Back at the house, she slept; when Dad arrived, we headed downtown to enter the stadium early to take it all in. My wife nudged her meeting to an early end, raced home, changed into ballgame clothes, and joined us in the bottom of the second. We were on field level, six rows up, and down the right field line. Imagine being at game seven of a World Series in your team's stadium with the people who matter most for you; it was surreal. Everyone was high-fiving everyone, like we all were best friends. In the ninth inning, leading 6-2, Motte came in to close it out. The stadium was shaking; the noise was louder than any sporting event I have ever been to. My ears were ringing, but I couldn't hear anything. Motte did his job; one, two, three. I lost my voice from screaming; confetti was shooting all over, fans were beyond crazy, everyone hugging. They brought out the podium for the trophy presentation as we'd watched on TV so many times; this time we saw it in person, and it was amazing.

When I look back on all that had to happen to get us all to that game, and the experience of seeing my team win it at home, *perfect* is the only way to describe it. The Cardinals may never go to another Series game seven again, so I knew it could be that once-in-a-lifetime moment. It will be an experience I remember and talk about until I go to my grave.

—Jerry Canaday
St. Louis, Missouri

***

In 2002, my son Holden was in the fifth grade. The only sports fan in the family, he often felt like a fish out of water, as no one else understood the appeal of team sports. The Giants had advanced to the World Series, and many of his friends were going to game five. Holden was dejected when I picked him up at school; my other kids had plans that day, so I looked at my sad boy and said, "I have an idea." I knew nothing about the series, but said, "Let's get some money out of the bank and see if we can buy tickets from a scalper. It's a long shot, but . . ." His face lit up, and he screamed, "Mom, you are the best!"

I withdrew all the month's extra money and we took the J-Church downtown; everyone on the train was going to the game, excited and wearing their tickets around their necks. As Holden's excitement grew, I began to realize the folly of my offer. We didn't have enough money; I'd gotten his hopes up—*Oy*, what had I done? As we neared the park, and crowd excitement grew, I tried to be realistic about our chances. Holden just said, "I know, Mom, but we're gonna get 'em, I just know it."

We arrived to a scene of wall to wall people, all yelling for tickets and no one offering any. It was intense. A guy near us held up his hand and said, "I have two tickets," and was immediately swarmed by a crowd of begging people, many with more money than I had. I looked at him, held up Holden's hand, and said, "I only have this much money." He said, "I want the little kid to get to go," and turned to me. Wearing a pale blue windbreaker, khaki pants, and a baseball cap, he looked like a SoCal golfer to me. I pulled out the money and handed it to him. There was no negotiating; I just gave it all to him. He said, "Take my phone number. Tell me how you like the game." He handed me the tickets and disappeared into the throng of people.

Holden was dancing and screaming, and then we looked at the tickets. They didn't look like anyone else's; they didn't say "game five," or even have a date on them. Everyone who we asked if the tickets were right, said, "They don't look anything like ours." Our hearts sank as we sat in front of the park, thousands of thrilled revelers smushing around us, and I started to cry. I was apologizing. I had no money left, knew nothing about baseball, didn't know how to negotiate, and had totally jerked my poor ten-year old's heart around. I realized I had the guy's phone number. Figuring it was a fake, I called; when he answered, I said, "You must be so proud of yourself, breaking a little kid's heart for a few hundred dollars. What'd you do? Print these out on your home computer?" He said, "What are you talking about?" I told him, "They're bogus tickets, and you suck!" He replied, "They are real, and they are great tickets, but if you want your money back, I'll give it back. Where are you?" I told him in front of the north gate. Holden was crying, but trying to reassure me, saying, "It's okay, you did your best." I felt like a fool.

I didn't expect to see him, but back he came through the black and orange crush. I couldn't believe he was returning to the scene of his crime. He pulled out my money and said, "These are good tickets, and you really should take them, but it's your choice." I was holding my money, he was holding out the (fake?) tickets. Should I repeat my first mistake? No one else was selling tickets. I had no idea what was true, or what to do. It was a lot of money for our family. The man looked earnest. I again gave him the money, and he again gave me the tickets, repeating, "Call me to tell me how you like it." In line, everyone was looking at our strange tickets. We neared the turnstile, holding hands in anticipation. The scanner beeped approval, and the entire crowd burst into applause. We were astonished. We were going to the game! As we walked toward section 105 along the first base line, Holden's eyes kept widening, and he hugged me and cried (a little!). We walked down the aisle to our seats in the fourth row, a few rows behind Bud Selig; I'd never heard of him, but Holden was going crazy. I called the guy and said, "Oh my god," and he replied, "I'm up here in the box with Willie Mays. Those are his seats. He wanted me to let a kid see the game. I'm his golf pro." We were sitting in *Willie Mays's* seats!

It was an amazing game. Dusty Baker's three-year-old son Darren, the bat boy, ran on the field to do his job at a very wrong time, and JT Snow, in an iconic baseball moment, snatched him up by his collar at the last second as Snow crossed home plate. He might have literally saved Darren's life. The Giants won the game handily, 16-4. Holden wrote a thank you letter to the guy, and received a letter and signed paraphernalia from Willie. What an amazing postscript to a wonderful, wonderful night.

—Jeri Taylor
San Francisco, California

***

It was a Sunday afternoon in 1982 when I decided that I was going to a World Series game. Growing up in Buffalo, we could listen to Yankees games on radio; they were the team we had to follow. In 1964, the mighty Yankees were playing the Cardinals. I had never heard of them, but I liked the uniforms; the white with red really showed up well. The Cards won that Series, and I was hooked for life; they were my team. I best remember the great pitcher Bob Gibson, and was also mesmerized by the speed and base-stealing of Lou Brock.

That fall day I was home waiting for game three of the National League Championship Series between the Braves and the Cardinals, potentially the clincher, with the Cardinals ahead two games to none. Winning meant a trip to the Series, and I decided I would get tickets to see the Cards in it. I sat down with a piece of paper that I have to this day, and called Atlanta Fulton County Stadium. The press box told me where the Cardinals were staying; with nothing to lose, I called the hotel, needing to talk to someone to tell them I'd been a fan since the 1960s. I focused on Red Schoendienst, their manager from 1967 to 1968, pulling together mental highlights. Shockingly, the hotel put me through to his room!

I began, "Mr. Schoendienst, this is Bill from Buffalo, New York, and you don't know me, but I've been a Cardinals fan since the mid-sixties." For the next thirty seconds, I crammed in as many highlights as I could before the anticipated hang up. I was so nervous yet so happy to be talking to this sports icon. He said, "Whoa, whoa, you're a fan, I can tell, but what can I do for you, son?" I said I wanted World Series tickets. He replied, "We have to win today's game first, and I don't have anything to do with tickets." My heart started to sink, but then he said, "Hang on and I'll get someone who does have something to do with tickets." Again, expecting the hang up, to my surprise, Lee Thomas got on the phone and told me he was involved in player development but also handled special ticket requests. He said Red told him to see what he could do for me. I could not believe my ears. He reiterated that they still had to win today's game, gave me his office number, and name of his secretary; he told me that if they won, I should call her at nine in the morning, and she would give me the details for getting the tickets. I thanked him profusely, and he said, "Just root for the Cardinals to win today."

I got off the phone not knowing what to do. I wanted to tell the world what I'd just done, but it would be meaningless if the Cardinals lost that game. I called my boss to beg for the time off on Monday. She thought I was nuts, but agreed. I was so happy, excited, and nervous all at the same time. The Cards won that afternoon, sweeping the Braves. Monday couldn't come fast enough. I packed the car, got out maps, and plotted the route to St. Louis, almost 750 miles, figuring it would take about twelve hours, with stops. On Monday morning, I called Mr. Thomas' secretary promptly at nine; she told me to come to the executive offices at Busch Stadium, and she would have tickets for me to games one and two—*and* six and seven! I then realized it would also be my first live Major League game. I'd seen AAA Buffalo Bisons games, including exhibition games against the parent clubs. But my first Major League game was going to be the World Series!

The long drive seemed like it would never end; I pulled into St. Louis around midnight, with the Arch gleaming in the moonlight. I was awe-struck. I parked near the stadium, and was amazed by the people lined up around it for a handful of tickets going on sale that morning. I admit I hoped I hadn't come all this way for nothing. Would there really be tickets for me? All these people from St. Louis were trying to get tickets. The next several hours were filled with more self-doubt than one should be allowed to have.

At nine, men in suits and brief cases started going into the executive offices as I sat in my Gremlin X in my beat-up Cardinals hat and green windbreaker, almost petrified to face the possibility of not getting the tick-ets. I pulled myself together, went in, and asked for my contact. She asked to see my identification, and returned a few minutes later with an enve-lope, telling me it would be eighteen dollars for each game. I paid with my credit card and asked her to thank Mr. Thomas for me. In that big white envelope were tickets to all four games. I had no idea where the seats were, nor did I care. Tickets in hand, I was the world's best Cardinal fan, and I deserved to be there. I walked out feeling like a million dollars. My efforts that crazy Sunday afternoon had paid off. I was going to the Series that night, and life couldn't have been any better.

I will skip most of the details of the game—not a good one for the Cardinals—as my story is as much about the journey as the game. I sat in the last row of the stadium, but right behind home plate. I saw the Clydesdales parade around the stadium and made a lifelong friend with a woman named Margaret, whose brother played handball with Schoendienst. The Cardinals forgot to show up and lost 10-0, but they won game two. I went back to Buffalo to watch the series on TV, where they lost two out of three. I would definitely head back for game seven.

As I walked around the stadium, taking in the excitement, thinking how lucky I was, a white limo pulled up, and a guy asked if I had a ticket, eventually offering me $800. I declined. The Cardinals won the game 6-3, and the place was bedlam. I had to get down to the field. By the time I did, everything was gone, no bases, hats, nothing but artificial turf, dirt, and police on horses trying to get the field cleared. I scooped three or four handfuls into my windbreaker pocket as police ushered several of us off the field. That third base dirt has been kept, almost religiously, in a small jar that has a red lid on it. It was triple wrapped in bubble plastic when we moved to Las Vegas from Buffalo, made the trip intact, and now sits proudly on my shelf. That dirt and the ticket stubs are truly prized possessions. I've told this story countless times, the short and long versions. It never gets old.

—Bill Hasbrouck
Las Vegas, Nevada

***

From 2000 to 2004, I went to college outside of Boston, but despite being a devoted baseball fan, it was the summer of 2003 when I finally made it to historic Fenway Park. It was worth the wait. That summer I was working in DC as a Capitol Hill intern. With a wedding to attend one weekend in Boston, I was going to miss my team, the Cardinals on an American League East inter-league road trip. They would be in Boston mid-week, and I was scheduled to land right after the last game. At lunchtime on Thursday, work was slow, and it occurred to me I would not be missed; if I got a standby flight, I might be able to make the game. I picked up the phone and got on the list. That was *almost* the last thing to go right.

Still in my suit, I grabbed my suitcase and ran out the door. The subway to the airport was delayed thirty minutes. I got to the airport with little time to spare, and the security line looked a mile long. I struggled to the front, begging forgiveness from the people ahead of me, knowing I couldn't make that flight otherwise. Through security, I thought I had a shot, when (I kid you not) a group of nuns and school children blocked the terminal. Now, I am a huge baseball fan, but running over nuns and children wasn't something I was willing to do. Begging forgiveness (again), I squeezed through, and finally made it to the gate. The door was literally closing, but I made it in time. There was one seat left on the plane. Home free. I'd have plenty of time to get to the game.

"This is the pilot speaking. We are experiencing some difficulties, and it looks like we will be on the tarmac for a little while." Figured. We landed in Boston an hour late, but if I hustled, I could still make it. I rushed to the T; I knew I would be late, but so what? I'd see most of the game. On the T, I looked around and realized I was surrounded by Cardinals fans. We are a geographically diverse fan base, so I figured I was surrounded by locals who were fans. Chatting with a few people, I discovered they were all in from Missouri, following the Cards down the East Coast from Boston to New York to Baltimore. What I knew to be true was overwhelmingly reconfirmed: Cards' fans travel, and these folks decided to make a vacation out of a St. Louis road trip to stadiums they don't normally see. I love being a Cardinals fan.

By the time I got to Fenway, the game had started. I didn't exactly have a ticket but thought I'd figure something out. I wandered for a bit, and found a scalper who offered a field level seat for thirty dollars. It was either a scam, or he just wanted to go home as the game had started. I figured what the hell, it was the second inning, and I wanted in, so I forked over the cash and headed to the gate. There I was, suitcase in hand, wearing the suit from work, sweaty, tired, standing in front of Fenway. I proudly walked over to the man in the yellow jacket, handed my ticket over, and slipped on my Cards' hat.

"Excuse me sir, there are no suitcases allowed inside the stadium." *You have got to be fucking kidding me!* What was I going to do? He pointed across the street to Gold's Gym and said they might store it for me. It was a ten-dollar fee; I had eight dollars left in cash. The man looked me up and down and took pity on me. He took the eight dollars and the suitcase, and told me to have a nice day. I returned to the gate and finally entered Fenway. Still in the second, with no runs yet scored, I figured I'd get seven innings out of my thirty bucks. Little did I know, I would get much more. The crowd was mixed; about a third were Cardinals fans (like I said, we travel), a third 1/3rd Sox fans, and a third Yankees fans who lived in Boston, and just liked to come watch the Sox lose. I happened to be sitting with the Yankee fans. The seat was great, five rows up from first base (worth way more to more than thirty dollars). I could practically have a conversation with Albert Pujols.

The game was an exciting one, the lead going back and forth until the thirteenth (I got eleven innings out of my ticket). It rained a little, but I loved sitting in it. 5-5 in the thirteenth, the Cards got a couple on with Jimmy Edmonds coming to the plate. He was not only a great player, but a great leader with a great attitude, and personified what I love about the Cardinals. With two on, Jimmy crushed a fastball to the opposite field, a towering shot arcing over the Green Monster and out of Fenway. I couldn't see where it actually landed, but the trajectory was right, and I could just imagine it landing on the roof of the Gold's Gym where my suitcase was sitting. The Sox got a couple in the bottom of the frame, but the Cardinals took the game. I was elated. It was a great game, and a great way to end what had been an insane day. It was all worth it. I spent the next few hours on Landsdown street near to Fenway at the bars chock full of Cardinals fans celebrating the win. The next day I got the suit a dry cleaning it desperately needed.

—Ari Stein
Oakland, California

(I know there were actually four stories here, not three, but three were about having to get to that Cardinals game. The fourth is a bonus.)

***

Sometime during the early 1970s, I was at a night game Candlestick Park, with the San Francisco Giants hosting the Pittsburgh Pirates. Bobby Bonds was on first, and the batter, whose name is forgotten with time, hit a line drive over Roberto Clemente's head. Bonds was going all out, digging for third. Clemente played the carom off the wall perfectly and threw a seed on a line to nip Bonds, one of the fastest men in the game at the time, at third. It was the greatest throw I've ever seen in person.

—Jon Leonoudakis
Los Angeles, California

***

During the 1971 Giants baseball season, I went to a game against the Pirates with a few friends. We witnessed the most amazing baseball feat I have ever seen. Roberto Clemente was playing right field for the Pirates. In the bottom of the seventh inning, Giants left fielder Ken Henderson came to bat. On a 1-1 count, he hit a line drive over the first base bag, down the right field line, and into the corner, the ball coming to rest right below the 335-foot sign. Clemente ran over, picked up the ball, and threw it from the corner all the way to Richie Hebner at third base without hitting a cutoff man. It was thrown on a straight line to Hebner, knee level, who applied the tag as Henderson slid into third. Henderson got up, dusted off his uniform, turned toward right field, tipped his cap, and went back to the dugout. We estimated the throw to be well over four hundred feet, but what amazed us was its accuracy. Never, before or since, have I seen a Major Leaguer make that kind of a throw! Everyone in the stands was completely astonished by what they had just seen; my friends and I talked about it for the rest of that night, and we are still talking about it today.

—Gary Siri
San Francisco, California

***

I was at Forbes for a Bucs-Houston Colt 45's doubleheader. Pirates hurler Bob Veale was coasting but got into trouble. With a runner on second, the batter hit a line shot to right, one hop to Roberto (Clemente). You could hear the third base coach immediately yell at the runner from second, head down, to stop. He rounded third and stopped. The coach was pointing to Roberto, standing with the ball, arm cocked for a throw. The runner took a step toward the plate, and Roberto fired a perfect throw to home. The crowd went nuts. The runner threw up his hands and went back to third. The coach was just shaking his head violently. I also saw Roberto make a throw from the exit gate in right center on the fly to home plate to throw out a runner! I spilled my lemon blend on that one. God, those were the days!

—Dan Lewis
Harrisburg, Pennsylvania

Just think how special Clemente was that three people would send stories about a throw

***

Unlike other outdoor sports like football and football (soccer), baseball will not be played in (heavy) rain, snow, sleet, tornadoes, etc. But it is often played in pretty miserable conditions, extraordinarily hot and humid in most of the country in the summer, quite cold in the northern states in the early spring and fall, and, well, conceivably any time in San Francisco.

It was a typically cold, foggy, windy night at Candlestick Park in the middle of the summer, 1976. Five of us went to Candlestick to see the Giants host the Mets in one of their two yearly visits. I was with my good friends Eric Gray, Lynn Rhodes, Alan Fram, and Beckie Marsh. As I said, it was cold. Bitter cold. We were sitting in the top section of the grandstand down the third base side. It was very cold.

After the third inning, since it was cold, I set off to buy hot chocolate for the group. Imagine, hot chocolate for a summer baseball game; if you ever visited Candlestick, you know exactly what I am talking about. Between the incredibly long lines and unbelievably slow service, I returned to my seat right about the time of the seventh inning stretch. I lost over three innings of the ball game at the concession stand. I didn't need that stretch. My friends, wearing winter coats, had also draped a huge warm blanket over them. I squeezed right into the middle, with my hot chocolate, covered with that blanket and surrounded by my friends. I don't quite recall if that hot chocolate was still hot when I got to my seat or, like the foggy, windy, air, it was already cold.

—Ira Cohen, as told by Eric Gray
Folsom, California

(My good, close friend, Ira, passed away four years ago. I wrote up this story with a little help from Lynn, and with permission from his wife Margaret, as Ira would have told it. I miss him deeply to this day. All our friends do. This story is for Margaret, Kayla, and Nathan.)

***

It was the hottest baseball game I'd ever been to, and I'm from Texas, so that's saying something. Washington, DC, Fourth of July 2011, eleven in the morning start time. It was me and the guys, my boyfriend, David, four of our friends, and David's father Eric, who was in town visiting (maybe to see us, maybe to see the Giants play the Nationals). Around the top of the second, we were all settled in, quickly warming beer in hand, and really starting to feel the heat. The sun was beating down on us and we could feel ourselves starting to roast. I was sitting next to Eric and I offered him some sunscreen. He squeezed the tube, and all of a sudden, a large blob arced toward the head of the woman in front of us. I think we both saw it happen in slow motion, but there was no stopping it; this woman was going to get sunscreen in her hair, or actually right on the small part in her hair. It made contact, stuck there, and the woman didn't turn around. She sat watching the game, clapping, seemingly completely unaware. We sat there slack-jawed, me also trying not to laugh hysterically, and Eric saying, "Oh my god, what do we do?!" At that point, I was thinking, "We?! I had no part in this!" but I had only known Eric for about four months, and I knew I should try to help. I told him we should probably tell this poor woman she had sunscreen that looked like bird poop on top of her head, and it was already beginning to congeal. Eric was too embarrassed. He said we should leave it and hope it evaporated. Now, I'm no chemist, but at this point I was thinking there was no way this congealing liquid was going to turn into a gas and magically let us pretend this hadn't happened. Eric would not be convinced. Instead, we spent the rest of the game sweating our butts off, rooting for the Giants who were under some sort of curse at the Nats' ballpark, and tortuously watching sunscreen dry and adhere to this woman's scalp. But hey, we were going with "maybe we helped protect her from cancer" . . . and at least Eric and I still have that bonding experience to joke about to this day.

—Lisa Allen
Washington, DC

(Yup, me again. I'm still going with the saved-her-from-cancer story. What a great way to really get to know my now daughter-in-law! This should have given Lisa a look into what she was in for with her boyfriend's family.)

***

Let me preface this story by saying I am a diehard sports fan, who does not leave until the last out is made, the buzzer or horn sounds, or the whistle is blown. On Friday, June 28, 1974, I was so looking forward to a doubleheader between the Cubs and Expos at Jarry Park. It was a nice summer evening, I thought, and I'd dressed accordingly. Game time was 6:05 p.m. After eighteen innings (four hours and fifty-five minutes later) and an 8-7 Cubbies' win, the temperature had begun to drop significantly.

The stadium was wide open and totally unprotected from the elements. Game two was now slated to start at eleven thirty; many fans decided to leave, as the cool winds started to howl. Not me; I loved my Expos, and was determined to stay until the bitter end. As it turned out, the second game lasted a mere two hours and twenty-two minutes, and the Expos took it 15-0. Despite the fact that I could no longer feel my extremities (it gets cold in an open field, even in June), and the organist chose to enhance the atmosphere by playing Christmas tunes, such as "Jingle Bells" (I appreciated the sense of humor), this is one of my most enduring baseball memories.

—Susan Heim
Richmond Hill, Canada

***

My son Eric Jr.'s birthday is May 12, the same as Yogi Berra's. My wife Rita and I took him to Yankee Stadium for his sixth birthday. On this day, the team put up a message on the video screen to sing happy birthday to Yogi . . . so thirty thousand fans were singing "Happy Birthday." When it got to the part where they sang, "Happy birthday, dear Yogi," my wife and I, sitting on either side of our son, yelled, "Dear Eric!" He was fifteen years old before he realized all those fans weren't singing happy birthday to him.

—Eric Schmidt
Bernardsville, New Jersey

***

If the Red Sox were at home on August 30 (my birthday), my mom and dad would take me to the game. August 30 is also Ted Williams' birthday, so it was a thrill to hear the crowd sing happy birthday, but when I was very young, I thought they were singing to me.

—James Gilcreast
North Providence, Rhode Island

***

My mother's birthday is September 16, 1937, Mexican Independence Day. One year on this day, I decided to take her to a California Angels game. I had box seats, and called the stadium to arrange for a birthday wish on the JumboTron. When the message came on the scoreboard, everyone sang "Happy Birthday." Mom's nickname is "Chi Chi Rodriguez," so everyone thought they were singing for the famous golfer. Mom and I knew who they were singing to.

—Mitzie Rock
Moreno Valley, California

HOME RUNS

And then there are the stories that are so unique, so amazing—some from just a wholly different place—that they cannot be categorized. They need to be, well, singled out as one-of-a-kind tales. Like with your children, you really don't want to pick favorites; there are many amazing stories throughout the book that could easily fit in this chapter, but I elected to put them in others because they better fit the theme. I had many great arguments with myself about which ones to place in this chapter, but in my book, so to speak, these are all grand slam homers.

***

I have so many favorite baseball stories befitting someone whose favorite thing is baseball. The game, and its inherent epiphanic highs and lows, is a road map of my emotional history. I fell in love with it as an eleven-year-old kid in Baltimore in 1975, and have grown into a man who lives and dies by what my beloved Orioles do each and every game for six months a year, forever accompanied by my 1968 "Angry Bird" tattoo. My early years following were filled with disappointment, which taught me the true meaning of "Baseball is a game designed to break your heart." Among my many cherished moments framed by the game, one stands out in its relatively low level of emotion, but steeped in the magic that can only occur in one of the thirty cathedrals of this true religion.

All I ever wanted to be when I was a kid was a baseball player or rock star. It never occurred to me to be both, and as neither actually came to pass, that's fine. I did come closer to one than the other; it was a much lower goal, and thus much less precious. I became a singer, guitarist, and benign despot of a band which, in the mid-nineties, had a record deal, and the perks that came with it. I, of course, spent those markers on free base-ball tickets from major label and associated law firm season ticket plans. That the tickets were for Dodgers games and not Orioles wasn't an issue, as I lived in Los Angeles, and any chance to go to any baseball game was still magic then. It actually still is.

By the late nineties, my band Lifter had run the course of releasing and touring for our first record. It certainly didn't make me a star, but I am proud of the damn beautiful concept of an album about *her*, and the heartbreak she ultimately wrought on me. Our deal with Interscope re-cords was tenuous at best, and we wrote and recorded demos for a second record, which never came into existence. But we still had access to those baseball tickets. The label had put us in the hands of a producer named Bob Marlette, a great guy with a fair amount of credits, but a metal and hair guy, not a good fit for my kind of songs. He was our connection to a possible second record *and* those important Dodgers tickets. By "our," I am including our drummer Tony, a die-hard Mets fan.

One day, recording songs in Bob's home studio, his friend John 5 stopped by. It turned out that this little rocker fellow was the guitarist for Marilyn Manson. This was not particularly my favorite band, but it was still pretty cool, and he was a nice enough guy. What I remember most about meeting John 5, and apropos of nothing, is his keeping his crazily overstuffed wallet jammed in his front pocket, looking like a tumor on his thigh. There we were, Tony and I, and two decidedly heavily costumed and adorned metal guys. We had four lower field level tickets to a Dodgers game for the next day, and it occurred to me to ask Bob and John if they wanted to go with us. Bob said sure, but John's reaction killed me. He literally lit up like some Christmas morning eight-year-old, eyes widened and mouth agape, and said, "Hell *yes*, I want to go!" He told us he had never been to a baseball game, which seemed crazy to me just on the face of it. How can any late twenties American male have escaped even a single trip to a baseball game? But his excitement was so visceral you just had to believe him.

Next day, we met at my place and headed to Dodger Stadium. Tony and I were simply transfixed by the level of excitement exuded by John 5. It was a perfect Los Angeles night, and we had great seats, and life was exactly as it should be. Then came the moment, the little baseball memory, that initially got me involved with this book. I have a lot of great baseball memories, with foul balls caught, and the one I didn't catch, which was all over the news broadcast. But this little story is about the pure stunned amazement of a guy, decked out in black heavy metal gear, attending his first Major League Baseball game, and a little stunt I pulled to put him over the top.

We arrived early enough to see the Dodgers taking batting practice, a must for me, and especially for John 5. The four of us were standing behind the seats on the foul side of the left field pole. Clearly it was up to Tony and me to gloriously guide John through this seminal moment in his life. I needed him to understand the emotional history and romance the game held for me. He needed to understand the heartbreak and the beauty and bittersweet sadness of the retired numbers on the outfield fences. He needed to understand that thirty-two was the wholly iconic number worn by the Left Arm of God (Sandy Koufax). And he also needed to witness the little moments of the magic of baseball. I pointed out different relics of my religion housed in this sacred cathedral, and then decided to screw with him a little bit. By now he was fully prepped, taking it all in the way you hope for anytime you take someone to their first real baseball game. His heavily metaled outfit made his childlike awe even more beatific to behold. I mean, this guy was just amazed in the purest sense, and brought none of the faux-coolness one would expect from a member of such a wildly different tribe.

I turned to John and told him to wait while I grabbed a ball, as if it was the most mundane errand imaginable. "How are you gonna do that?!" he asked, looking like a little kid, save his Slayer T-shirt and that inane wallet on his thigh. With no idea of how to actually end this joke, I said, "I'm just gonna walk into the seats and grab a foul batting practice ball." I made a big show of inspecting the rows of still empty seats, ascertaining exactly where to stand to get the next ball. "Ahh! Right there should do it," I said, casually walking into a row of left field foul seats. Tony was just watching and humoring me as he took in the incredulous wonder of John's face, not wanting to miss any of this. I got to my chosen spot, and of course, baseball being the magical game that it is, the very next ball bounced about twenty feet in front of the wall, a ground-rule double in a game, and then perfectly, magically, epically into my hands.

The true religious aspect of the moment is that I was divinely granted a moment of inner strength that allowed me, instead of giving in to the sudden flood of adrenaline and literally shitting myself, to simply turn to the guys and say in a soft, almost lazy voice, "Okay, I got one, let's check out our seats," to which John, transfixed like he'd seen God, bellowed, "Get me one!" I told him I was sorry, but it really only worked for one ball a game. He was crestfallen, but still riding on the rush of a glimpse of the beautiful unknowable. Tony whispered to me, "Just how in the hell did you do that?" I was literally shaking as I told him to just keep cool, and we turned to walk towards our seats.

We watched the game with our newly converted baseball fans, explaining the rules and traditions of the sport as the game unfolded. The chance to share this beautiful alchemical mix of magic, exultation, heartbreak, and epiphanic punishment and reward with someone utterly new and open to its experience is a truly rare gift to those of us already shackled by its soul-wrenching power. To be able to give away what makes this game so intensely romantic and perfect is ultimately why we keep coming back. It's a transformative experience, the opportunity to guide a new soul through the open gates of being consumed by a love of the game. We can feel the wonder of our first game, maybe with our dads, maybe someone else, anyone else acting as a shepherd of the magic of baseball. For that night, I was the eight- or nine-year-old little boy who sat and watched an early 1970s Oriole game from the cheap seats up above the first base line. And I was the kid who, before life would ultimately lead me away from—and finally back to—the game I loved, before all the rock music and drugs and darkness set in, I was just a kid filled with wonder about what was unfolding on that beautiful green field so far below me.

What happened on the field, and who won the game, is of little importance. What mattered was sharing the night with a guy who simply should not have been there with me. I gave John the ball and silently hoped that he'd been infected by the baseball fans' affliction. We stayed until the end, not the norm at a Dodgers game, and headed back into a world of un-listened to demos and the slow dissolution of a band. But still a world where the game of baseball makes even the worst days livable. And whether or not John 5 ever watched another baseball game in his life, I know I got a chance to share magic with him in the form of a ridiculously lucky caught foul ball. And I got to feel like a little boy again.

—Mike Coulter
Eagle Rock, Los Angeles, California

***

Back in the late fifties, I was playing semi-pro ball in the Cascade League in the Seattle area. The team I was on was Nick's Indians, and we were having a so-so season. On a three-day weekend, we were playing the Cle Elum Tigers, and one of our players was a Snohomish Indian named Bobby Parks, a pretty good player. Bobby was in the midst of a horrible slump, around 0-28. He was beside himself, because he was a solid .290 hitter. We played the Friday night game and got our butts kicked, something like 12-3. It was at a small-town field and the locker room was a little more than ten by twenty feet—including a toilet, sink, and a shower. Floors were concrete, as were the walls; there were a couple of small windows and a few benches with a long rod to hang clothes on. Immediately after Bobby went 0-4, he went into the shower with his uniform on (keep in mind, in those days the material was wool), and proceeded to soap himself up, uniform and all, rinse off, remove the uniform, and hang it up to dry. Several of us looked at him like he had gone over the edge; finally, someone asked why he had done that. Toweling himself off, he replied, simply, "Washing away the evil spirits." Saturday was a day game, and he went 4-4- with a homer, and five or six RBI. We won the game, and immediately, three other members of the team showered with their uniforms on. We won again on Sunday, with those three players combined for of eight hits. We just had to pay attention to the Indian signs.

—Gary Weaver
Medford, Oregon

***

In July of 2002, our family went to Yankee Stadium to take in the sights and watch a baseball game. It was a hot afternoon, and the stadium was packed. Our seats were in the third deck on the first base side, and in the section to our right was a family of about fifty-plus people, ranging in ages from new born kids to elderly grandparents. I know they were family because I spoke, pre-incident, with one of the characters.

During the game one of the family members kept dipping his fingers into his beer and dripping it down the pants of one of his relatives sitting in front of him. At one point, I said to my daughter Lisa (who was twelve, and very innocent and naïve) and sister-in-law Kathy that this was not going to end well if the "beer dripping" kept up.

Sure enough, around the sixth inning, the "drippee" had enough. He stood up (visual: lots of tattoos, shorts that were down below his butt, and multiple piercings), turned around and landed a right hook onto his relative's jaw. At that point, the majority of the family of fifty-plus started fighting, kids included, pushing and shoving each other down the rows, piling up at the cement wall at the first row. My first thought was, *Wow, the holidays must really be something at their house.* My second thought was, *these people are going to fall over the edge and end up on the two hundred level.*

At this point tattoo man lost his shorts; they completely came off along with his boxers, right in front of twelve-year-old Lisa. She saw everything, and I do mean *everything*! Next, the police, as well as numerous security people, arrived and pushed me, Lisa, and Kathy out of our seats and into my husband, Larry. Larry, my brother Mark, and my two sons (Brian and Kyle, aged twelve and fifteen) had no clue what was going on. Larry told me to sit down and watch the baseball game. I told him I could not sit because the police had taken over our seats. He was clueless to the brawl that was taking place because he was watching the game. Ultimately, the whole section was ejected from the stadium for fighting; some were even arrested and taken away in handcuffs.

This is a baseball memory that is engraved in our family's memory bank forever (especially Lisa's). I think the Yankees won the game that day. We regularly attend Seattle Mariner games, and have never witnessed anything close to this. Yankee baseball at its finest. It must be an East Coast thing.

—Marie and Larry Toedtli
Kirkland, Washington

Go Mariners !
Marie
History from Yankee
the old Stadium
Larry

***

I am not a fan of any sports. I have been to a few baseball games, but only when I would get free tickets and go for the experience of drinking beer, eating stadium food, and just having a good time with friends. It's not that I don't like baseball; I just don't know much about the game, who the players are, or many of the rules of the game.

I was in Chicago for a Job Corps conference (mid 1990s), and meeting my friend Pearl Broecki in the bar of the hotel where I was staying. When I got to the bar in the late afternoon, there were just a few people there, but not Pearl. An older gentleman was sitting alone at the bar, and I felt it would be safe sitting next to him, as I preferred not to sit alone. I asked him if I could join him while waiting for my friend (who was notorious for always being late). We had a few drinks and chatted about life, my job, the fact that I liked working with young adults, and that I was excited to see my friend who I hadn't seen in for quite a while. He shared little about himself; I was just glad that I felt comfortable with him, and that we could sit there together. Once Pearl showed up, I turned to the man and said that it was nice to meet him, although we didn't know each other's names.

I introduced myself, and he said, "Nice to meet you, Sarah, my name is Ernie Banks." We shook hands, and I went to sit with my friend.

My friend, a native Chicagoan, asked me who I was talking to. When I told her, she started to shake a little, and asked me if I knew who Ernie Banks was. "Well, yes, it's the man over at the bar!" I answered.

"That's Ernie Banks! Mr. Cub! You must go ask him for his autograph. He's the most famous Cub player ever!" she replied excitedly. So, I wandered back over and said, "Mr. Banks, my friend over there tells me I need to get your autograph. You are Mr. Cub? You must have been one great basketball player."

Well, that sure made him laugh, and he said it was great to be in Chicago having a casual conversation with someone who had no idea who he was, and by the way, he played baseball with the Cubs, not basketball. He gave me an autograph and wished me luck. Oh, the questions I could have asked, the things we could have talked about! Yet it wasn't a missed opportunity. We had a good conversation, a few laughs, and fun moments as two strangers keeping each other company on a slow afternoon in the bar. How many people can say the same?

Everyone to whom I tell that story laughs as soon as I mention Ernie's name, and they can't believe I had no idea that the Chicago Cubs were a baseball team. I still have that autograph somewhere. He even wrote "Good luck with Job Corps."

—Sarah Wuest
Minneapolis, Minnesota

(I worked with Sarah back in the nineties. We had not seen each other in many years, and when we did, catching up on our lives, she asked what I was going to do in retirement. I told her about the book, and she said she didn't have a story for me. She sure did the next day. Now, how many of you figured out the older gentleman in her story would turn out to be the legend, Ernie Banks?)

***

As a long time Giants fan, it was a thrill to hear I would get a chance to be a "Ball Dude." A relative recommended me to those who assigned people to sit down the foul lines and retrieve balls hit in those areas. You get a crash course in what to do (and not to do), so as not to embarrass yourself, or interfere with the game by touching a ball in play. There are a few instructions that come with the honor of being a Ball Dude, one of which is pretty much a no- brainer: "Hand the ball to a kid. Don't throw it up in the stands. Hand it to a young fan." We all know what would happen if you tried to toss a foul ball in the stands: chaos. Having umpired Little League and high school baseball, I felt confident in not making a mistake that would put me on the don't-invite-him-back list, or an ESPN highlight, but I didn't figure on being touched emotionally. Positioned on the first base side, I used my dad's glove, an old three-fingered Wilson from the early forties. It is always a topic of discussion. I was just proud to have a piece of my dad on the field, and with my son "ball duding" along third base, it was like having three generations out there.

I got a couple of easy grounders and caroms, which I tossed to little guys sitting in or near the front row. Then I looked around to see if there were any young fans sitting a little farther up who might be "worthy." I found a likely candidate, and hoped I would get another foul ball hit my way. I'd been watching the whole family for a little while, anticipating a chance to surprise them; they appeared to be grandma, mom, and dad, and a little girl about four or five years old. The "girls" all had on identical pink jackets, and they were enthralled with the little girl who was having as exciting a time as I had ever seen a young fan have. She would get so excited every time something would happen, and the crowd would get loud, and she would stand and clap her hands and cheer along with everyone else. She was adorable. I had to get her a ball.

Sure enough, it happened. A nice three hopper hit, well, right into Dad's old faithful glove. I looked back to the stands to locate my young recipient. People were standing, yelling, reaching and begging for the ball; I couldn't see my little fan. I pointed towards the area, about fourteen or fifteen rows up. Mom and Dad sort of realized I was pointing their way, and in a questioning look, pointed to their little girl and mouthed "Her?" I gave a nod, and waved her down. They leaned over and sent her on her way. It was obvious she was too excited to describe, but there was one thing I can describe: She had Down syndrome. Her smile and enthusiasm told me that while it may have affected her physically, she was not hindered emotionally. She knew she was going to get a baseball. When she got to me, I placed the ball in her hand, and just touched her on the head. Her joy and happiness multiplied. She started to jump up and down and cheer, as if she had just caught the final out of a big game. She looked back at me with the brightest eyes and said, "Yea! Yea!" and ran back to her seat.

The whole crowd in that area gave an audible "Awe," and many stood to watch and applaud. I couldn't take my eyes off of her. When she got back to her seat, she was still as excited as could be. She showed it to grandma, and then mom, getting big hugs from them. Mom looked at me and you could see her eyes starting to tear up. She mouthed a very slow and grateful thank you. By now, both mom and grandma were wiping away the tears. She showed the ball to dad, who gave her a hug, and then turned and looked at me, making a gesture I'll never forget. Pointing to me, he formed the words "You're the man." I reached up and tipped my cap, like the players of old would do.

In that split second, I had a rush of emotion I still feel today when I talk about it. People were applauding and cheering, and in that moment, I felt like a big-league baseball player. I never expected that. I gave a baseball to a little girl, and made her and her family jubilant and emotional to the point of tears. They thought I had done something extra special for their daughter. But what they did for me can't be measured. To be able to receive praise from hundreds, if not a thousand or so, baseball fans for a simple—and to me obvious—act performed on the field, let me feel for a moment like a star. I'll never forget that feeling, or that family. Or what it's like to feel like a Big Leaguer.

—Gary "Frano" Fralick
Stockton, California

(One game, in our eighth-row seats, between innings, I was minding my own business, just looking out at the field, when an attractive young woman, scantily dressed, walked down to the ball dude who sat on a stool and fielded ground balls. I was watching her talking to this very senior citizen, when suddenly she pulled up her shirt and bra, exposing her breasts. My friend Rosie immediately covered her teenage son's eyes. I gasped for breath, assuring my wife that I just needed a moment to recover from this possibly life-altering experience. Several weeks later, I went to talk to Gary, the ball dude for the game I was now at, told him this story, asked if he had an interesting one, and this is his. I have read and told this story literally hundreds of times, and I tear up and get goosebumps every single time. Frano and I have become friends, and that means a lot to me.)

***

My son Eili was born without three fingers on his left hand. He had a slightly larger thumb and a stub of a pinkie. But it never stopped him from doing anything in thirty-nine years and counting (well, except the time in elementary school when a misguided gym teacher tried to make him climb a rope). Anyway, Eili liked baseball, and wanted to play Little League like all his friends, but he couldn't catch a ball with the glove that the hospital's orthopedic department had modified for him. They had inserted a plastic piece so he could strap his hand to the glove; the glove did stay on, but he couldn't catch a ball with it.

One day, when he was about eight, Eili was sitting on the stairs fidgeting with my glove I had left there. It was for a lefty, so he put it on his right hand and just kept squeezing it. I got his attention, and said, "Catch this," tossing a ball at him. He caught it, and his whole face lit up. (It still makes my eyes moist when I recall or retell this incident). That was it; the glove with the plastic insert went in the trash. And did he start playing baseball! With a vengeance. He wanted to be a pitcher, so I had to buy a catcher's mitt because I found that I really needed one if I didn't want to have my hand stinging after each of his hard pitches. He would pitch by holding the end of the glove between his thumb and pinkie on his left hand and throwing with his right. As soon as he released the ball, he would quickly slip the glove onto his right hand. It took him a while to master this, but soon it was seamless, and he would be ready to field before the ball reached the plate. People at first thought this was odd, and the first time he pitched in a game, all the batters, at the behest of the coach—adults can be cruel—tried to bunt. They stopped doing that after Eili threw out the first six batters at first.

What really made him feel good was the day we went to a Red Sox game in Boston. Jim Abbott was a pitcher for the Sox's opponents that day, the Angels. Of course, Abbott had a good career as a pitcher, even throwing a no-hitter, despite only having one hand. I learned that he always tried to meet with kids who had arm/hand "differences" before a game. About forty kids showed up that day (who knew there were so many kids just in the greater Boston area with "hand differences"?) What impressed me was that no press or cameras were permitted in the area where we met him. Once again, the smile on our son's face said it all. Jim Abbott may not be Jewish, but he was, and will always be, a mensch in my book.

Eili's baseball career? Well, he played through freshman year of high school, but that little sphere called a hardball got faster and faster as it came towards home-plate. He switched to running track.

—Burt Klein
Newton, Massachusetts

(For those not familiar with Yiddish, the word "mensch" means a person of integrity and honor. It is a true compliment.)

***

When the beloved Tigers' announcer Ernie Harwell passed away in 2010, I heard that people were going to the site of former Tiger Stadium at Michigan and Trumbull Streets to play catch to commemorate him. I joined the group on Mother's Day, but didn't feel excited; the field was in terrible condition, full of trash and weeds. I remember thinking that I had a lawn mower, and made plans to organize a clean-up. This was the spontaneous beginning of a six-year project to clean up, renovate, and maintain this field, and we became known as the Navin Fields Ground Crew. It was an incredible group of volunteers.

As I went about my work, I had so many great opportunities to think about my history with baseball. I grew up without a father, but Mom arranged for me to have a Big Brother, Dennis Boufford, who took me to my first Tigers game in 1971, when I was eight years old. I saw my favorite player, Norm Cash, and Mickey Lolich pitched that day. On July 15, 1973, Dennis took me to another game, and we saw Nolan Ryan, he of a recently tossed no-hitter, warm up right near where we stood, the sound of his fastball popping into the catcher's glove. Dennis said, "We might see a no-hitter today." Sure enough, we did. Cash is infamous for, after already striking out twice in that game, coming to the plate in the ninth inning with a table leg. Home plate umpire Ron Luciano sent him back to get a bat; Cash asked why, noting he wasn't going to hit him anyway. He did make contact, popping up to end the game. I didn't understand why people were cheering since our Tigers were being shut down; of course, as I look back, I see the significance. Harwell called it the most dominating performance he had ever seen.

Looking back became a theme as we worked that field. As I rode my John Deere mower to cut the grass, I recalled games I attended, and how baseball had become so important to me. In left field, I recalled that Willie Horton, number twenty-three, was positioned there. In center and right, I imagined Speaker and DiMaggio, Ruth and Kaline. My fellow volunteers felt the same way, as did the thousands of fans who came to our new field, with license plates from many states. They stood on the pitcher's mound and imagined Walter Johnson and Satchel Paige. They stood where Babe Ruth and Ty Cobb roamed the field. They reenacted Kirk Gibson's home run from the last Tigers World Series title in 1984. Every day, people come to relive their baseball memories, historical or personal. People have scattered loved ones' ashes there. Some married there. I got married there, to Sarah. On August 3, 2014, Sarah rode out from center field on a lawn mower, got off at second base, and walked to home plate under an arch of bats. We were wed in front of friends including, of course, my fellow volunteers.

SARAH, TOM AND FRIENDS

Because this group was willing to devote so much time to remove rubble and debris and take care of the field, what would have been a trash dump with no baseball future became a destination where people came to relive their memories and revel in baseball history. I am so proud of what we did for six years.

—Tom Derry
Redford, Michigan

(Tom wouldn't boast by telling you that he won the 2016 Hilda Award, given by the Baseball Reliquary, for distinguished service to the game by a baseball fan. Google "2016 Hilda Award Recipient Tom Derry." Google "Navin Fields Grounds Crew." Congratulations, Tom.)

***

Nick Anitole was a teammate on my Ponce de Leon Baseball League team. All the players in the league, whether in our thirties, or now, when some of us are in our sixties, are seeking some small taste of our youth. Unlike Ponce himself, our quest drives us to play baseball, typically early on spring and fall Sunday mornings. Sadly, Nick passed away at forty-three in 2010 after a battle with cancer. Having him as a teammate has given me my two greatest baseball experiences in a life happily filled with many, outstanding baseball memories as a young player and "old man" player, as a son and father, as a coach and as a fan.

First, the "baseball" experience. Nick took a hiatus from playing after receiving his diagnosis, but there was no keeping him off the field. After surgery, enduring treatments and regaining some of his strength, one Sunday morning Nick came back. We were all thrilled to see him, happy to have his wise-cracking, self-deprecating good humor back in the dugout. I don't know that anyone expected that he would play in the game that morning, but with his father, George, and sister, Katherine watching apprehensively from the bleachers behind home plate, Nick took his turn each time through the batting order, and even played an inning or two in the field. It was inspiring just because he was there, playing baseball again, joking as he always did with his teammates. But that was not enough for the baseball gods.

Our team was down by one run with two outs in the bottom of the last inning. With runners on second and third, the tying and winning runs, it was Nick's turn in the order. He stepped into the batter's box. Although the level of play at Ponce de Leon League games is by no means high, it is competitive. Nick's at-bats earlier in the game had been about what you would expect under the circumstances. He reached base once because he was unable to avoid being hit by a pitch, prompting worry on the bench and in the bleachers. His simply being on the field was heroic; no one expected anything more. The punch line is obvious: After falling behind in the count with two strikes, Nick hit a looping fly ball into shallow right field that nestled softly onto the grass barely beyond the reach of any fielder. Both runners scored easily, and while it was no sure thing, Nick was able to amble safely to first base before the opposition realized that attempting to record the final out there might have been the best option. Everyone on our team was incredulous, exhilarated, speechless, and euphoric. As sports journalist Red Smith famously wrote in an entirely different baseball context, "Reality has strangled invention. Only the utterly impossible, the inexpressibly fantastic, can ever be plausible again." Nick, his father and sister, and most of his teammates were in tears. It was a special, most memorable baseball experience for all who were there.

But there is more, the "life" experience. Over the years since Nick's passing, nearly every Sunday, whether in the ninety-degree heat of an afternoon game in June, or at a bitter cold eight-in-the-morning game in late fall, George and Katherine, are at our games. They are our most loyal fans. In fact, they are just about our only fans. About seven or so of us who were Nick's teammates remain on the team. For them, and for us, our connection is baseball and Nick.

Most recently, in the spring of 2017, Nick's wife Dahlia and seven-year-old son Nicholas joined George and Katherine at our last game of the season. It was the first time Nicholas attended one of our games since he was an infant, shortly after we lost Nick. We won a championship on that day, but the highlight for everyone was seeing Nicholas, and hearing him talk enthusiastically about playing baseball.

—Bill Blier
Washington, DC

***

I've attended hundreds of baseball games in my life, starting in the early 1970s at Candlestick Park in San Francisco, plus many more contests at about a dozen or so other major and Minor League parks over the years. I've seen a bevy of Opening Days, thrilling walk off hits, a handful of exciting post-season contests, one all-star game, and a no-hitter. I've only caught one live foul ball, but I've snagged countless others in batting practice. A certified baseball geek, I am.

When asked recently if I could identify my favorite in-person game, there was no shortage of candidates. Selecting one would be right up there with asking Julia Child which soufflé was her pièce de résistance. After careful consideration, no single game burned brighter memorably than any of the other gems. But then, it hit me.

I cannot remember what I had for dinner the night before last, but if you want to know what happened at Candlestick Park on Sunday, May 4, 1975, I can help. You see, I was at the 'Stick that day, a day when the one millionth run in Major League Baseball (MLB) history was scored. Not many can claim witnessing this historic event. In fact, only 9,450 fans besides me can truthfully do so.

A fifth-grade classmate invited me and half dozen others to his eleventh birthday party, an event his father graciously said would be at that upcoming Sunday Giants game. Imagine the cost of such a party today; the poor man would have to take out a small loan to finance the undertaking. The day before the party, the weather gave us an added surprise thanks to a rare rainout, so that game would be made up the next day as part of a good old fashioned, two-for-the-price-of-one doubleheader, not a day-night doubleheader as is common today. So now, we would be attending two games instead of one.

The next day, we all piled into my friend's family station wagon and headed up Highway 101 on a dry, but brisk and partly cloudy Sunday morning to see the Giants play a pair against the Houston Astros. We arrived early, and took our seats in the upper box seat section above the first base line and watched batting practice (BP). One thing that caught my eye immediately was the new-look, flashy rainbow uniforms the Houston players were sporting. Another oddity I spotted as I gazed across the vast green AstroTurf field, was an unusual message on the left field scoreboard. Normally, the pre-game message read Welcome, or the out of town scores were displayed. But on this day, massive letters that couldn't be missed, spelled out: "Runs needed to reach the million mark = 23."

Very interesting. Giants' radio announcer Al Michaels had mentioned something about this "millionth run" business on Friday's KSFO 560 AM radio broadcast that I'd tuned in to some thirty-six hours earlier. At that time, the countdown number was in the three figures, so I didn't think much of it. However, with the current "23" displayed on the board for all to see, coupled with the fact that this figure was being reduced by a factor of one every few minutes or so thanks to East Coast games in progress, I began to wonder. Adding my fifth-grade math skills to the equation, along with some deductive reasoning and a side dish of estimating tactics, I concluded the following: Not only would the magic number be eclipsed on this day, I just might be witness to it.

When BP ended, the countdown number read ten. At the conclusion of the National Anthem, it had dwindled to a measly five. In the top of the second inning, the figure was even closer to the magic mark, when Bob Watson and Jose Cruz each drew walks to lead off against Giants' starter John "The Count" Montefusco. Up to the plate stepped Houston catcher Milt May, and as he dug in, the number on the board read one. May then got a pitch he liked, took a mighty swing, and connected. *Crack!* He sent a high, deep drive over the right field fence, and when it landed, it rattled around in the vacant, folded-up football bleachers.

My first reaction was, "Oh crap, my team is down three-zip, just like that. Not good!" But a conflicting emotion then came over me: I was thrilled. The number one was still on the scoreboard after May's homer sailed over the fence, which meant the millionth run was about to score, before my own eyes.

Candlestick message board relayed the situation as Houston's Milt May slammed three-run homer off John Montefusco in second inning of opener. Bob Watson, shown taking his lead off second base, touched home plate with the historic run. For the scene seconds later, see page 46.

Sure enough, Watson, the runner at second, began sprinting for home instead of leisurely jogging in, as is the norm after a batter just knocked in a teammate via the big fly. But this was no ordinary run Watson was about to register. He knew what the countdown number was, so he took off at top speed, crossing the plate with the game's first run, and with it, MLB's one millionth run.

A moment of recognition commemorated the event, memorialized by an official proclamation on the message board. After the ceremony, the countdown was removed from the scoreboard, and the focus returned to baseball, more baseball, and nothin' but baseball. And we got lots of it. Each game took over three hours to complete. Pitching was not sharp. The day saw forty-two bases on balls issued, twenty-six in game two alone, and runs were almost as plentiful. The Giants came back to win game one, 8-6, but dropped the nightcap, 12-8.

After the game, home plate was removed and sent to Cooperstown. That night, I heard an account on the news that reported a sensational story of timing. At nearly the same moment May had homered, Reds' shortstop Dave Concepcion also went yard, about 2,400 miles away in Cincinnati, and sprinted around the bases, only to find out he crossed the plate a hair after Watson did.

As for the party, we all had a good time. One kid ate six hot dogs all by himself; another overdosed on cotton candy and peanuts; two others spent much of the day fascinated by how far their loogies could sail in the infamous Candlestick wind swirls. But we all got to see the one millionth run in Major League Baseball history cross the plate.

Hmmm, now then, what *did* I have for dinner the night before last?

—Nevin Duerr
Foster City, California

***

I had lived and died as a Giants fan since I was a little boy, both when they hailed from New York, and then when transplanted to California in 1958. I was shocked and dismayed on a December night in 1996 when I learned all-star third baseman, Matt Williams, my favorite player, had been traded to Cleveland for three players—Jeff Kent, Jose Vizcaino, and Julian Tavarez—who at the time fit the "journeymen" label.

Urged on by my wife, Mary Beth, I wrote an angry letter to Giants President Peter Magowan. Complaining that baseball fans were feeling unappreciated and sick of greedy owners, loyalty-challenged players and endorsement-happy agents, I decided to "divorce" the Giants and find a new team to root for. I also mailed back all of my Giants' team paraphernalia collected over more than forty years—uniforms, jackets, figurines, baseball bats, foam fingers, and even my car's license plate holder.

I wrote a business letter to all Major League and some Minor League (MiL) teams asking why I should make theirs my favorite. I asked which player they would offer as a role model for my young sons to emulate, and which was more important, gate receipts or fan loyalty. Were they developing talent at the MiL level, or interested in only buying high-priced rental players each year? I cc'd major sports news outlets, who reported on my team search, and they soon dubbed me the "Free Agent Fan." I began appearing on major news shows, such as Good Morning America, the Today Show and NPR, and in the Washington Post, the New York Times and USA TODAY. My message in each story was clear: Fans are the most important part of the game of baseball, not profits, salaries, and ticket sales.

Teams began contacting me to speak to their officials. The Orioles gave me a tour of Camden Yards, and let me pitch from the mound. The Mets invited me to a clinic for kids, and had me play catch with manager Bobby Valentine at Shea Stadium. The Marlins flew me to their Winter Fan Fest and gave me a tour of Pro Player Stadium with mascot Billy the Marlin. The Durham Bulls invited me to dine with their owner to learn about his team. Some teams sent autographed baseballs from their Hall of Famers and other mementos in a blatant attempt to bribe me to pick them. I donated the trove of treasures to a charity and told all teams to answer my business letter if they wanted my consideration.

More than thirty teams contacted me, and I chose the Philadelphia Phillies as my new favorite Major League Baseball team because of their exciting home-grown talent and a letter from their promotions manager John Brazer, who wrote, "To be a Phillies fan, you must have hope in your veins, fealty in your heart, comfort in your soul, and a lump in your throat!" I chose the Durham Bulls as my favorite Minor League team, partly due to their commitment to helping the less fortunate in their community.

In 2008, my fandom was rewarded, with the Phillies winning the World Series and the Bulls winning their (MiL) championship equivalent.

—Michael J. Volpe
Falls Church, Virginia

***

In 1942, as a sixteen-year-old high school student in LA, my family, with many other Japanese-American families, was sent to the Manzanar Relocation Center internment camp in California as the US entered the war against Japan. I don't wish to begin a political discussion about how wrong it was to treat loyal citizens in that fashion, but rather talk of the power of baseball to help us normalize our lives during those years.

Looking back, I now have a different perspective than I did then. It is perhaps astonishing to me that I can say that I had some of the best times in my life in the camp. We couldn't leave, and were certainly subject to many rules; in that sense, we were prisoners. At first, we were scared at being taken from our homes with no reasonable explanation. However, as a teenager, my friends and I had a great time enjoying each other's' constant company. We were safe and fed, we ate at different block mess halls with friends instead of family members, and we were carefree. We enjoyed our lives. Because of lack of family sitting together for meals, the typical Japanese paternal authoritarianism that my father would have exercised if we were at home went out the window.

Soon after we arrived, we were told about women's softball teams. Some of the players on the Dusty Chicks, the camp champions, asked me and my best friend Pee Wee to join. Most of the players were older than us, as much as four years; with most of the positions on the field filled, I played catcher—at first without a mask! Some of the girls really knew how to play, and I had to learn quickly. The camp newspaper—*The Manzanar Free Press*, a rather ironic name—featured stories about our games. By playing on this team, I had the chance to meet people from all over the West Coast, places like Sacramento, Stockton, Fresno, LA, and San Diego. I had not had the chance to travel as a kid, so this opened doors for us. I think US Senator and author, S. I. Hayakawa had a good point when he wrote, "Perhaps it was the best thing that could have happened to Japanese-Americans of the West Coast . . . the relocation forced them out of their segregated existence . . . opened up possibilities for them that they never would have known." I feel this helped us integrate into mainstream American society after the war.

Camp administrative staff were, of course, all Caucasian; their own team challenged the Dusty Chicks to a game, played in front of many spectators. I don't recall many details of the game, but I remember Pee Wee making a running catch of a ball hit very far. Best of all, we won that game by one run.

My story is not one of specific baseball memories, games, or plays. It is about the experience of how baseball helped many of us cope with imprisonment. What seemed to a sixteen-year-old as a fun time with friends has taken on a different perspective as I have aged. It was extremely cold in the winters and sizzling hot in the summers. We were not treated brutally; we were fed, and had social activities, but we were prisoners, nevertheless. For many of us, baseball was more than just a recreational diversion. The Japanese-American community, both the Issei, people who were first generation in this country, and the Nisei, my generation, had played and loved baseball before we were interred, and this gave us an opportunity to hold on to a very important element of our lives before the camps. After the war, walking down First Street in "Little Tokyo" in LA, Issei men would come up to me and tell me how much they enjoyed watching and rooting for the Dusty Chicks. So, I guess we left an impression.

Every year we have reunions for survivors and their children. I have often spoken at seminars, and to high school students, about the camps. It was a terrible time in this country's history, but this provides an opportunity to teach people and provide hope that something like this never happens again.

—Rosie Maruki Kakuuchi
Las Vegas, Nevada

(There have been several stories that I really searched for: Bartman; the ball bouncing off Canseco's head for a home run; the Mets first perfect game; and others. When I first learned several years ago about how baseball was an important way to try to "normalize" life in the internment camps, I knew I needed to have such a story. Thanks so much, Rosie, for this wonderful memory.)

***

Growing up, one of my prized possessions was a silver Sears transistor radio my dad gave me for my seventh birthday in 1959. When I asked where he got it, he told me that he found it at the thrift shop on the Air Force base where he worked, saying, "It had your name on it, so how could I resist?" It was the best present I could have wanted. Mom and Dad did wonders with his Air Force paycheck; there were presents whenever they could find excuses to give us gifts, especially when Dad came home from a trip. In my case, that meant a sports magazine or book, as they knew how crazy I was for baseball and football. My library grew with the years, as Dad was away from home a lot in the sixties. Always nearby was my trusty radio. If it was summer, I was listening to Great Falls Electrics baseball, a Class A farm club of the LA Dodgers. There was one really special event that I kept to myself for a number of years.

Nights on the Montana prairie, with wide open spaces and few local radio stations, meant programs ranging as far east as Minneapolis, St. Louis, and Dallas, Calgary, Vancouver, and Winnipeg in Canada, and west to Seattle and Portland, and finally, California, Phoenix, and Denver. Night after night, when the neighborhoods kids were done playing baseball or touch football, I sat on our porch glued to my buddy, the radio. One hot night, thumbing the dial, I found "KFI Los Angeles." In my ear were Vin Scully and Jerry Doggett doing Dodger Baseball! So exciting, Major League Baseball on a Montana August 1960 night. The signal faded; after an eternity, it returned as strong as before, and Vinnie was describing a Willie Mays home run hit to the right center field recesses of the LA Coliseum ball park. Baseball in a football stadium? Just then, Mom called me in for bedtime, and I hid the little magic radio under my pillow so she wouldn't see it. Later, I turned it on low, so my parents wouldn't hear it. There were Vin and Jerry again; Drysdale had just brushed Cepeda back with an inside fastball and the dugouts emptied. The signal disappeared; when it returned, Vin was asking the fans to yell out "Happy Birthday" to Frank Secory, that night's home plate umpire. Fifty thousand voices rose as one to serenade him. I was probably one of the few kids in Montana to witness this. Later that summer, a writer from *Sports Illustrated* said that it was truly baseball history being made, thanks to Vin Scully. Thus began a lifelong tradition in my family; decades upon decades of sports happiness poured out from radios in the houses where my family resided, a tradition proudly passed from father to son. There was, however, one time when my silver radio almost got me in more trouble than a young man could ever understand.

I took my trusty friend with me when I was sworn into the US Army, in 1975. My drill sergeants at basic training never knew my radio was my constant companion, nights and weekends. I got through basic and AIT Tech Training with the secret intact. When my unit traveled cross-country in the fall of 1975 to participate in a war games exercise, it went along in my pack. These were exciting times in the sports world; the plucky Boston Red Sox were matched in the World Series against the powerhouse Big Red Machine, the Cincinnati Reds. We arrived at Fort Bragg, North Carolina in time to hear games three, four, and five on a radio that one of our cooks brought out to the field. There was even popcorn and Kool-Aid in our chow tent! By the night of game six, however, we were well involved with maneuvers. My job, with one of my friends, was to hunker down in a foxhole and watch for "enemy activity." When it occurred, we were to call it in on our two-way radio to our company headquarters. The night passed on rather silently, save for the little silver radio . . . which picked up game six on a local station. We took turns holding my radio in the back of the foxhole, while the other pulled sentry duty.

Around midnight, all hell broke loose. Carlton "Pudge" Fisk came to bat in the bottom of the twelfth inning, and socked a home run off the foul pole at Fenway Park. The Red Sox had won, 7-6! The Series was tied at three games each, game seven to be played the next night. Boston fans went wild with joy; unfortunately, so did I. From somewhere down deep in my gut came a war whoop that could wake the dead. And it did, for hundreds of feet in every direction on that "battlefield." Sirens went off, powerful searchlights turned on; the battlefield became a parade ground full of intensive activity. Soon, a jeep full of officers pulled up in front of our foxhole. A rather severe-looking full bird colonel jumped out of the jeep, followed closely by our unit commander and first sergeant and a wargames umpire. They proceeded to give me the chewing out of my life! Bluer language was never spoken by so many officers to one lowly private dogface soldier. When it was all over, my first sergeant turned to me and said, "I want that radio. *Now!*" I handed my friend to him; he marched us to our company area, telling us to bed down for the night.

By morning, cooler heads had prevailed. The colonel wanted me charged with Dereliction of Duty and busted with loss of pay, but my officers found out about the mystery of the Little Silver Radio and asked him to let them handle how I would be punished. He reluctantly agreed, after ordering my commander not to let me back in the war games and keeping me out of his sight for the rest of our stay. My punishment for bringing my radio to Fort Bragg was to write a five-hundred-word essay on "The Importance of Signal Intelligence and Security in Army Maneuvers." In addition, I was restricted to the company area for the balance of our time there. I wrote my essay that night in the chow tent, munching popcorn and listening to game seven on our cook's radio (the Red Sox lost). Later that night, the first sergeant entered the tent, walked up to me, and handed over my little silver radio. Top winked at me, did an about-face, and marched out of the tent, whistling "Take Me Out to the Ballgame." I had learned my lesson. Baseball and war games don't mix, and be careful who you share your secrets with!

—Dale Chenoweth
Maynooth, Ontario, Canada

MICKEY, CAN I HAVE YOUR AUTOGRAPH?

I met my political idol, Hubert Humphrey. I have met some singers whose work I love, but who are, regrettably, not household names. Except for running into Russ Ortiz in a supermarket, and asking Jeff Kent to pose for a picture with my daughter during spring training, I have never even met a ballplayer, much less had a conversation. Okay, I did recently meet Dusty Baker and John D'Aquisto, two really good guys and ballplayers, at book signings. I guess at this point I don't really care about meeting stars. I'm not that star-struck, but I always hear friends talk about the players they've met in all kinds of places, and the conversations they've had. Oh, to have met the Mick, or Tom Terrific, or Stottlemyre or Bouton, or . . . This is the chapter for which I had the most stories to choose from, and it was agonizing. A lot of coin-flipping was involved. Here are some wonderful stories from people who did meet players- whether their personal idols or not—in, of course, a rather interesting cross-section of ways.

***

On the way home from the hospital with our two-day-old brand-new baby girl, we made a quick stop at Wrigley Field. At the time, my husband was the manager of a gift shop inside the stadium. It was March, and Opening Day was a few days away. Wrigley had always been like a home to me—I had spent so much of my childhood there—so I didn't give a second thought about the wisdom of walking down the concourse with a newborn.

A familiar figure came towards us. I would recognize Sweet Swingin' Billy Williams anywhere. Part of the reason I fell in love with baseball was because watching him bat was a joyously beautiful event. "Hey, Billy," my husband proudly said, "want to see my new daughter?" Billy came over, gently pushed the blanket away from baby Jane's face, and kissed her forehead.

Thirty years later, Jane is an amazing young woman. No doubt it is because she was "blessed" by the legendary Hall of Famer Billy Williams.

—Amy Rubin
Chicago, Illinois

***

The most memorable time I've had at a ball game happened last year. My special needs daughter, Dani, loves Angels' outfielder Mike Trout. One day, with her mom's help, she wrote Mike a letter, and posted it on Facebook. Responses encouraged us to try to get that letter to Trout. Several folks with connections to the Angels tried to help, but with no luck. About that time, Dani and I were invited to a sports clinic at the stadium to work out with some Angels' training staff and players, hoping, unsuccessfully, that Trout would be one of them. Still, Dani had a great time meeting, playing catch with, and talking with players. I brought a copy of Dani's letter along with a photo, adding my email address at the last minute. I approached the Angels' head trainer, told him about our efforts, and asked if he could put the letter in Trout's locker, and he said he absolutely would do so. I did not tell Dani in case nothing ensued. However, within a couple of days, Dani received an e-mail from the Angels office.

Hello Dani,

My name is Andrea Hagemann and I am contacting you on behalf of Mike Trout. Thank you for reaching out to Mike, and

for the well wishes. He would like to set up
a batting practice visit and tickets to an upcoming game for you and your family. Our
next homestand starts on Monday, August
25, and ends on Sunday, August 31. Let me
know which day works best. Thank you,
Dani. I look forward to speaking with you
soon.

I sent that email to my wife Sue, and she forwarded it to the friends
who had tried to help. It was a tear fest. We picked the date, and were given
instructions on when to come and where to go. We were all so happy that
this was coming true for Dani, but still did not tell her anything more than
we were going to a game. First, we stood on a mound area between big
Angels hats outside the stadium. As the cameras started rolling, we finally
told her what was going on. She was in shock. We then entered, credentials
around our necks, the bowels of the stadium. We walked down a corridor,
and could now see the light from the field. We popped up behind home
plate and walked onto the field among a group that was escorted to a stag-
ing area next to the dugout. The Angels came out for their warm ups and
batting practice (BP). Dani could not take her eyes off of Trout; soon he
was in the batting cage. Some players came over to give autographs. We
talked to manager Mike Scioscia, and got a great group photo with him
and some players. Then, an Angels' PR guy asked for the "Trout group";
Sue and I looked at each other, and said that was us, not knowing what
was to come next, a meet with Trout, perhaps an autograph. We followed
him to the big *A* painted behind home plate. After Trout was done with
BP, they started walking over to us. Holy cow! We were going to be alone
with Mike! He was the most genuine guy you could ever hope to meet.
Dani was still in shock. He said he had read the letter, and was happy to
meet her. We talked, and took photos with him, and he signed her jersey
and other things for about fifteen minutes. Now we were all in shock!
Dani's dream came true. She will never forget that day; she still looks at

the photos and videos almost every day. The best photos have been blown up, put on canvas, and hang above our fire place.

MIKE TROUT, DANI AND HER FAMILY

—Eric V. Bergeron
Fullerton, California

***

My story did not happen at a ballpark or field, but at a corner store then called Sun Valley Dairy in San Francisco. It was 1970 or so, and as a twelve- or thirteen-year-old boy, I was of course curious about the female body and its many mysteries—as perceived by a twelve- or thirteen-year-old boy! I was with a friend, and he dared me to open the cover of a *Playboy* magazine at the back of the store, because he said that, on a particular page of the magazine, there was a close-up picture of a woman's . . . vagina. I didn't believe him, of course, but I looked around the store, saw no one in sight, and after a few seconds of nervous anxiety, took the bet. I walked quickly down the narrow aisle, bent down to the floor level shelf on which the magazine was displayed, and frantically opened it up. There it was—yes, a close-up of the aforementioned body part—although mostly a lot of pubic hair. I wasn't even sure what I was looking at; I was mostly in disbelief, pretty much as a twelve- or thirteen-year-old boy would be.

I quickly regained some of my composure, although sweat was probably dripping off my brow, and I closed the magazine. I got up from the floor and, though I hadn't heard or seen anything during my surreptitious look at the magazine, there was a person right next to me. He certainly startled me when I rose from the floor. I said, "Hello, Mr. DiMaggio!" I knew it was him, even though he looked older, grayer, and more wrinkled than I remembered him. But it was Joe DiMaggio. He said something like, "Well, hello, son." I put my hand out, we shook hands, and then I walked away as quickly as possible. I never knew if he had seen me peruse *Playboy*. I didn't want to know.

—Anonymous

(The author of this story wished to remain anonymous. I know him well and will attest to his credibility. This is the secret we share!)

***

When I was a boy, about nine or ten, living in Cleveland, my dad would always take me to see the Yankees when they came to town. In those days, there wasn't much security around the ballpark, or even guarding the players. One day in 1932, we were able to just walk into the Yankee clubhouse. My dad recognized Babe Ruth, and amazingly, we were able to walk right over and shake his hand. Eighty years later, I still remember it clearly. How can you ever forget a day like that?

—Howard

***

Tom Seaver has always been my number one, my ace. Growing up in Brooklyn and Long Island from 1962 to 1980, well, there was no baseball player more important than Tom Terrific. When the Mets traded him to the Reds in 1977, it broke my heart. I realized I loved Tom Seaver way more than I loved the Mets. At that moment it became clear to me that the game was the players, and the teams, uniforms, logos, etc., all property of the owners, was simply noise. I began following players and baseball as a whole, a truly liberating moment for me, and one that completely reshaped how I viewed the game. For nearly forty years, I've enjoyed the game without the drag of team-based misery when someone loses, or hyper-euphoria when someone wins. I recommend it to everyone.

In the fall of 2003, a few months after we moved from Chicago to Cooperstown, and years before I became mayor and meeting my baseball heroes became commonplace, Tom Seaver came to the Bullpen Theater in the Hall of Fame, a small venue to begin with made more intimate by the presence of only fifteen people. My first Seaver sighting was when he poked his head through the cutouts in the right side wall to peek at the crowd. When he came in to sit for his interview and Q and A, Seaver was about five feet in front of me. As I expected, his answers to the questions were smart and informative. I particularly enjoyed his story of telling the younger Jon Matlack to set up a great curveball with a crappy one. When it worked during a game, Matlack looked to the dugout and shrugged in disbelief.

When it was time for questions, I was ready. I began by telling Seaver how much he meant to me, and showed him the scorecards for his three hundredth win and his return to Shea as a Red. (I brought them to demonstrate my worship. "No autographs," I was told, but that wasn't my goal.) Then I said that I could go on and on. He said, "Go ahead." So, I told him my story (see paragraph one). His trade led to my liberation, and I thanked him. It was a rare experience to be able to tell a man whom I hold in such regard how I felt.

Afterwards, pictures were allowed, and my wife Karen stalled so I could spend extra time talking to Seaver. I showed him the scorecards up close, and we talked a bit about Dick Schaap, for reasons I can't quite recall. Karen told him she had never seen me in such a state, and Seaver said, "Keep him under control." In the previous pictures, Seaver sometimes stood apart from the other person, sometimes shook their hand. My picture with him was very different. I take it as a sign that perhaps I had gotten through in a different way from the average fan, and that still makes me feel good.

When we left, a woman who may have been one of Seaver's daughters said that what I said was very eloquent. Years later, I chatted with Seaver at an induction weekend cocktail party. That was surreal and marvelous, but less out of the norm these days; as mayor of Cooperstown, I can't really be a fan first. Not so that first time, in October of 2003, when my hero put his arm on my shoulder and smiled for the camera.

—Jeff Katz, mayor and author of *Split Season*
Cooperstown, New York

***

In the early sixties, down in Southern California, my friend, Jack Pritchett, and I were passionate fans of Hank Aaron. We figured anyone could identify with Willie Mays' greatness; Hank was our guy, with his incredible consistency and all-around skills. The first thing we did each day was discuss Hank's line in that morning's box score.

One night—I guess I was around thirteen or fourteen years old—we were at Dodger Stadium with the Braves in town. We went right down to the very first row next to the visitor's dugout. Aaron was playing pepper with Warren Spahn and a couple of other teammates, wielding the bat. He must have sensed our presence, because as the pepper game ended, he turned ever so slightly and flicked the ball in our direction. It was floating like a feather—couldn't have been dropped. My friend cradled it, and our night was made before the game even started.

—Bruce Jenkins, author of *Shop Around: Growing Up with Motown in a Sinatra Household*
Montara, California

***

On April 20, 2007, my parents and I were in town to see our beloved Red Sox take on the Baltimore Orioles at Camden Yards. Wandering around Baltimore's Inner Harbor with my mother on a clear sunny spring day, and ready for lunch, we passed a Cheesecake Factory; I not so subtly nudged Mom, saying, "Mom, look, Jason Varitek is eating here. We have to go." We chose the outside seating option for the weather, hoping to see the Sox captain. We shook hands with Orioles infielder Brian Roberts and Red Sox pitcher Kyle Snyder, and were seated at the table next to Varitek and his friends. My fourteen-year old self was trying to contain his excitement and maintain civility and dining etiquette. My intentions only waned when Mom abruptly blurted, "Oh my god, Jesse, it's David Ortiz." I was wearing my Red Sox number thirty-four jersey, Ortiz's; as he passed by, he patted me on the shoulder and said, "Nice shirt, man." This was turning into quite an afternoon! Big Papi was seated at the vacated table next to Varitek's. Imagine this uncontrollably excited fourteen-year-old Red Sox fan and his mother, simply seeking a place to eat lunch, now sitting in a table triangle featuring two of the most popular Red Sox players in recent memory.

As we ordered and chatted about our nearly fantastical scenario, fans started imposing on these stars' space, asking for autographs and pictures. I just sat and watched. Mid-meal, I nearly spat out my lunch—my Cheesecake Factory favorite, orange chicken—and quietly exclaimed, "Mom, Manny Ramirez is here." He sat down with his Dominican pal Ortiz. So, the table trifecta had grown: Varitek and friends, Manny and David and friends, and fourteen-year-old Jesse and his mom. I could barely eat, trying to prolong this experience by ordering dessert, asking for more time, more water, anything. I watched every move the players made, even ignoring Mom, trying to eavesdrop on their conversations. When the waitress asked Big Papi for his order—this is no lie—he turned to me and asked, "What did you have?" I replied immediately, "Orange chicken." He said to the waitress, "I'll have four." David Ortiz had just asked me what I was having, and ordered my meal! This day could not have gotten any better! Mom was in total disbelief. We decided not to notify my dad of these unbelievable goings on until we left the restaurant.

Varitek had gone; I had shaken his hand and wished him good luck. It is imperative to know that Ortiz had just come out with an autobiography (co-written with Tony Massarotti, then of the *Boston Globe*) that Mom had bought me in hopes of getting it autographed in Baltimore. I approached his table and said, "I'm not going to ask you for an autograph, or to take a picture. But I bought your book recently and have tickets to the game tonight, and was wondering if I brought it tonight, would you sign it?" He said, "Yeah, buddy, bring it by tonight." I said thank you, and at the last second said, "Hey, Manny," after entirely forgetting that another one of my all-time favorite players was next to me as well.

We had to get to the ballpark when the gates opened at five o'clock for a 7:05 p.m. first pitch. With resounding success receiving autographs, I had my secrets and maneuvers for getting prime position. For two hours I stood, front row, near the Red Sox dugout, and where the players warmed up and stretched. Ortiz completed his pre-game routine without even an acknowledgement. We watched the game from our ticketed seats, but I only lasted eight innings. The game would end in a Red Sox 6-2- win, the big hit a bases clearing double by none other than Big Papi. In the ninth, I slipped past security and sat right next to the Red Sox dugout, book in hand, hoping to catch Ortiz on his way into the clubhouse. Once the final out was recorded and handshakes completed, we locked eyes and he nodded his head at me. I was in. The butterflies in my stomach became full-fledged hummingbirds. But the Sox sideline reporter pulled him away for a post-game interview. The air within me was deflated. So close, I thought, but I did not give up; he still had to make his way back to the dugout. The interview concluded, and he acknowledged me again. I stuck my book over the railing for him to sign. I grabbed the Sharpie that belonged to the kid standing next to me. "I need this," I think I said, and there it was. He signed his book. As he handed it to me, I mentioned, "It was the orange chicken for that big hit tonight," alluding to the lunch we had shared that afternoon. He pulled the book back, smiled, wrote something else, and handed it back to me for good. I read what he had written. On the inside cover, his autograph, and underneath, a note that read "nice orange chicken." I looked up to say something, but he had disappeared into the clubhouse. It was the only autograph he signed the entire night. It was the orange chicken.

That is my favorite Red Sox/baseball story. I've lived and breathed Red Sox baseball non-stop since I was four. I've been to World Series games, seen walk-offs, and a no-hitter. But this one tops my list.

—Jesse S.
Hampton, New Hampshire

***

I was twelve when I went to the opening game of the Yankees/Tigers series, September 28, 1984. It was my first chance to see Chet Lemon, my favorite player, play in person for the first time in three years. I wore a White Sox jacket; despite their having traded him to the Tigers for Steve Kemp, they were still my number one team at the time. (My baseball loyalties have taken me down some weird paths over the years, perhaps a story for another time.) All I remember about the game is that the Tigers won, and that Lemon was thrown out at second trying to stretch a single into a double. At that point, he was thrown out again . . . for "bumping the ump" while arguing the call. This happened late in the game; as I was there mainly to see my hero, I decided to leave the stadium and wait outside in hopes of meeting him.

When the game ended, I spotted him near the players' parking lot. I can't remember if he was alone, but there weren't many people around, so

I approached him to tell him he was my favorite player and how much I admired the way he played. (I also hoped he noticed my White Sox jacket.) I made sure to address him as, "Mr. Lemon,"; he graciously shook my hand and said, "I didn't get your name." I then realized that I was so nervous I'd forgotten to introduce myself, which I then of course did.

I stood in awe of the man whom I had idolized and tried to emulate since I was twelve. I was so touched that he showed such genuine interest in me, a kid he just met outside a place that wasn't particularly hospitable to visiting teams. I don't recall much else about our conversation, except that somewhere along the line I asked for his autograph and he signed a small piece of paper for me. I recall that after a while, his teammates started to appear, among them Lou Whitaker, Larry Herndon, Willie Hernandez, and the late Aurelio "Señor Smoke" Lopez (whose cologne was so strong that I thought he must have bathed in it). The five of them congregated, as if ready to hang out that night; I could see that it was about time for me to head home. As I departed, I'm sure I told "Mr. Lemon" again what an honor it was to meet him.

I was giddy all throughout my walk from the stadium back to East Harlem (I loved walking to Yankee Stadium in those days, even if there wasn't a game); even the unmentionable comment made by a stranger I excitedly told of the thrill of meeting my idol couldn't bring me back to Earth. At least my mother appreciated hearing all about it.

Believe or not, the next afternoon was even better. I went back hoping to see Chet again, and I did. This time I didn't attend the game; I just timed my trip to arrive in time to see the players exit, and there he was, surrounded by friends and family, and a stadium hot dog vendor. This time I couldn't approach him, as I was behind a barricade, but I got his attention and he remembered me—by name! Someone in the group around him presented him with a portrait of Lemon, his face super-imposed over his uniform number (thirty-four). I remember thinking the sketch wasn't such a great likeness, but I'm sure he was pleased to receive it just the same. I also recall him saying to an overly friendly female admirer, "I'm a married man, miss," and that he had two of his uniform caps with him (which he gave to the hot dog vendor).

Finally, they started to leave, and Lemon took a few steps to join his teammates. All of a sudden, he stopped in his tracks, turned to the hot dog vendor, and said, "Give one to Shannon." The vendor complied; I suddenly became the little kid featured with "Mean Joe" Greene in the famous Coca-Cola commercial. I said, "Wow! Thanks, Mr. Lemon!" My day—possibly the rest of my year—was made!

—Shannon Rhett
New York, New York

***

When I was sixteen, a buddy of mine and I drove to St. Louis and stayed at the Chase Park Plaza to catch a few games. The Cubs were in town to play the Cards, and were staying at that hotel. Many fans would stop and ask the players for autographs; we didn't. Saturday night we ate at Stan and Biggie's Restaurant, and Stan Musial came to our table. Sunday morning there was a long line for breakfast at the hotel coffee shop. When we finally got to the front of the line, the maitre'd told me he had a table for four, but we were only two. A gent behind me tapped me on the shoulder and asked if they could share our table. It was Leo Durocher with Billy Williams. It was the best breakfast of my life.

—Jim Johnson
Overland Park, Kansas

***

As a regular traveler, I spend a lot of time in the Delta Sky Club. During a morning "hang out" I sat next to a middle-aged gentleman with a young son, and we sparked up a conversation that lasted extra-long, since our flights were both delayed. Our talk was often interrupted by people saying hello to him. I assumed he was a popular Salt Lake City businessman. One interruption ended with him signing an autograph, so I decided to ask him what line of work he was in. He responded by saying the sports industry. We continued to talk, about kids, politics, the weather, etc. After a dozen or so more interruptions, I finally just said, "Who the heck are you?"

I hung out with Johnny Bench for two hours, and never got his autograph! I got Benched at the Sky Club!

—John Pedersen
Salt Lake City, Utah

***

My son, Elijah, was eight years old when we were at the San Diego Airport. Mr. Padre, Tony Gwynn, was taking his San Diego State Aztecs Baseball Team to New Mexico. We saw Tony, and he stopped what he was doing to speak to us. Elijah had been telling me he was going to play for Tony, and now was his time to make a connection. Elijah had the biggest grin as he told Mr. Padre all about Tony's "stats" and his career. Tony told Elijah that he knew more about him than he did himself!

Tony Gwynn will always be Mr. Padre to my Elijah and me.

—Merry Andrus
San Diego, California

***

News of Bobby Murcer's brain tumor started up my Movies of the Mind machine this week. If being a class act in life has anything to do with beating this cancer, I am betting on Murcer.

It was 1985 when I met this Yankee. An entrepreneur named Max Shapiro put a week-long camp together, headed by the likes of Mickey Mantle, Whitey Ford, Hank Bauer, Tom Tresh, Tom Sturdivant, Moose Skowron, and Murcer. At check in, sixty excited, over-age campers were gossiping in the lobby of our Deerfield Beach Hotel when a buzz came through the crowd. A Yankee bluish black steamer trunk came bustling into the lobby, the white NY logo leaving no doubt that a legend was about to enter.

It wasn't Mantle. Or Ford. An average-looking man, youthful and smiling, appeared behind the crash of bellhops and bags. He might not have been the royalty we were waiting for, but he was still Bobby Murcer, and we welcomed him warmly. Unlike Mantle, he was comfortable with the adulation and banter. Over the next several days, I got to know this gentle man. He always had a smile on his face and made time for anyone who asked. Unlike many campers, I never rushed for pictures with the stars of the week, Mantle and Ford. Two of my favorite photos are with Bauer and Murcer, Bobby and I standing with our bats on our shoulders, the November sun at Fort Lauderdale Stadium, former winter home of the Yankees, lighting up the backdrop.

One afternoon during this amazing week in my life, my dad visited the clubhouse as my guest. Dad opened his mouth, and these words flew out, directed to Murcer: "We had high hopes for you. Your career was such a disappointment." Talk about disappointment. If there was a hole in the ground in the Yankees clubhouse, I would have volunteered to be swallowed up and taken my dad along with me. Murcer kept his class. He smiled, excused himself, and sought out another, more uplifting conversation.

In the Yankees versus the Campers game over the weekend, I found myself on the mound facing my boyhood heroes. I was doing pretty well, and then up came Murcer. He swung at my first pitch and almost removed my ear; the ball came back so quickly I didn't even have time to duck, whistling past my ear. That buzzing remained with me for an hour or so. I glanced at Murcer, classy as ever, standing over at first base and grinning. He mouthed some words at me, but my hearing hadn't returned thanks to the buzz from his bat. He might have said, "How's your dad?"

When George Steinbrenner dealt Bobby away in the 1970s, he realized his mistake and brought him back to the Yankees so he could end his playing career with the team he most identified with. In the past twenty years, George kept Bobby close. As an assistant general manager and as a broadcaster, Bobby continues to this day as part of the Yankee family. Bobby Murcer is one class act.

Sixty former campers and millions of Yankee fans are rooting for Bobby just as hard now as we did when he was playing center field and hitting home runs. He might not have been what some fans were expecting when he was encumbered with the Ruth-DiMaggio-Mantle-Murcer succession. But he was Bobby Murcer.

And that was pretty damn good.

—Steve Tarde
La Mesa, California

***

My boyhood idol was Robin Roberts. When I was eight or nine (1952 or '53) my dad took me to a game at Connie Mack Stadium to see him pitch. After the game we waited outside of the Phillies locker room. In those days, there was minimal security. It must have been April or May, because I was wearing a leather jacket with buttons. Robbie came out and I was in awe. I said, "Hi, Robbie." He came over, asked my name and age, and thanked me for being a fan. Then he actually buttoned my jacket and said it was cold.

Fast forward to 1989, and Robbie was at an autograph signing with Steve Carlton in Cherry Hill, New Jersey. I went up to him with a colored photo I had purchased at Cooperstown. With tears in my eyes, I related the story of meeting him as a child. He was sixty-three at the time, and he simply said, "Well, I'm just glad to still be alive so we could meet again." It still gives me chills. That memory is so typical of a starry-eyed kid who gets something "precious" from just a few kind moments from a baseball idol, especially with my dad present. Thinking back at my reaction in '89, maybe it was typical for an adult who meets his idol, too.

Dad was a hard worker who worked seventy hours a week managing a liquor store. Sunday was his only day off, and when I was young, he would take me to see the Phillies, or we watched them together on TV. In 1980, the Phillies finally made it to the World Series. The father of my daughter's babysitter was an executive with Exxon, and he gave me two tickets to game one. I was married, but my wife understood my need to repay my father, who by this time had had a heart attack and was disabled.

"Dad, wanna watch the game with me today?" I asked on the phone. He said, "Sure, come over and we'll watch it." "No, Dad, get dressed. We're going to the game. I got tickets." I could hear him choking up over the phone. He had a tough time walking up the long ramps at Vet Stadium, but there we were, in the two-hundred-section—great seats. They were so good that Irv Cross, former Eagles safety and broadcaster, sat behind us. The Phillies won their first Series game since 1915 after a dramatic three-run homer by Bake McBride, and they held on to win. He was as excited as I was in 1951 when he took me to my first game.

It is amazing what a bond baseball can create, not just for sons and fathers, but fathers and daughters and moms, too. It can cement loving re-lationships. My dad was not an openly loving person. He never kissed me, only shook hands. He never said he loved me, but I knew he did. He just couldn't say it. But we had that bond of the Phillies; for that very special day, we were truly father and son.

—Harold Kasselman
Vorhees, New Jersey

***

My parents took me to see the Houston Colt .45s play the San Francisco Giants at Colt Stadium on May 11, 1962. I was thirteen years old. Prior to the game, I stood outside the Giants' clubhouse with a piece of paper look-ing for players to give me their autographs. I was able to collect signatures from Felipe Alou, Harvey Kuenn, and Don Larsen. Kuenn signed without a word and walked onto the field. Larsen sat down on a chair near the clubhouse door as a long line formed to his left, appearing to enjoy the at-tention of the autograph seekers. I approached Alou as he walked towards the field. He took my pen and paper, and as he signed, asked me where I was from. I said San Antonio, and he asked me if I had seen his brother Jay Alou playing Minor League ball there. I later learned that Jesus played for El Paso in the Texas League that season, so he might have been with El Paso when it played in San Antonio. This was the only time I ever heard him referred to as Jay. Alou's easy friendliness made a lasting impression on me. I was a Felipe Alou admirer from that day forward.

Satisfied with my Giants autographs, I took my seat with my parents, and watched Dick Farrell pitch a masterful 7-0 shutout. Willie Mays doubled in the fifth inning, one of six hits Farrell scattered in his complete game gem. The Giants' starter was a rookie pitcher named Gaylord Perry, who entered the game with a 2-0 won-loss record. In the fifth inning, Merritt Ranew and Farrell hit homeruns off Larsen who had relieved a wild Perry in the third. The Colt .45s tagged Perry with his only loss of the season. I can still see Farrell's home run, a mammoth shot over the left-center field wall in the deepest part of the park. I recently learned that the ball had to travel more than 410 feet to get over the wall in that spot. Farrell dominated the eventual 1962 National League World Series team that day. I still have my program from that game.

Maybe I sought out Giants' players for autographs knowing I'd have opportunities to pursue Houston players. Ironically, they ended up as the only autographs I ever sought at a ball park before I turned forty.

—Mark Wernick
Houston, Texas

***

Watertown, in northern New York State where I grew up, was home to a short season Class A ballclub for the Cleveland Indians. A baseball fanatic, I applied for and got a second job as an usher at the ballpark, not knowing I would end up meeting and interacting with many players I had watched on television as a kid, such as Manny Trillo, Buzz Capra, Bump Wills, and Sandy Alomar Sr., as well as older veterans like Bill Monboquette. I saw future stars come through, like Steve Kline and Brian Giles. I also got a wonderful opportunity to interact with front office personnel from the Cleveland organization. Some were also former Major League Baseball players, such as Johnny Goryl who was the director of Minor League player development during the time I worked for Watertown. We would chat before and during the games, about baseball in general or what was going on in the organization.

My fondest memory was of Monboquette, an instructor for one of the teams. I met him before a game, we chatted briefly, and I got his autograph on a game-used bat, my most cherished piece of memorabilia. We talked baseball, of course, about the way it used to be and his playing days, which is what I enjoyed the most about our encounter. I am old school about baseball, and a bit of a historian, so listening to him was a thrill for me. Monbo acted like he was no better than me, just so friendly and open, when players today seem so distant. He made me feel like he truly cared about the fans, and was glad someone knew of and wanted to listen to him.

I was at work the next day at the mall in Watertown, and who should come walking by but Bill. He remembered me from the night before and stopped to talk for almost an hour. He had to be one of the funniest former players I ever met. That will stick with me always.

The three summers I worked for the Indians affiliate, 1991 to 1993, were the three best of my life.

—Mark Morrison-LeMay
Solvay, New York

***

My dad was an usher at Fenway Park. He would get to the park about ten thirty in the morning for a one o'clock game. He often brought me and my brother Joe along, and as you often hear from people, the sight of coming up from the bowels of a stadium, seeing the gem of a field, with green grass from here to the moon, was just an unforgettable sight. One day, in 1948, when I was four and Joe was five, we had on our Red Sox uniforms, and were playing around on the field. Dad's section was in the box seats right behind home plate, and Ted Williams came by. Dad called Ted over and he took a color photo, with Joe and I propped up on the railing, and Ted in the middle with his arms around us. Dad thanked Ted, of course, although with us being so young, we probably did not know how special this was.

As I grew up, I started to play and love baseball. I was a pretty good player, with excellent hand-eye coordination, and other skills that either come naturally or not; they cannot be taught. I was drafted by the Kansas City Athletics, stayed in the system through their move to Oakland, and was called up during the 1970 season, playing with such great players as Reggie Jackson, Catfish Hunter, and Rollie Fingers. I was traded to the Washington Senators, who promptly moved to Texas and became the Rangers, managed by . . . Ted Williams.

My dad sent me the picture of Ted with Joe and me, and I went to Ted and asked if he would sign it. His first reaction was "Who is that?" When I told him, he called the press, and another photo was taken, kind of a then and now. Williams and Driscoll revisited almost twenty-five years later. What a memory!

—Jimmy Driscoll
Tamworth, New Hampshire

MY TIME ON THE FIELD

I walked on a Major League Baseball field once or twice, for a Giants fan fest. That's pretty much it. I didn't throw a first pitch, or play alongside Major Leaguers, or throw batting practice, or conduct official business. I never even fell on the field trying to catch a foul ground ball. These folks have had some wonderful experiences that would make many of us wish we could walk in their cleats.

***

On June 8, 1969, I was at Yankee Stadium when, between the games of a doubleheader with the White Sox, the Yankees retired Mickey Mantle's number seven. Ironically, I was not a big Mantle fan, having much preferred Roger Maris. However, I was at this game with my college girlfriend, Sandi, who was most definitely not a baseball fan. The ceremony was between the games of a doubleheader against the White Sox. As Mantle was being driven around the stadium in a golf cart, acknowledging all of the admiration and applause, I remember thinking that the driver of the cart must be the luckiest person in the world. After the ceremony, even before the actual game started, Sandi asked if we were going to leave. She'd had enough. Of course, the answer was no.

Several decades later, when working for the San Diego Padres, I was charged with making all the arrangements for the ceremony and celebration of Steve Garvey's retirement. It was held on April 16, 1988. I had first gotten to know Steve when he played the Dodgers, and really liked him. We became lifelong friends. Steve was always at the top of the list for cooperating with whatever was deemed necessary with the front office, the media, and the fans. For that day, I coordinated and delegated every aspect of the ceremony. Except one. Remembering that day almost twenty years earlier, I decided that I would drive the cart so that I could experience what it was like having a ball park shower a player with admiration and appreciation. I felt like the luckiest person in the world.

ANDY AND STEVE GARVEY

—Andy Strasberg, author of *Baseball Fantography*
San Diego, California

***

My first memory of Major League Baseball is coming home from school, seeing the end of the seventh game of the 1960 World Series on our black and white RCA TV, with Bill Mazeroski hitting the Series-winning home run to beat the Yankees. I was hooked! Ironically, I became a Yankees fan mainly because Yankees second baseman Bobby Richardson was from my home state, South Carolina.

Coming full circle: At an Old Timers game in Atlanta in the early nineties, I was pitching batting practice. Former Braves' skipper Billy Hitchcock, managing the Braves' old timers, asked me to coach first base. The first batter up was Hall of Famer Eddie Matthews, who singled to right. Coming down the line to first, Eddie signaled to me that he needed a pinch runner. I tried to get Hitchcock's attention in the dugout, to no avail. Eddie then said, "Here, you run for me. I'll coach first." The next batter hit a grounder to short, and I slid into second base right into none other than . . . Bill Mazeroski. As I jogged off the field after they turned the double play, I couldn't help but think back to that day in 1960. When I crossed the line at first, Matthews said, "You can coach first again." Ahhh, memories.

—Larry Livingston
Atlanta, Georgia

***

On April 30, 2008, my wife, Yurima, and I got great seats for a San Diego Padres game at Petco Park. We were invited to go onto the field for batting practice (BP). Ryan Howard, Charlie Manual, and Davey Lopes of the Phillies were behind the cages watching the other players hit. Ryan kept looking over at us. He really was checking out my wife, and he came over and started talking to her. He was really polite and charming, and I think he thought I was just a friend or something (a lot of people think that, as she's a pretty gal, and I'm just some goofy-looking dude). Dave Winfield, then working in player personnel with the Padres, came over and began talking to her as well, just flirting away. The thing about it was

I didn't even care; in fact, I was so awed at the two legends that I let it go on just so I could meet and talk to them. Yurima and I still joke about it whenever they air the Subway commercials with Howard. Howard and Winfield are classy guys, and are/were great players, and meeting them that day, and getting their autographs, was awesome. The best part is that Yurima proved to be a perfect diversion as Chris Young of the Pads beat the Phillies that night 4-2. Ryan was 0-3 with a walk and a strikeout. Perhaps he should have been concentrating a little more on the pitchers, rather than Yurima, during BP!

—Joey Banet
San Diego, California

***

When I first started to go to big league games, I was already eighteen. I grew up in Iowa, and all we had was Single A ball. However, I quickly made up for it, going to about forty games my first summer in Chicago. Most were at Wrigley. My normal routine was to roll out of bed around noon, stroll to the ballpark, grab a bleacher seat, drink beer in the sun, go home, pass out, and then hit the open mic. The next day would be the same. This lasted most of the summer, until I finally exhausted my Bar Mitzvah money and had to start doing temporary office jobs.

My favorite memory of those times happened one night, a couple weeks before the season started. I was playing someplace a couple blocks from Wrigley, under the El tracks on Addison. I'd noticed there was scaffolding up, as they were doing some last-minute work on the ballpark. After midnight, fortified by a few Old Styles, I walked up to the corner of Addison and Sheffield, climbed up and over, and was in. I had Wrigley Field all to myself! I sat in the dugout and the press box, ran the bases, and made "catches" in the outfield against the ivy-covered wall. I've been to hundreds of games since then, but I'll never forget the night that Wrigley Field was mine.

—Dan Bern, singer/songwriter, *Doubleheader*
Santa Cruz, California

(Dan is another great songwriter and storyteller. Check out this CD)

***

In 1998, I served as the number-two guy in the Tampa Bay Devil Rays' media relations department. This was the team's inaugural season, and the job was wonderful, but for personal reasons, I decided late in the year that I would return home to Nashville after the season was over. Rays' manager Larry Rothschild knew this, and he gave me the best going away present possible: the chance to take batting practice (BP) at Yankee Stadium during the team's final road trip. I borrowed catcher Mike DeFelice's bat—I had never used a wooden bat before, having grown up with the aluminum kind—and stepped up to the plate to hit off of Frank Howard, the legendary former slugger who often threw BP for the Rays. As Wade Boggs and other players looked on, I squared to bunt at the first pitch, just as all the real players did. Howard held up just as he was going to release the ball. "Just swing the bat, son!" he bellowed. I got to hit for what seemed like ten minutes. I didn't hit any homers, but I didn't swing and miss, either, which to me was a victory. And then the best of all: Pitching coach Rick Williams let me walk across the Yankee Stadium grass out to the bullpen with the starting pitcher for his pre-game warm-ups. As we walked across the field, I got to experience a true New York moment—fans were heckling the pitcher mercilessly. I closed my eyes for a few seconds and imagined they were yelling at me. It felt great.

—Andrew Maraniss, author of *Strong Inside: Perry Wallace and the Collision of Race and Sports in the South*
Nashville, Tennessee

***

Sometime in the last ten years or so, I received a letter of invitation to throw the first pitch at a Giants game. Now, to be honest, I am not much of a sports fan; the only kind of ball that I have really had any experience with is a bowling ball. Often, while on the set during the evening news, while my co-anchors were talking and laughing with the sports guys, I would doodle on blank pieces of paper, really not interested in the scores of whatever sports they were talking about. One time, just before the holidays, my partner grabbed the piece of paper I was writing on, and showed the viewing audience "Belva's Christmas dinner shopping list." I was a bit embarrassed, but it was all in good fun.

When the appointed game day came, I had to suppress my fears and anxiety, and walk out to the mound like I knew what I was doing. I really did not know how to throw a ball, even a tennis ball. My twelve-year-old nephew, Marco, offered this one comment: "Auntie, please don't throw like a girl." Even knowing what that meant would have been something. I just knew Marco, and I wanted it to be a strong throw. So, I—all of my five-one-and-a-half frame— took the ball, wound up, and . . .

I won't go into the details, to some degree forgotten. I won't tell you if I poured in a strike, or threw a thirty-five hopper to home plate. I will leave it at it was a great honor to be asked, and a real challenge to overcome my fears.

—Belva Davis
San Francisco, California

(Belva is very modest. While I cannot comment on her actual first pitch, I do know she's an award-winning, groundbreaking newscaster in the Bay Area. I'm honored that she would contribute a story for my book.)

***

In the early 1960s, my dad developed and marketed headrests for cars, long before the auto companies started to install them as a safety feature. In 1965, the Minnesota Twins won the American League pennant, and Dad got the inspiration to use that as part of a marketing campaign for his headrests. Because my sister Joan and I were identical twins, he decided that we naturally fit into this idea. He dubbed the pair of us the "Safety Twins," and struck an arrangement with the Twins for them to promote his headrests. So, in the late afternoon of a very sunny and steamy summer day, adorned with tiaras and sashes that announced our imagined title, we were brought on to the field to meet and be photographed with the Twins. We were only nine years old and quite mortified about the whole thing. That aside, I remembered feeling a little star-struck to meet the players, who were very sweet and nice to us. In addition to the professional pictures that Dad had taken that day, Joan and I were given Polaroids signed by Harmon Killebrew, Camelio Pascual, Tony Oliva, and Mudcat Grant, one of my favorite players. While I found the whole experience embarrassing at the time, I now appreciate having the pictures to look back on, and realize what a special day that was for us.

JOAN AND NANCY AND THEIR FATHER, SHERMAN, ON THE RIGHT

—Nancy Blumstein
Minneapolis, Minnesota

***

Last night, my family spent a beautiful summer evening on the field at an empty Comisky Park (fine, US Cellular) playing catch, taking batting practice (BP) and warming up in the bullpen, facilitated by the team's coaching staff. This once-in-a-lifetime experience (or in our case, once a year!) is all thanks to my father who, many years ago, became a partial owner of the White Sox. This special night is open to all owners' families. This is one of many perks we've had access to through the years: attending the occasional spring training, having a nice indoor dining room we can escape to when games get rained out, and even tickets and travel with the team when they were in the 2005 World Series. I am always slightly embarrassed to admit, however, that I am not really a White Sox fan, or a huge baseball fan at all, for that matter. In many ways, while I appreciate these perks and highly coveted access, I know that they are largely wasted on me.

However, this one night each year, out on the field, I understand what it feels like to be a true baseball fan. The night plays out pretty similarly each year. We suffer through horrendous Chicago rush-hour traffic to make it to the stadium by six o'clock, get our colored Sox T-shirts and hats that will all be worn that evening and then shelved until the kids need a particular colored shirt for a Color War day, and then head out to the field to join the activities. The first view from the field never ceases to take my breath away: the hyper-green turf, the vastness of empty seats, kids playing catch in the outfield, and then scattering when an in-shape dad happens to really knock one out during BP.

We take part in all that we can, depending on the relative ages of our kids that particular year. We warm up a bit in the underground batting cage off the tunnel behind the dugout, hoping that by the time we make it to out to the real deal (hitting from home plate!) we are the ones to make the kids scatter in the outfield. Hasn't happened for me yet, but I have been impressed with how many times I've been rewarded with that resounding *crack* when bat hits ball, an extremely satisfying sound, and a good reminder that at forty-one, I'm not quite old yet.

What I have come to realize, however, is that the most important and memorable part of this yearly ritual actually has nothing to do with baseball. It has everything to do with my father and the joy he gets out of watching his children, and now grandchildren, run around the field, take pictures with Southpaw the mascot, and eat hotdogs with abandon, all thanks to an investment he made over forty years ago. Yes, he invested in baseball, but what he really invested in was his family. And his return comes not in money or championships, but nights like last night.

Update: Several years later, the stadium is now Guaranteed Rate, *and* my batting has greatly improved!

—Amy Haggarty
Highland Park, Illinois

***

On April 2, 2016, my Navy buddy Eddie Espanol and I took in the final pre-season game for the San Diego Padres against the Chicago White Sox at Petco Park in San Diego. As we walked through the gate, a young lady named Jennifer, a member of the entertainment committee, asked me, "Would you like to throw out the ceremonial first pitch today?" At first, I thought she was joking, but when she started giving me the details, I knew she was serious. I said, "Sure, I'd love to." She led us down through the stadium and onto the field, gave me a baseball with the Padres logo embossed on it, and I waited for my opportunity to walk out to the mound after the National Anthem. Surprisingly, I wasn't nervous, but I was concerned about throwing the ball over the plate without it bouncing. I can honestly say that I didn't disappoint either myself or the crowd in attendance that day, as my pitch went hard and fast right into the catcher's mitt. Afterwards, the catcher and I greeted each other, and he gave me the ball.

Since there was no batter at the plate, I can honestly say that my pitching debut was a—wait for it—"no-hitter."

—William Jones
San Diego, California

***

I've been very fortunate, with many great memories and moments with the San Francisco Giants. My husband Heath and I have been to playoff and World Series games in each of the even-year championships. We witnessed Matt Cain pitch a perfect game. I even bought Eric, (the author of this book), one of his first beers at a ballgame. But one particular memory is very unique and special to me: I sang the national anthem on the day Barry Bonds broke the all-time home run record.

By day I practice law, and consider myself a fierce litigator with an appetite for winning arguments and staying true to my principles. But, by night, and on weekends, I balance the stresses of my work with singing. I will sing to whoever will listen. Martuni's was a frequent Friday night happy hour bar of mine, with a live pianist who payed backup like a sophisticated jazzy karaoke jukebox. I eventually joined a band called "Bella Ciao", founded by famous accordionist Tom Torriglia, which played retro-Italian pop hits and similarly styled originals. While Italian should have been the greatest challenge, more challenging was looking the part. Despite my Chinese-Vietnamese heritage, a large bouffant wig and red and white polka dot dress usually did the trick of deceiving native Italians into at least wondering whether it was my father or mother who had passed on my Italian genes (I've been told that in my full-face makeup everything about me screams Italian except for my nose). In any event, my efforts must have worked because at several gigs, I gained the approval of grand-mas to wed their single, available - and of course, highly desirable – Italian grandsons. I am, of course, Italian in my heart.

In late July, we got the call to sing the national anthem and a couple of other songs on August 7, 2007. It was, after all, Italian night at the park.

Of course, we said yes. As my bandmates tried to figure out which instruments they would use while standing on the field, I secretly panicked. The anthem is a difficult vocal solo; its range tests the upper register of even the most seasoned singers. And then there are the words. I panicked at the thought that I might butcher them in front of 40,000 people.

As fate would have it, there was another energy building at the same time: Barry Bonds was about to break Hank Aaron's home run record. The stadium was constantly abuzz with excitement; it wasn't a question of *if* he would do it, just a matter of *when*. I remember seeing people with buttons showcasing which number home run Barry hit, evidence of the time that they were witness to a history- in-the-making game.

Within a week of show time, I developed bronchitis. Not just a seasonal cough, but the kind of voice-stealing, raspy, mucus-in-your-lungs and nose bronchitis cough that would make any singer panic before a show. There was no way I would cancel, or let a replacement take my spot. I went to the doctor and bought every herbal remedy Whole Foods had to offer, including one called "Singer's Saving Grace." It tasted horrible, but I needed every bit of help I could get. I remember trying not to practice—to save what little voice I had – but also trying to sing the high notes to test how badly I might crack. It would come down to a game day. I prayed to the singing gods.

When the big day came, I bundled my nerves and elixirs with me into a taxi and headed for early sound check. The driver thought I was insane, humming to myself in the back seat and randomly blurting out notes in my upper register to check my range and warm up, while trying to save my voice. I sheepishly explained I had a singing gig at the ballpark, but that I was sick – I'm sure he'd heard stranger things in his years driving a cab. I kept telling myself I was prepared, but I wasn't for what was about to happen.

I was the only one from the band at sound check; it was important for me to get acquainted with the two to three second delay that I knew would distract me if I was unfocused. But as I walked onto the field, there they were - The Giants. **Every single one of them**. I scanned their jerseys – a sea of cream-colored shirts and black numbers, moving effortlessly and routinely through the motions of baseball. I wanted to note who I could spot, but in the moment, my nerves couldn't take it all in. In my head I knew I'd sing in front of 40,000 people, but I hadn't accounted for a private show for the team. All I could think was how embarrassing this sound check could be.

Of course, this was routine for them, listening to vocal rookies and professionals wailing and crooning during batting practice. But I remember thinking "Are they going to hear me sound check? Can't they go somewhere else? WHY ARE THEY HERE?" My escort handed me the mic: "Go for it" she said. My inner voice panicked. What do I do? Just talk? Should I sing? As I nervously started uttering the words "Check,...check", I could feel all of them looking at me. I'm sure they weren't, but at the time it felt like they were all watching. Oy vey. You could hear the proverbial pin drop, like the DJ record scratch, followed by crickets. No one was talking. Only the sounds of bats cracking balls could be heard.

As I opened my mouth to sing, my voice boomed over the Public Address system. The delay and echo were surreal. I could feel my brain fight to keep time as I sang fast but in time. When I hit the high notes – no cracks. What a relief, but that was short-lived when I realized I had to replicate this performance in just a few hours. My escort asked if I wanted another go; "No way" I said. Under ordinary circumstances I would have loved to continue testing the mic, but in front of the players, I felt as though I had just survived a shark tank. I was already embarrassed from doing well, and could only think how mortified I would feel for uttering a wrong note or word in front of the whole team. As we walked past home plate, a couple of the players gave me some compliments and said I sounded great and would be great later on. It was so sweet. I have no idea to this day which players spoke to me, but their encouragement was something I'll never forget. I blushed and walked off the field.

As the hours passed, the night turned into a blur. Waiting for show time, in the moment, felt like forever, but then it was time in a flash. With adrenaline pumping through my system, we walked onto the field. I knew my parents were in their seats, but I couldn't see them in the crowd. With a hot mic in hand, I sang. Positive mantras filled my head. As I hit the high note, I could hear the cheers. Relief. A genuine small hit my face. Yeah, I was a little nasally sounding, but I didn't butcher that note. I don't think anyone could tell that I was sick. I messed up one note at the end, but I tell myself that's what I get for making artistic edits to a song with a concrete melody. I hate that I did that, but I know for certain no one cared as much as I did.

MICHELLE

Of course, what made that night special was not that I sang the anthem; that night Bonds broke that record hitting 756. We sat in our regular seats near left field—which happened to be where he played. My joy from singing well was dwarfed by my excitement that Bonds did it – and that I was there to witness it. Because of my performance, my mom and dad came, armed with their video camera. My parents and I had never been to a game together. But for my gig, they would not have come, and we would not have captured it all on film (on a camera, not a phone). Dad captured the hullaballoo of Bonds' achievement. The game was stopped; Willie Mays gave a speech. People around us screamed and cried and cheered.

As we looked back on dad's video footage, we caught another serendipitous thing. While I sang the anthem, the camera panned the backs of all the players, all wearing black jackets with no numbers. You could not tell who was who. Except Bonds. In the lineup of players paying allegiance to the anthem, you could see only one jersey plain and clear: number twenty-five. I like to think that if I didn't have bronchitis, and didn't do what I did that day, maybe fate would have been different for Bonds that day. I guess it was just meant to be.

—Michelle Full
Walnut Creek, California

(Michelle, the beer you bought was my first ever at a ballpark. The next day, we went to another game, and Lynn tried to recreate and cultivate my astonishing new enjoyment of beer. I didn't care for it nearly as much; it must have been the company of a new friend! We had the partnership tickets for the game at which you sang, but we were out of town, and sold them to you so you could bring your folks to watch you sing. It all worked out well!)

***

I played ball at Northeastern University in the mid-1970s. As a nineteen-year-old, I had the opportunity to pitch against the Red Sox at Fenway in late April 1977, hurling the first four innings against the regulars, with only one ball leaving the infield on a line. It was a great experience, but sometimes the worst thing that can happen to a young man is having a little success at an early age. I spent subsequent winters in Florida spending my savings at baseball schools, seeking tryouts chasing the dream of playing pro ball.

Nine years later, getting ready for my start in the Boston Park League, I read in the sports section of the *Boston Globe* that the Red Sox were desperately seeking a batting practice (BP) pitcher because Walt Hriniak, a coach for the Sox, was sidelined from that duty while recovering from a rotator cuff injury. Being the madman that I was, I couldn't contain myself, so I called Jack Rodgers, the traveling secretary, and told him I was interested. I blew off my amateur team that night and showed up at Fenway the next morning, at nine o'clock. The Angels were in town, and Tommy John would start for the Halos. By this time, I was a pretty polished amateur, able to emulate Juan Marichal's high-kick pitching motion. I stood atop the bump, throwing two seam fastballs, one after another, with nary a breath in between, to the bench players who hit before the regulars. By the time the third sub was getting in his hacks (I think Marty Barrett) all the regulars came over to the screen, hooting and hollering at the subs as one high eighties two-seamer after another came burrowing down on them; the madman on the hill was taking no prisoners. Not one ball even found the wall that early morning. The fellas were a little intimidated by me; after all, it wasn't your typical lazy-ass BP session. Later in the clubhouse after showering, there were a lot of eyes looking at me. Jim Rice came over (I had pitched against him nine years earlier in that exhibition game) and told me I did a good job, but that I needed to take more time between pitches. I know for a fact that they never saw anyone work so fast, so furious, and so extreme with that crazy leg kick; needless to say, they did not ask me back. Neither did my amateur team, since I had blown them off the night before.

The dream, playing professional baseball, dies very hard. I had to be content coaching college ball at Suffolk University, and then at my old high school, Boston Latin, for twenty-eight years. I was happy to be a student of the game, and then, in turn, impart my knowledge and passion for baseball to anyone and everyone who was willing to listen. So, in a way, the dream continued!

—Charles Peterson
Boston, Massachusetts

***

My brother Brian and I played baseball endlessly in the backyard of our home while growing up in the 1970s. Listening to Vin Scully on a transistor radio was our routine, with rare televised games to bring it to life. We played a game called "double play," where we threw a crazy bouncy ball and tried to turn an imaginary double play. In 1999, the Dodgers sponsored "Think Blue Week," a fan promotion for which they selected fans to sing the National Anthem, be groundskeepers for a day, do an inning of play by play, and play in a softball game prior to that night's Dodger game. I had written in telling of our love of the Dodgers and our desire to play together to relive that memory. Eighteen regular players were selected, along with two fantasy umpires; I surprised Brian with the news that we made the team!

On the day of the game, we got to dress in an alternate (old) Dodger dressing room. The Dodgers provided us with jerseys, pants, stirrup socks, and hats to keep. "Just bring your shoes and gloves," they had told us. Softballs and bats were provided. Sides were chosen. Brian and I played on the same team, and batted consecutively. We played six innings and used regulation bases. I recall stepping out of the Dodger dugout, warming up in the on-deck circle, listening to the Public Address announcer call my name and position (first base, like my hero Steve Garvey; I play first to this day in my adult softball league). I strode to home plate to bat, with a few dozen players and family members sitting in field-level box seats cheering us on. I backed out of the box, looked around, and took in the moment, trying to envision fifty thousand screaming fans, and imaging how it must feel to step up with the game on the line, or as a rookie about to bat for the first time. It was exhilarating and breathtaking. I went 2-3 at the plate.

However, the highlight occurred in the second inning. As had always been the case, I was playing first base, and Brian was at second. With one out and a runner on first, Brian fielded a ground ball to the left of second, took a step or two to his right, tagged the bag, and threw on to me at first to complete the double play to end the inning, fulfilling the fantasy that had been played out literally thousands of times during our childhood. I tossed the ball onto the mound and slapped gloves with him as we ran into the dugout with sheer joy at sharing the moment with him on the field where we had watched our heroes for years. I have always loved and treasured that moment with him.

A few nights later, the Dodgers gave us tickets, invited us to the field, announced our names, and showed game highlights to the whole crowd, including our double play. Brian could not attend the game that night, but he was there in spirit.

—Bruce Rokos
Moorpark, California

***

The San Francisco Giants held a contest asking for photos of the Giants' Orangest fan. I submitted one of my daughter Alexandra and her Friesian horse, Gabriel, decked out in Giants' gear for a Halloween horse show. She won the contest, and a team representative asked if we could bring our horses for a victory ride around the ballpark during an evening game. We trailored Gabriel and my horse, Uiltje, to the park in the afternoon to practice, and let the horses get a feel of the park. We returned that night, and with some forty thousand fans cheering and waving orange rally rags, the horses (our trainer Rachel Burke was on Uiltje) took the field to great reception. The horses were on their very best behavior, and the whole thing was perfect from beginning to end. After they left the field, fans came to the area where we were parked and asked for autographs on baseballs. It was a magical evening at AT&T Park for us all.

ALEXANDRA ON GABRIEL AND RACHEL ON UILTJE

—Gina Sierra
San Francisco, California

***

Before a Phillies game in the summer of 1985, they introduced a bunch of guys who had played at the Phillies Dream Week, when folks pay to train and play games, guided by old Phillies legends. They were bald and pot-bellied old guys, and I thought that I had to do this (even though I was neither of these).

I participated in Dream Week for the first time in January 1986 in Clearwater, Florida, where the Phillies conducted spring training (ST). I reported to the locker room, and our unis were hanging up, ready for action. I played catch with Tony Taylor, the great second baseman for the Phils. I went through the stretching regimen, and Jim Bunning, the Hall of Fame pitcher and manager of my team, put me in charge of the pre-practice and game stretching routine one day. During one at-bat, Bunning gave me the bunt sign. I missed it, but I got a single. That didn't matter in the long run, because I caught hell when I got to first base.

FRANK AND JIM BUNNING

I caught every inning of every game for the five days of the program. One of the managers was Larry Bowa, who was very aggressive, and wanted to win every day. Lee Elia, one of the coaches, said he would pay a hundred dollars to anyone if they beat the crap out of Bowa's team and shut him up.

At the end of the week, I was very banged up. I lost a toenail from running into a fence. My arm was yellow, black, and blue. My knees and groin were hurting from blocking all the balls in the dirt, and I had a bloody nose. In addition, when I got off the plane coming home, I had a 102-degree temperature. My wife greeted me by saying, "What happened to you?" I replied that it was the greatest week of my life, and couldn't wait to go back next year. It was a week of hell, and a friend of mine said, "And you paid money to do this?"

Prior to my fifth and last Dream Week, I trained very hard. I continually threw a ball against a mattress on the wall in my basement to get my arm in shape. I did a million knee bends for my legs. That spring, at the age of fifty-seven, I caught three doubleheaders, and picked a guy off first base. The pros let me catch batting practice. Greg Luzinski, the Bull, was one of the managers, and I golfed with him and outfielder Del Unser. Phils announcer Chris Wheeler lent me his clubs.

The Phillies 1991 Yearbook listed me as the MVP of my team that year's Dream Week. I started my days in the hot tub, finishing with Motrin to kill the pain, and ice bags, with the trainer rubbing hot, soothing ointments on my back. I immediately retired, going out right on top. Now I go to ST every year with *no pain*, but great memories.

—Frank Brodsky
Wynnewood, Pennsylvania

***

I was a member of the Philadelphia Phillies grounds crew, the first to ever dance with a mascot, the original Phillie Phanatic, Dave Raymond. Starting in the mid-seventies, the stadium organist Paul Richardson would play a song from the Gong Show called "Gene, Gene, the Dancing Machine." It was the one played when the *unknown comic* came out to do his act. So, at the stadium, during the fifth inning, when we went out to smooth the sliding pits and sweep the turf, the Phanatic would circle the bases and "knock us down" one by one. At that point, we would all dance to the song. On many occasions, we danced with paper bags over our heads, as was part of the Unknown Comic's shtick. I know the Yankees crew became famous for doing the Macarena, but we were doing this before they did.

—Mark "Froggy" Carfagno
Philadelphia, Pennsylvania

FAMOUS, HISTORIC, AND MEMORABLE GAMES

Some games are famous, perhaps infamous. I don't mean just because it was the last game of the World Series. No, they are famous because they are just recognized as something special. Maybe it is a certain play that occurred, rather than the whole game. Mazeroski's World Series-ending home run. Babe Ruth's home run point. Mantle's leg being ripped up in his first season. Robinson's steal of home. Schilling's bloody sock. There are so many games that baseball fans know about, even if they happened decades before they were even born. They are part of baseball lore. Here are the accounts of some special, memorable games.

***

September 26, 2016, should have been just another baseball game, the Mets visiting the Marlins. But it no longer was. It was the day after Marlins' ace, Jose Fernandez, was killed in a boating accident. As I drove to Marlins' Park with my friends Evan Katz and Andrew Shield, we wondered how they would memorialize Fernandez. After all, Jose wasn't just a great pitcher; he was a joyful, joyous man who loved the game, touched so many in the community, and whose story about coming by boat from Cuba and rescuing his mother from drowning was so well known and admired. We figured correctly that there would be video highlight tributes celebrating his accomplishments and life between innings.

It was a better-than-usual crowd for a Monday night, about twenty-seven thousand. There was an eerie sense of quiet in a stadium that is usually loud and echoey, even with small crowds. All the Marlins wore jerseys with number sixteen and the name Fernandez. There was a moment of silence before the game as the whole team gathered on the mound; you could see the empathy and camaraderie from the Mets players who seemed to be equally hurting. We sat in section twenty, near the Marlins' dugout. Two ten-year olds near us were bawling their eyes out; it was interesting to see the impact that Fernandez had even on little kids.

Left-handed batter Dee Gordon led off the bottom of the first; he stepped into the batter's box from the right side, emulating Fernandez's stance for one pitch, a ball. He then turned around to the left side; we wondered if it was even legal to change sides in a count, but Mets pitcher Bartolo Colon certainly had no problem with it. On the third pitch, he blasted a deep home run, his first of the season. As he circled the bases, you could see the tears stream down his face; you could just feel his hurt, and he received a hero's welcome from all of his teammates. My heart seemed to jump out of my chest at Gordon's blast, and the emotion I felt then I now again feel as I write this story; the hair on the back of my neck just stood up. I will remember this moment my whole life.

I could go on with all the emotion, and individual tributes given to this great ball player and role model. No need to do that; you can look it up on-line. Suffice to say that after the game, a Marlins' 7-3 victory, the team assembled on the mound, each of them placed their hats on the ground, and Manager Don Mattingly kissed the ground. It was an extraordinary tribute to an extraordinary man.

—David Clemmer
Coconut Creek, Florida

(I met David and his friend Karla at a Giants-Dodgers game in San Francisco. He told me that he had been at this game, and I gasped—I really wanted this story. Ironically, earlier in the year, I had been to another Marlins-Mets game in Miami, featuring Matt Harvey and . . . Jose Fernandez.)

***

October 14, 2003, Wrigley Field, was a night that will live, as the expression goes—and really is true here—in infamy. I was there with my wife Mary Beth, and daughter Jennifer. The Cubs were hosting the Marlins in the sixth game of the National League Championship Series. Ahead three games to two in the best of seven series, they were leading this game 3-0 in the eighth. Just one win away from the World Series. Every Cub fan knew we needed just one more win, and it would probably come tonight. We were primed.

People will say the loss of that game wasn't really Steve Bartman's fault, and they will lay out their case. But I was there, and I'm telling you that it was a definite turning point. Cubs fans, and Cubs players, had a psychological thing going on. We knew that anything could go wrong at any time, and that it probably would. And the Bartman thing was it. Once it happened, there was just a negative feel to the rest of the inning and game. The air came out of the place; after we lost that game there was not a shred of confidence that we could win game seven, even if it was at home in the "friendly confines" of Wrigley.

We were sitting about fifteen rows behind Bartman, and I can still see the whole thing playing out in slow motion. It was a very catchable ball heading toward the stands, according to what we saw and other photos, but we also saw Bartman moving into position to catch the ball. It seemed like the entire stadium was yelling, "Noooo!" and thinking, "Don't do it, you idiot! (Pictures reflect that interference should have been called.) And then the Marlins scored eight runs. That was the game; that was the series.

After the incident, thousands of people were yelling at the little guy in the Cubs hat and a blue sweatshirt with the headphones on. I'm not proud of myself, but I'm sure I was yelling, "You stupid ass," along with many others. Not much later, I stepped out to go to the restroom, and saw Bartman being escorted out of the stands, and I think out of the stadium, for his own safety. I remember seeing people in the walkway above him throwing stuff and yelling at him. Poor bastard. And poor Cubs.

But now we've won it all, and we can forget about Bartman. Personally, I'll never forget that night.

—Rich Pope
Northfield, Illinois

***

I was a rookie reporter in 1988, when the A's played the Dodgers in the World Series. The A's were heavily favored, with the "Bash Brothers" of Jose Canseco and Mark McGwire leading the way. In game one, Canseco hit a grand slam in the second inning, and the A's got the lead to Hall of Fame closer Dennis Eckersley for the ninth inning. Eckersley had been so good that year that the A's surely would win.

The World Series is such a big event that the press box cannot accommodate all the reporters. I was in temporary seats, in the top deck at Dodger Stadium. I grew up going to games at Dodger Stadium and sitting in the top deck, so I knew exactly how to get down the stairs, all the way to the clubhouse. Most reporters did not, so they left their seats when Eckersley came in, to get down to the clubhouse before the elevators got too crowded. So, they missed it—and I saw it—when Kirk Gibson hit his famous home run.

Bill Shaikin, sports columnist, *Los Angeles Times*
Los Angeles, California

***

I attended a Friday twi-night double-header at Candlestick Park, the Giants hosting the Dodgers, on July 26, 1988. "Hosting" is a kind way to put it, at least from the fan's perspective.

The first game took three hours; the second went into extra innings. There was a total of seven hours of baseball played, with a break in between. That gave the fans plenty of time, with no excuses needed, to drink beer. By the time the second game was over, there were bonfires in the center field bleachers. There were brawls, particularly between Giants and Dodgers fans. Fans scaled the fences and threw batteries and whiskey bottles at Dodgers' left fielder Kirk Gibson. It was a zoo. Oh, did I say there was drinking?

The result of this night of baseball was the new California requirement of suspending beer sales after the seventh inning. The Dodgers swept the doubleheader. So much fun.

—Will Durst
San Francisco, California

***

I can't remember if it was a Saturday or Sunday day game, but it was a crisp autumn day, October 1, at the end of the 1961 season. I was twelve years old, and my uncle Armando was taking me to the movies. On the way to the subway, I asked if he instead would take me to Yankee Stadium to see the Yankees play the Red Sox. A budding baseball fanatic, I wondered if Maris might just do it—hit his sixty-first home run. Armando, also a big Yankee fan, had also wondered whether that would be the day. He agreed, and off we went to the stadium, not knowing if it would be packed that day, or if we could get tickets. It turned out there were plenty of tickets; the stadium seemed to be less than half full. Maris had missed hitting his sixty-first within the 154 games that Babe Ruth hit his sixty, so purists felt it didn't matter. Except that it did, because until then no one had ever hit sixty-one homers.

We sat on the first base side on the first level. It was a pitching duel, with rookie Tracy Stallard pitching for the Sox. On that last day of the season, Maris batted, swung, and hit the ball on a not particularly high-arc towards right field, plopping into the seats in right-center. The fans went nuts, we went nuts, and Maris, a shy, retiring sort of guy, had to come out of the dugout twice to acknowledge the cheers. I saved the scorecard and ticket stub for years, only to lose them at some point. But Armando and I still talk about the day that he didn't take me to the movies, and on a whim, we got to see Roger Maris hit his sixty-first homer on the last day of ironically, the 1961 season.

I have no idea what movie we were going to see.

—Sonia Gulardo
New York, New York

***

April 27, 1947, I attended Babe Ruth Day at Yankee Stadium when Ruth made his farewell speech. It was a cold day, and the Babe was wearing a camel's hair coat and a "cabbie" cap. His voice was very hoarse, something he mentioned in his speech. I don't remember exactly what he said, or anything about the game; it is a matter of record, and can be found on the internet. I just remember the thrill of being at that game, and seeing the love bestowed upon perhaps the greatest player of all time by sixty thousand fans.

—Jules Organ
Boynton Beach, Florida

***

October 17, 1989, my husband Steve and I drove to the game with friends. They had left three children at home, the oldest able to babysit. Our kids, Matt (eleven) and Shelley (five) were with us. It was a very warm night, and everyone was in a festive mood. This, of course, was not just any game. It was the third game of the World Series between the Giants and the A's. We were in our seats on the third base line, waiting for the game to begin, when the earthquake hit. You could see the seats undulate in waves. We watched everyone in centerfield clear out of the stadium. We stayed in our seats unsure of what to do. A fan in front of us had a portable TV; as we looked over his shoulder, we saw that the Bay Bridge had partially collapsed. We made our way to the parking lot to meet up with our friends who were already in the car, but the police were not letting us leave the parking lot. I think they were letting VIPs exit first. After twenty minutes, Steve said he couldn't wait any longer, and got in line for the porta potty. Suddenly, the police insisted that we start moving; I told our friends it was okay to leave Steve behind. They were frantic about their children; pay phones weren't working, and of course there were no cell phones. There was an incredible traffic jam leaving the park, but we eventually made our way home. About ten minutes later, Steve arrived! He said that he realized what had happened and started walking. In the chaos, he caught a taxi and got home quite quickly. Our house had no damage. There was some irony about the only item in the house that moved. My son had a collection of mini-helmets from every team on his dresser; the only one that fell to the ground was the Dodgers.

—Roz Itelson
San Francisco, California

***

My wife Ellen and I thought that it would be interesting to stroll around Memorial Stadium before the start of the last Orioles game on Sunday, October 6, 1991, and reminisce about the thirty-seven years we'd been watching baseball there (they'd arrived in 1954 when we were six years old). I still remember a Styrofoam baseball my father brought me from their Opening Day parade. After circling the stadium, we'd started back to our car, when a man came up to us asking if we'd like two tickets (the game had been sold out for a long time). I asked how much, guessing that because the game was ready to start, the price might be coming down. He said that they were free; he either felt sorry for us, or feared that we were undercover cops. In either case, we accepted his offer and sat down to watch a dreary game. The Orioles straggled to a 67-95 finish in 1991, and in this game, they quickly fell behind the Tigers. It dragged on, as everyone waited for the post-game ceremonies, which had been kept a tight secret. With one out in the bottom of the ninth, Cal Ripken came up. It occurred to us that if he hit into a double play, he would be the final batter at Memorial Stadium—he did, and he was.

The ceremony started out as uninspired as the game, as the grounds crew slowly dug out home plate and put it in a limo to be transported to their new home at Camden Yards. The field then emptied as everyone wondered what was next. The magic began as the theme music from *Field of Dreams* started and a middle-aged Brooks Robinson, in his old Orioles number five uniform trotted out to third base. He was followed by his "brother," number twenty, Frank Robinson, heading out to right field, number twenty-six, Boog Powell, to first base, and number twenty-two, Jim Palmer, to the mound. They were followed by over a hundred former Orioles, not just stars, but also semi-forgotten, middle-aged, and older players back on the field in their uniforms one last time. Together at shortstop were Cal Ripken, Mark Belanger, Luis Aparicio, Ron Hansen, and even Willie Miranda from the 1950s. I don't think there was a dry eye in the crowd. At the end, all the players gathered in a circle in the infield as a 360-degree camera took a panorama.

Post script: This was not the final game at Memorial Stadium; it did not go gently into that good night. In a bizarre turn, it became, again, a football home for a decade. Demolition started in 2001, ten years after the Orioles played their final game there. On 9/11, the planes hit the Twin Towers, and everything shut down. My office closed, and as I headed home, it felt right to pass by Memorial Stadium. All that was left was the iconic memorial façade, stating that "Time will not dim the glory of their deeds." A few days later, even this was gone.

—Stephen Luckman
Baltimore, Maryland

***

In 2013, the all-star game (ASG) came to NY; the city covered in the orange and blue, the city embracing the Mets rather than the Yankees, was one of my favorite parts of the week. I attended all game-related festivities and enjoyed each one. I expected the main event to be just another ASG, as the players enjoyed the adulation of the fans. I was excited to see Matt Harvey start alongside Mets captain David Wright. Harvey did not disappoint, striking out three in two innings of work and Wright went one for three, making the hometown fans proud. I was excited to see one other player with a chance to play but with no guarantee as he was a relief pitcher. One Yankee I really respected and loved watching was Mariano Rivera, and this was his final season and last ASG. What happened was something no one expected. With the American League leading 3-0, Rivera started warming up; it was clear that he would be coming in for the eighth, not the ninth, inning. (Joe Nathan actually pitched Mo's customary final inning.) I figured there would be some acknowledgment that this was Rivera's last game, but what occurred on the field sent ripples through the whole crowd. As the bottom of the eighth inning was starting, Rivera came out of the dugout to jog onto the field with his teammates, but as the other players came up the steps they stopped, clung to the railings, and allowed Rivera to take the field by himself. He looked back and realized what was happening, as we slowly did, too. He took the mound, standing on a field all alone, with players applauding him from both dugouts, and the fans erupted. We stood and gave Rivera a long standing ovation, which literally gave me goosebumps, and still does thinking about it, an incredible tribute from the fans, but more importantly from all the players who showed Rivera just how much they respected him and what he had done for the game they all love. He acknowledged the crowd and the spontaneous display by the other players with grace and dignity. He was clearly moved, and unafraid to show his emotions before pitching his typical 1-2-3 inning. That moment is one I will remember forever as one of the things I love best about baseball.

—Leslie Heaphy
Canton, Ohio

***

My wife (then fiancé) and I sat in the rain in our ninth row, third base seats, wearing ponchos, because the seats were so expensive, I was going so sit there every minute I could. Everyone's emotions were high. There was an Elvis impersonator, but "Elvis" wasn't the only celebrity. Tom was there, and Doc, Bud, and Rusty, among others. It was September 28, 2008, the last baseball game to be played at Shea Stadium.

Watching Tom Terrific flip off the metaphoric light switch on his way out made me cry a little. Seeing so many of the '86 team that I had watched in that year's post-season was incredible, and brought back wonderful memories of my youth. Some of the '69 Amazins were there too. My wife bought me a brick from Shea and a brick on the fan walk at Citifield.

The Mets lost that game 4-2 to the Marlins, knocking them out of contention for the Wild Card game. It was a little disappointing that when the game ended, the team didn't stick around for the ceremony, or greet and thank their fans. A loss is always tough for the team, but it's work for them, where it's more of a passion for their fans who stand by them. Still, I needed to be at that last game at my favorite childhood stadium. It was such a wonderful experience.

—Matt McCauley
Vernon, New Jersey

(For the unfamiliar, that is Tom Seaver, Doc Gooden, Bud Harrelson, and Rusty Staub.)

***

How does one decide which baseball game to attend? I choose based on dates and Giants giveaway items. I picked one several months in advance, as my sister and her family were going to be in San Francisco. They live in Pittsburgh, and her husband decides when to visit based on when the Giants are in town so our families can go to a game together. It just so happened that the Pirates were scheduled to play the Giants during their 2002 visit. What could be better than that? For whatever reason, I bought tickets for a Friday night game. It must have been fate.

It was August 9, in the year when Barry Bonds was likely to hit home run number six hundred. As the season progressed, he hit homer after homer. My co-workers kept asking what day my tickets were for. I replied, saying maybe, just maybe, we would be there. As the day of our game neared, it looked as if he could hit that magic home run on our night. He hit number 599 on Wednesday, August 7, so he was due for another one, right?

We got to our seats in Section 308, row twelve, the former Snow Pack section for JT Snow. The ticket price was nineteen dollars for a memory of a lifetime. We watched the game with great anticipation, not wanting to say anything for fear of jinxing it. Every time Bonds batted, the stadium lit up like a laser light show. Everyone had cameras ready to take pictures of every pitch. It wasn't until the sixth inning that we got our wish. As Bonds hit that homer to center field, the clicks on the cameras were so loud you could hear them over the roar of the crowd. My nephew got into it, and has a photo of the ball as it approached Bonds. Everybody at that game got their ticket stub stamped as they exited the stadium, with the words in green BONDS 600. We also got a special pin that says the same thing.

The Giants ended up losing the game to the Pirates. Who cared? What better way to share event than with a family of Giants fans glad to have Bonds and another family from Pittsburgh that was glad he had left the Pirates. An historic event and evening.

—Janet Reves
Pacifica, California

***

For many years, while cutting my teeth on baseball, I heard stories about the Dodgers' early years in LA when they played in the venerable Memorial Coliseum. Hardly an ideal baseball venue, it served its purpose as a temporary home until Dodger Stadium opened in 1962. I always felt a special connection to the hallowed Coliseum, having been born just a couple of months after the Dodgers won the 1959 World Series when I was in the baseball womb, so to speak. While I attended other events there in my life, I always regretted that I'd never been able to see a baseball game at the Coliseum.

I jumped at the chance to buy a ticket when the Dodgers and Red Sox announced that they would play an exhibition game there on March 29, 2008, in commemoration of the Dodgers' fiftieth anniversary in LA. The cavernous stadium configured to quirky baseball dimensions, e.g. short fences; it felt surreal to actually watch my beloved team play on that field, even in a meaningless pre-season game, surrounded by 115,000 fans of all ages and backgrounds, some old enough to share recollections of games played in the 1958-1961 era. Several original LA Dodgers were on hand for the event. The Dodgers' organist played songs from the late fifties, and Vin Scully was there to call the action, as he had in 1958. Even the ghost of Roy Campanella was on hand, as the special night the Dodgers staged in his honor in 1959 was recreated on this evening.

The Red Sox won the game, 7-3, but I was awestruck. I've been to my share of World Series games but had never experienced anything like this—a game that counted for nothing but meant so much to so many, played in a unique setting. We experienced a magical, memorable evening that united generations of fans; the Guinness Book of World Records recognized us as part of the largest attendance ever at a baseball game. It's a memory I'll treasure forever. For a few hours, I almost felt like I was back in the womb—being born to baseball all over again.

—Linda M. Wilson
San Diego, California

***

What Cal Ripken Jr. means to Oriole fans can only be understood by those who have been blessed to have a great player and person as their hometown baseball ambassador for so long that he becomes like family.

His final season was the end of an era, and cause for celebration, but the nostalgia of Cal's victory lap came to an abrupt end on September 11, 2001. When play resumed, the schedule had been completely rearranged and as the games ticked away Cal couldn't seem to make contact. Maybe his hands were sore from signing autographs and shaking hands, or the endless interviews were depriving him of rest. Maybe it was the emotion of it all, the World Trade Center, the fans, his career, his family. All of it, all at the same time. The country was heading off to war, and here we were, having a retirement party. The bat looked like a chunk of cement sitting on his still broad shoulders, bowed but not broken. He was sprinkling around random singles, but his power was gone, and that sprinkling had turned to vapor with only three games left.

In Cal's first at-bat against Frank Castillo of the Boston Red Sox on Friday October 5, he lined out unceremoniously to center in the second inning. Castillo had a no-hitter until Luis Matos poked a single up the right field line in the fourth. In the fifth, Cal popped out weakly. The Sox scored four quick runs, and the game began to slip away. In the bottom of the seventh, with two out, Castillo faced the Iron Man again, and Cal hit a ground ball between short and third for only the second Birds' hit of the night. Camden Yards shook. It was only a single, but you'd have sworn it was a grand slam. I just knew when I saw it. Castillo was on fire that night, but Cal had somehow punched one through. It was a small piece of dignity for him and the team he cared about so much. My eyes got misty as I sighed deeply, taking in the moment of closure. The scoreboard flashed "Career hit number 3,184." After a moment I said, "That was it." The lady standing next to me sighed, "Yeah." And then we both smiled through the tears.

—Ken Mars, author of *Baltimore Baseball: First Pitch to First Pennant*
Parkville, Maryland

***

In 1968, LA Dodgers' pitcher Don Drysdale pitched a Major League record six consecutive shutouts on his way to a total of eight. His statistics that year are often overlooked when compared to fellow National League pitcher Bob Gibson, but Drysdale pitched a then-record fifty-eight and two-thirds consecutive scoreless innings pitched over the course of a month. I was at that record-setting game. There was a play in which the runner appeared to score, but the batter, in running to first, appeared safe but was called out for interference, nullifying the run and prolonging the scoreless streak. Ironically, years later I was at the game when Orel Hersheiser broke Drysdale's record by a third of an inning, and I have a signed Hersheiser ball with a photo of my dad asking for the signature.

—Mark Hertz
San Jose, California

***

In Bryan Adams' song "The Summer of '69," one line says, "Those were the best days of my life." In my case, it was one of the best years of my life. I had a summer job getting paid for playing ball with guests at a Catskill Mountain Hotel. That got me a chance to go to Woodstock. Neal Armstrong landed on the moon, and I met my first ever girlfriend. Everything was perfect . . . almost. The one bummer: The Mets were nine and a half games behind the Cubs in August after showing unprecedented success earlier that year.

Suddenly, things started to change. The Mets started to win; the Cubs started to lose. The Cubs came to New York for a series against the Mets, and a black cat ran onto the field in front of the Chicago dugout. Leo Durocher, the Cubs manager, got thrown out of the game, and the Mets kept on winning. They eventually won the division in the first year of divisional play. The words "Mets" and "champions" had always been mutually exclusive, but they were National League East Champs. Could they beat Atlanta and go to the World Series? Atlanta, the team previously from Boston, and then Milwaukee, known for the saying "Spahn and Sain, and bring on the rain." The Mets had "Seaver and Kooz and bring on the booze!" And they did. The Mets swept Atlanta, and would face Baltimore in the Series. I didn't care what it would cost or take; I was going, too! A friend and I grabbed our sleeping bags, got on the 7 train and camped out at Shea Stadium the night before tickets went on sale. We were fifteenth or twentieth in line. We got our tickets.

The series began in Baltimore. The girl I'd met that summer had come to New York from Cherry Hill, New Jersey, to visit. As an eighteen-year-old kid going to college in New York City, and living with my folks, I didn't have the luxury of privacy; that's why we walked down Fifth Avenue listening to game two on a transistor radio, instead of watching on TV with the folks. She thought I was a major nut job when I started jumping up and down, running around in circles when Donn Clendenon hit a home run to give the Mets their first ever World Series game lead. They'd lost the first game when Baltimore pounded Tom Seaver. I damn near started my own ticker tape parade when they won game two in Baltimore.

The series moved to Shea for game three, and my first Series game was special. The sense of anticipation, the media coverage, it was all what people were talking about. The Mets, prior to 1969, had given new depth to the word "horrible." If one would state, "They stink," that would be an upgrade. Now they were three games from being world champions. The games in New York had fantastic pitching, great catches, dramatic home runs, shoe polish-stained baseballs. The Mets won games three and four. In game five, Baltimore lead early, 3-0; the Mets took the lead in the bottom of the eighth. With two outs in the top of the ninth, Davey Johnson hit a fly ball to left field. It traveled slowly up and very slowly down.

Cleon . . . do not drop the ball. Cleon Jones, the Mets left fielder caught the ball, got down to one knee, and looked up. It was over. The Mets were the world champions!

The notion of that 1969 reality was, and still is, preposterous. As long as men and women compete, in any sport or endeavor one chooses to name, there will never ever be anything as special as that group of athletes. They proved to the world that anything is possible. I ran down to the field at the end of that game from the very top of Shea; I carried a piece of turf from the Shea's infield to Washington Heights. People on the subway offered to buy it. They wanted to touch it. It lived in a box for eight more years, but that final out, that atmosphere, is the stuff that baseball is all about—dreams turned into reality.

—Ron Baum
Mill Valley, California

MINI-CHAPTERS: A SNEAK PREVIEW

Here are a couple of stories from a couple of chapters that will be in the next volume, coming (B)at-tractions, if you will (these stories won't be in the next book, but the chapters will). This is like how you feel when they bring up that number one prospect in late September, giving fans a little glimpse of what they can expect to see next year. The chapters will include, in addition to those sampled below, Coaching, Umpiring, Stories Handed Down, Good and Bad Behavior, Mickey, Willie and the Stars of the Golden Age of Baseball, Television and Radio Stories, and Just Another Day at the Park.

MY FIRST GAME

In July of 1971, my Cub Scout troop rented a school bus from Sunnyvale to bring us to Candlestick Park to watch the Giants play. Their opponents were the Pittsburgh Pirates, led by Willie Stargell, in the year after the incredible Roberto Clemente died in a plane crash delivering humanitarian supplies in Nicaragua. There was also an "old-timers" game right afterwards, which was pretty interesting. Anyway, this was Dave "King Kong" Kingman's second game in the Major Leagues. He had pinch-hit for the great Willie McCovey earlier, because the Giants were getting blown out. In the seventh inning, Kingman was up with the bases loaded. Dave hit a grand slam and was 2-3, with five RBI's that game. It was exciting to see someone so young doing so well. The Giants came from behind and won 15-11.

It was the only baseball game I ever saw with my father.

—Andrew Berger
Fremont, California

(This was the first and only game Andy saw until he came with me to a Giants game during the 2015 season. I noted earlier that this is the story that started this book; it hit me like a proverbial shot. I have received many even more emotional stories, but this was the first—an early indication this would turn out to be as much a human interest book as it would be play of the game.)

***

My first baseball game was when I was twelve years old. All the way to the 'Stick in the car, my dad was telling me how much we don't like the Dodgers. "They are our sworn enemy," he said. We're in a tight pennant race, and the Dodgers can't win. This was August 22, 1965.

Juan Marichal and Sandy Koufax were on the mound. It was very exciting to be in the stands with my dad watching two aces battle it out. The Dodgers scored a couple of runs, and then Marichal hit Maury Wills in his second time at bat. I remember Dad saying something like, "This could get ugly," but I just wanted to finish my hot dog and take in the game.

When Marichal came to the plate for his next at bat, Roseboro threw the ball back to Koufax really hard from directly behind Juan, nicking his ear. Marichal looked back at Roseboro and said something. Then Johnny took his mask off, and all I remember is Juan swinging his bat at Roseboro's head. It all became a blur. Benches emptied, and for fourteen minutes, there was my first real baseball brawl, live and in person. Marichal was ejected, and Roseboro exited the game with a bloody towel held against his head.

I was pretty excited, although not in a good or happy way, and I realized how much we really don't like the Dodgers. I've kept that rivalry alive ever since, but of course without the fighting.

Dad continued to take me to Candlestick, often bringing his dad with us. I remember my grandfather sitting with his small transistor radio glued to his ear. He had lost his sight by this time, and told me you didn't really need to see baseball to enjoy it. The sound of the ball hitting a glove or a bat, the smell of the grass and hot dogs, and Russ Hodges and Lon Simmons were all you needed to enjoy the game.

It's because of these two men, and that one fantastic day at the 'Stick, that I have my fervent love for the San Francisco Giants.

—Debi Durst
San Francisco, California

***

"USHERS AND VENDORS AND BALL BOYS, OH MY"

In December 1957, I wrote to the Baltimore Orioles telling them of my desire to be a bat boy. It's a long tale, but suffice it to say that at the age of fourteen, I got that job, progressing from a clubhouse guy, who did the laundry and cleaned shoes, to ball boy to bat boy. I worked there from 1958 to 1960. April 25, 1958 was my first game working as a bat boy. After the game, in which the Orioles beat the Yankees, Brooks Robinson, who was as great a person as he was a third baseman, went bounding up the steps from the dugout to the clubhouse, four at a time, and I heard him say, "Who says we can't beat those fucking Yankees?" It was shocking and great at the same time.

—Warren Sollod
Baltimore, Maryland

***

I was seventeen years old, in my third year as a guest services staff member for the San Francisco Giants. I was serving as the press elevator operator, which in a way sounds dull, but gave me a great opportunity to meet famous people. One day, one of those celebrities rode up and down several times, and finally, he looked at me and said in a deep but friendly voice, "Hello, my name is Orlando"—long pause— "Cepeda." I looked at him and smiled sheepishly; then, with a big ear to ear smile on my face, I replied, "I know who you are." He replied, "And what's your name?" I looked at him for what seemed like hours, although probably only ten seconds, and nothing came out of my mouth. I finally looked at my name tag, and said "Rachel." Ever since then, he just calls me "Baby."

—Rachel Gray
San Francisco, California

***

I was about ten years old, growing up in New York, when I discovered baseball. My mom, who was from St. Louis and a big Cardinals fan, was my most important baseball influence. In 1961, my parents decided to take our family to spring training (ST) during my spring school vacation. We drove through the night to St. Petersburg where the Cardinals and Yankees trained. Hard as it is to believe these days, my parents would drop me off at the stadium in the morning, and come back to get me later. On my first day there, I was standing around with my autograph book, among a group of kids, just looking at ballplayers and the field. It was a magical feeling to me, as I had only seen ballplayers from afar or on baseball cards.

Suddenly, the clubhouse attendant came up to this cluster of kids and asked *me*, "Want to be a bat boy today?" I was stunned, and he took the dazed expression on my face as a yes. He took my hand and walked me into the visiting clubhouse of the Milwaukee Braves. There I was among stars like Warren Spahn, Hank Aaron, Eddie Matthews, and Lou Burdette. He told me my duties, both on the field and in the clubhouse. That was the beginning of my ST bat boy career.

The next day I connected with the Cardinals, and was their batboy for the rest of my two-week vacation. I struck up a friendship with pitcher Ernie Broglio, who after that would always leave tickets when his team came to New York. Broglio, of course, is notorious for the lopsided trade that brought Lou Brock to the Cardinals, but to me he was a hero. I got to know Julian Javier, and he would practice his English-speaking skills with me while we rode the bus for road games. In 1963, I was a ST bat boy for the Mets, and I have a picture in my Mets uniform, with Casey Stengel, who signed that picture. In 1964, I got individual day jobs with the Cardinals, the Pirates, where I saw Roberto Clemente up close, and the Dodgers, where I saw Sandy Koufax pitch while I was his bat boy. What more could a young baseball fan ask for?

—David "Batboy" Moriah
Lawrence, New Jersey

CASE STENGEL AND DAVID

"TO CATCH A BALL . . . OR NOT"

I've snagged lots of baseballs in the stands at Major League games, including Mike Trout's first career home run and Alex Rodriguez's three thousandth career hit—but there was a steep learning curve for me at the beginning. The first foul ball I ever got during a game was hit by Expos catcher Darrin Fletcher at Shea Stadium, way back in April of 1992, when I was fourteen years old. I was sitting on the third base side, and when the ball landed in a thick crowd of fans several rows behind me, I did the only thing I could: I turned around and looked at the ground in case it trickled down the steps. To my surprise, that's exactly what happened, and I lunged under an orange railing and grabbed it. This was my big moment —a lifelong dream turned into reality. I wanted to celebrate as I'd seen countless other fans do on TV, but unfortunately I forgot about the railing, so as I jumped up to show off the ball, I whacked the absolute crap out of the back of my head. Total jubilation mixed with intense physical pain are an odd combination. I wish I could say I learned from that silly mistake, and never got hurt again after that, but no. In the process of chasing baseballs at more than 1,600 Major League Baseball games, I've sprained an ankle, cracked a rib, and gotten a black eye. I've also been ejected six times, but that's a story for another time.

—Zack Hample, author of *Watching Baseball Smarter*
New York, New York

***

Various moments define me and my life; my first car, first house, first wife, my kid. Some may not think that is a good thing, but I am proud to say—nay, mighty proud to say—that I still have them all. However, . . .

I have attended Major League baseball games all my life. I have no idea how many I have been to, but "they" say I went to a few games at Seals Stadium, in the two years before the 'Stick was ready for the Giants. My grandfather usually took me; it doesn't seem that long ago that I was sitting with him along the first base line with his best friend, Harry Jonas. The two subjects of discussion I still remember were trying to guess the attendance, and my consumption of mass quantities of food. When I got full, Grandpa would turn to me and say, "You done?" If the answer was yes, he would then joke, "I guess it's time to go." I have honored him with a tile at McCovey Cove that reads "To my grandfather, Lester Levy, who taught me to love the game." However, I have been saying, for years, that I have never been close enough to a foul ball even to shift my weight to the balls of my feet!

The evening of August 27, 2007, Steve Melikian invited our new circle of friends, including Tim and Bob, to a Giants game in his club level seats on the first base side of home plate. The Giants were playing the Rockies, but I was there for the camaraderie, not the game. Before we left for the stadium, I put into motion an elaborate plan to bring in the makings for martinis, a story for another time. I got my hooch past the heightened security of AT&T, and we proceeded to our seats. There to greet us was the daughter of my "newest best friend," Eric Gray. Rachel's been working for the Giants for quite a few years, but I had never bumped into her at a game, at least not in a professional capacity. After the requisite hassling of a good friend's progeny (Man Rule Number Thirty-Four), and a picture to send to Eric, we went to our seats, drank martinis, and ate copious amounts of peanuts, shells all over the floor under our seats.

In the top of the seventh, all of a sudden, someone yelled, "Here comes a ball!" I think it was off the bat of Bengie Molina. Sure enough, an easy-to-see ball was completing its gentle arc from home plate up to our seats. I immediately jumped to my feet, realizing that, because of the steepness of the seating, there would be no competition to catch the ball. I didn't account for the peanut shells covering the smooth cement floor under foot. As I got up, I slipped on the shells, my hand pulled down just a bit; the ball glanced off the inside of my right thumb, and then hit my head. I found out that it had hit Tim's hand, either before or after my headshot, popped up in the air, and ended up in the hands of the kid to my left. I was bummed, but not terribly upset. It was the first time in forty-seven years of attending games that I had even bothered with the aforementioned weight shift, let alone contacting a ball on the fly. I waved off the usher's offer of medical attention and went back to paying non-attention to the game.

A couple of batters later, Kevin Frandsen popped one back that bounced off Bob's hand. The ball went under the seat to his right, and as he reached for it, he inadvertently pushed it my way, just under the seat to my right. I noticed the guy in front of me reaching straight back, so following the direction of his arm, I reached down to where his hand would logically have been. I felt the ball in his hand, but not firmly enough that I couldn't rip it from his grasp. I am making this sound as if I was more of a brute than I was; it wasn't as drastic as I have described. But it was mine! After calming down a bit, I posed for a picture with my treasure, and another mocking the guy with whom I was competing. As we left the concourse, we paid our respects to Rachel, showed her my ball, and headed down the stairs. Writing this, I just realized I never saw Rachel working at a game before, never caught a ball before. Hmm.

Was this yet another milestone that helps define my life, who I am, why have I been put on this earth? Dunno. To those reading this now, and when I am gone, who would say that I needed to get a life, I *have* got a life—and now, my ball!

Oh, somewhere men are laughing, and you can hear the children call.

The planets must have been well aligned, 'cause Greenberg's got his ball.

—Steve G.
San Francisco, California

AFTERWORD AND ACKNOWLEDGEMENTS

I hope you have enjoyed this book, smiled, teared up, remembered something from your childhood, or even last week. Let's begin a dialogue. If you want to contact one of the story authors, I will try to put you in touch. Let me know the stories you particularly liked, the ones that got to you. Please send me your topics for debate (pace of game), your favorite players (Mickey Mantle), baseball books (absolutely Ball Four by Jim Bouton) and songs (Chuck Brodsky's *"Letters in the Dirt"* about Richie Allen). Email me about anything you want to say about baseball. I encourage you to send me your stories at eric.baseballstories.com.. You see the range that they cover, far greater than anything I could have dreamed up. Ask your friends, co-workers, moms and dads, uncles and aunts and grandparents, your kids and their friends. I will be starting volume two soon. There's not that much time between the games of a doubleheader. Well, there wasn't before it became an opportunity to charge two separate admissions.

I know it's dangerous to single out people when so many have contributed and given me strong encouragement, but here goes. Andy, of all people, go figure, this book is because of your story. Kevin, Eric L., Chuck and Sheldon, you take the prizes for the number of people who sent me stories because of your encouragement, used or not. Sherri, you sure did your best, asking everyone you knew. Steve, your constant ragging on me for engaging everyone I meet for a story on two continents (I won't state here what you call me) was your way of supporting me; Gary, you have given me so much advice on the ideas of book formatting and what to look for in a publisher, and always listening, often forgetting, but always encouraging and urging me to finish the project. You two, my "brothers" from different coasts, have now become friends *despite* this project. Cheryl, we see you almost every week; rarely does the subject of the book not make some appearance in our conversation. Barry, you have seen me in action, tracking down people for stories, more than anyone except for Lynn. Thanks for putting up with my disappearances at all those spring training games. Hilary, I don't know what to say. A softball teammate I had not spoken with in six years, you jumped in, and without asking, developed a Facebook page for me. Whether that netted a hundred stories, or none at all, doesn't matter; it was your willingness to do this unsolicited that means so much to me, as it is the many of you who tried to connect me to friends, ballplayers and others. Ronnie, thanks for giving me my first reading opportunity. Ian K. and Cam, you opened some great doors for me. It was an unbelievably hard task to finally come up with a title for the book. Oh, boy, the options and nuances. DJ Warren, Cindy, Jeff and Lynn, you all helped me come up with the final decision (and many others weighed in as well). Thanks to everyone at Palmetto who helped me through this process. Jack, thanks for taking this on, even though you are not a baseball fan, for having faith in the project, and always checking in. Abbey of the creative team, thanks for what turned out to be a beautiful result. Lindsey, you edited this, guided me in making sure that it all came out right. I hope that I did turn you, at least somewhat, into a baseball fan.

Everyone thanks their family, and it is certainly all warranted for me. Dad was not a huge fan, but he always took my brother and me to games because we were. He resuscitated his limited interest to keep track of everything that Jeff Kent did because he was Rachel's favorite player. Mom was always there to take us to our hundreds of Little League games (even if I was one of those whose baseball cards were tossed). Lisa, the newest member of our family, your efforts to help me find a publisher and always give suggestions and opinions have been greatly appreciated. I totally love that you asked me if we could go to spring training, and that you share our family enthusiasm for baseball. Rachel and David, your love of this great game immeasurably heightened and sustained my love for it, and ultimately this project. The times we have spent at games, and especially those two baseball road trips, have been special. Lynn, you have had to endure seven years of my moaning about people not getting back to me and my child-like excitement when another great story came my way. You are my own personal tech guru, ball park seat mate, sounding board, story reviewer and assistant editor, and all-around advisor/consultant (and I am only referring now to this project). For that, I will forgive that obnoxious "Whoop!, Whoo!" that people in our section, including you, taunt the visiting teams' relief pitchers with as they warm up. As for almost everything in my life, thank you.

As the bio on the back cover says, baseball fans, all of us. See you at the ball park.

ERIC, RACHEL, LYNN

LISA, ERIC, LYNN AND DAVID

This is a list of all the story contributors whose stories just wouldn't fit into this book. Some are already slated for Volume 2. Some of you may not see this list; some may not even remember our exchange. I just want to sincerely thank all of you for taking the time and effort to send me a story. I've enjoyed reading every single one of them. Please forgive me if I have left someone out or misspelled a name.

Aarons, Burnie
Aaronson, Steve
Ackerman, Carl
Acquilano John
Adams, Carl
Adkins, Joshua
Akin, John
Alioto, Carl
Allan, John
Allen, Scott
Alphin, Marcus
Altman, Rodney
Amine, Kassem Hamze
Appling III, Thomas C.
Arabino-Madonna, Margaret
Arnsdorf, Eric
Aubert, Brianne
Aulenti, Jim
Avise, Jim
Azucena, Blanca
Baltz, Doug
Barbee, Debi
Barning, Frank
Barrett, Chris
Barrington, Reese
Barton, John
Beck

Beckerman, Scott
Beerman, Adam
Beneke, Brad
Benesch, Brad
Benizon, Kyle
Bennett, Jim
Benninga, Steve
Benson, Anne
Bentivegna, Tony
Benz, Mark
Berger, Paul
Berry, Rhonda
Bessette, Curt
Best, Jack
Biskar, Neal
Biskobing, Brandon
Bitely, Adam
Blackwell, Allison
Blackwell, Olena
Blakeman, Shawn
Blom, Ellis
Blustein, Richard
Bobrik, Michael
Bolden, Lise
Bondurant, Matt
Boone, Bret
Bowers, Lee

Bowman, Dave
Breslin, Ken
Brody, Joshua Raoul
Brost, Billy   Brown, Errol
Brown, Richard
Browne, William
Buchko, Chris
Burrill, Kevin
Busch, Stephen
Busch, Pamela
Butch, David
Cahill, David
Caine, Gary
Calvo, Pete
Cangelosi, Linda
Capps, Patrick
Chartier, Chris
Casella, David
Chernak, Greg
Clairmont, Matt
Clancy, Jay
Clark, Will
Clarke, Fred
Clevenger, Lori
Cody, Chris
Cohen, Carolyn
Cohen, Mitchell
Cohen, Ron
Coleman, Richard
Collins, Eric
Cook, John
Cook, Niles
Coombs, McKay
Copsey, Brandy

Crawford, Nathan
Crehan, Herb
Csorba, Alex
Cuadra, Gretty
Cullen, Bob
Cusack, Shawn
Cusey, Melissa
Dale, Barry
Davis, Vicki
De Ceuninck, Kevin
Dean, Nancy
DeGrano, Richard
Deluna, John
Denton, Mike
Devigal, Lourdes
Devlin, Charles
DiSclafani, Paul
Distel, Dave
Doherty, Marnie
Donahue, Gary
Dorin, Robert
Douglas, Steve
Dow, Bryan
Doyle, Kevin
Dulkin, Jerry
Duncan, Erika
Ecker, Diane
Eisenberg, David
Elias, Johnny
Elliott, Laura
Emerich, Melvin
Enochson, Donald
Famularo, Jared
Farrar, Mike

Feinberg, Alan
Fillingham Reichart, Linda
Fine, Ben
Fisher, Paul
Flannary, Tim
Floyd-Nelson, Rachel
Folkmanis, Dan
Fouty, Allen
Fox, David
Foxwell, Len
Fram, Alan
Friedman, JD
Fung, Lawrence
Gagas, Nick
Gallo, Christopher
Gardella, Kathy
Giboney, Paul
Gietschier, Steve
Gilman Redburn, Cindy
Gilroy, Gary
Gilroy, Leslie
Godfrey, Andrew
Goldberg, Matt
Goldman, Joel
Goldman, Scott
Goldmark, Joe
Gomes, Terry
Gomez, Adan
Gonzales III, Victor J.
Goodman, Ford
Gorback, Bill
Grant, Alexander
Grant, Greg
Gray, Andy

Gray, David (uncle)
Green Maglish, Nina
Green, Jon
Green, Jonathan
Greenbaum, John-William
Greenberg, Richie
Gregory, Quinn
Griffith, Steve
Guay, Adam
Guay, Richard
Gutherie Troy
Hagan, Shelby
Hall, Michael
Hall, Norman
Hamilton, Linda
Hammer, Hali
Harner, Andrew
Harraghy, Jack
Harris, Sherry
Harter, Lisa
Haskett, Nancy
Hatcher, Tyler
Haus, Katlyn
Hausmann, Jerry
Hawks, Emily
Hayden, Tom
Heeringa, Kevin
Hernandez, Henry
Herron, Gary
Hershenson, Rich
Hershoff, Steve
Hill, Bradley
Hilton, Irene
Himelstein, Jason

Himmel, Jason
Hinds, Bob
Hoffman, Marilyn
Holman, Kenny
Holman, Paul
Holmes, Nancy
Hoover, Deborah
Hopkins, Karen
Hornbaker, Mark
Howell, Kathy
Howell, Kenny
Huddleston, Tom
Hughes, Mark
Hulett, Ric
Hunter, Bruce
Hunziker, Darlene
Huser, Sue
Huth, Ronald
Hylinski, Bee
Im, Terry
Insinga, Jan
Iorlano, Joe
Itelson, Steve
Jacobs, Bob
Jacobs, Joshua P.
Jacobsen, Lawrence
Jackson, Craig
Jeffs, Brian
Jenkins, Victor
Jensen, Eric
Jew, Andrew
Joblonski, Suzane
Jody
Johnny WBZ

Johnson, Bob
Johnson, Paul
Jones, Derrick C.
Joseph, Will
June, Jay
Kahn, David
Kalb, Lewis
Karp, Richard
Keene, Fred
Keeny, Greg
Keiter, Cathy
Kelly, Gerald
Kemp, Allan
Kempster, Doug
Kendrick, Bob
Kerby, Damon (dad)
Kerby, Damon (son)
Kilbride, Lisa
Kindberg, Karl
Kivatanos, Ron
Koba, Harry
Komjathy, Jim
Korral, Josh
Kretchmer, Robert
Kyger, Ernie
Lacki, Tanner
Lampman, Jon
Landry, Brian
Lang, Rich
Lanzalotti, Mike
Lardy, Steve
LaSalle, Mick
Lau, Don
Lawhorn, Vicki

Leahy, Jim
Lear, John
Leavy, Laurence
Ledbetter, Jayne
Leerar, Philip
Lehrman, Jeremy
Leibin, Ira
Leibin, Jay
Lentz Patterson, Susan
Leonard, Ed
Lesonsky, Rieva
Levin, Mark
Levin, Steven
Lew, Christopher
Lieberfarb, David
Lim, Euell
Limon, Ray
Lindberg, John
Lokey, Dennis
Long, Rodger
Lowenthal, Ira
Luecke, Greg
Lufrano, Richard
Lum, Donna
Lust, Michael
Macho, Emma
Macho, Kevin
MacLean, Donna
Maier, Howard
Mandelberg, Rob
Margolies, Mike
Marinec, Greg
Marmet, Connie
Martin, Kitty

Martineau, Peter
Marweg, Dan
Massocca, Mike
Matteson, Scott
May, May
Mayberry, Bob
Mayer, Lucas
Maywalt, Tim
Mazza, Dr. John
Mazzella, Tony
McAleney, Patrick
McBrayer, Wayne
McClure, Jane
McCormick, Kathy
McCray, Gale
McGlasson, Tim
McPalmer, Richard
McSweeney, Gary
Mead, Bob
Medina, Jackie
Meier, Paula
Mena, Roxann
Mendillo, Matthew
Mendlovitz, Dan
Middlebrook, Matt
Migdal, Joel
Milden, Neil
Milo, Anthony
Mire, Beverly
Mires, Larry
Molinari, Elaine
Montgomery, Wynn
Morgan, Mimi
Moutzouridis, John

Mulligan, Martin
Murphy, David
Murphy, Mike
Murphy, Pat
Museus, Shelley
Nakata, Lauree
Narolewski, Steve
Nerger, Law
Newbold, Andy
Nezamis, Gregory
Nichols, Peg
Noche, Celeste
Noller, David
Novick, Bob
O'Brien, Maureen
Oakes, Zan
Oberman, Michael
Oleson, Stephanie
O'Malley, Mike
O'Neill, Patti
Ordman, Marc
Orozco, Pete
Ottley, Gale
Ouellette, Ashley
Owen, Stephen
Parber, Anthony
Parker, Helen
Parks, Jr., Roger
Partridge, Glenn
Paskach, Brendan
Patel, Ameeta
Patel, Shivam
Patterson, Joanna
Pepper, Andy

Perez, Jr., Ernie
Peri, McKenna
Perkins, Mike
Peterson, Darcy
Peterson, Ross
Pfaltzgraf, Andrew
Phipps, Sheryl
Pisciotta, Mike
Plonsker, Jeffrey
Potthoff, Mark
Pressman, Mike
Price, Deon
Price, Joseph
Purden, Austin
Purtill, Matt
Pyburn, Nancy
Quaid, Tom
Rabin, Paul
Rachmany, Eric
Ramirez, Joseph
Rapagna, Paul
Raskin, John
Rascoe, Ric
Rastrullo, Jon
Ray, Gary
Rea, Bob
Rey, Dave
Reyes, Juan
Rhein, Eric
Rhodes, Judy
Rhomiller, Ryan
Rico, Gilbert
Riddle, Clinton
Rinaldi, Joe

Ripert, Benoit

Risley, Rick

Ritter, Dave

Rivette, Adam

Roberts, Jay

Roberts, Mike

Rodgerson, Warren

Roeder, John

Rogers, Patti

Rose, Derek

Rosenbaum, David

Ross, Barry

Ross, Scott

Rowe, Andy

Russo, Vince

Sablesak, Bill

Sachs, Stuart

Savarese, Ted

Schear, Abe

Schechter, Joel

Scherf, Hank

Schiff, Sam

Schimaneck, Michael

Schleter, Dan

Schneider, Mike

Schuster, Claudia

Schuster, Gerry

Schwartz, Julie

Seabury, David

Sebastian, Nick

Sered, Allen

Shea, Mike

Shibuya, Parker

Shinfeld, Jerry

Shrum, Kirk

Signer, Ray

Simon, Matt

Sines, Ben

Sisco, Paul

Smith, Darryl

Smith, Jay

Smith, Rick

Smith, Timothy

Snyder, Kelly

Sobel, Stan

Spahn, John

Sparks, Craig

Spencer, Rick

Spinner, Howard

Stein, David Z.

Stein, Ellen

Stenstrom, Kerwin

Stertz, Phillip

Stewart, CJ

Stodder Jr., John

Stoll, Lyn

Stoyle, John

Sudow, Tom

Sugerman, Mike

Suzuki, Eric

Swanson, Jesse

Tavill, Robb

Tennant, James

Terrizzi, Mike

Thorn, John

Thurm, Wendy

Tiell, Bob

Tiell, Scott

Tinneny, Helen
Tobler, Doug
Tomsick, Tom
Topaz, Mark
Trujillo, Gary
Turbitt, Lisa
Turgeon, Jeffrey
Unterberger, Richie
Upin, Ben
Van Zant, Jonathan
Vanderlans, Jim
Vaughn, Laurie
Vaught, Dennis
Vendramini, Mark
Vieira, Mark
Vinay, Jo Jo
Vitelli, Al
Walcoff, Rich
Walton, Dianne
Walton, William
Walz, Carrie
Wambach, Rich
Wang, Tova Andrea
Waters, Larry
Watkins, Lee
Watts, Ed
Waugh, Deborah
Weiner, Evan
Weintraub, Rob
Weiss, Adele
Welborn, Michael
Welch, Bob
Westerfield, Elizabeth
Westerfield, Khaki

Westling, Craig River
White, Tom
Wiens, Jeff
Wilkins, Douglas
Willson, Tim
Woerner, Warren
Wong, Pandora
Wong, Randy
Wood, Bruce
Woodruff, Tim
Wulf, Doug
Yoshida, Kristin
Zambrano, Michael
Zayat, Liliana